Speaking Truth to Power

SPEAKING TRUTH TO POWER

Essays on Race, Resistance, and Radicalism

Manning Marable

Westview
PRESS

A Member of the Perseus Books Group

Copyright © 1996 by Westview Press, A Member of the Perseus Books Group

Published in 1996 in the United States of America by Westview Press, 5500 Central Avenue, Boulder, Colorado 80301-2877, and in the United Kingdom by Westview Press, 12 Hid's Copse Road, Cumnor Hill, Oxford OX2 9JJ

A CIP catalog record for this book is available from the Library of Congress.
ISBN 0-8133-8827-9
ISBN 0-8133-8828-7 (pb)

The paper used in this publication meets the requirements of the American National Standard for Permanence of Paper for Printed Library Materials Z39.48-1984.

10   9   8   7

PERSEUS
POD
ON DEMAND

Contents

1 Black Liberation in America

2 The Third World and the Politics of Peace

3 Radical Democracy and Socialism

Acknowledgments and Dedication

Many people contributed to the development of this work over the past decade. The editors, newspaper publishers, and radio station managers who have distributed my commentary series, "Along the Color Line," permitted me to interact with thousands of people who directly shape and influence my political work. The editors of the political journals and publications where many of these essays first appeared, including *Black Scholar, Southern Exposure, Monthly Review, Forward Motion, Rethinking Marxism*, and *The Progressive*, frequently helped me present my arguments thoughtfully and creatively. I owe a great debt of thanks to my political colleagues and friends in the black freedom movement, in the American Left, and particularly in the Committees of Correspondence.

All intellectual and political work involves the collaboration and assistance of many people who contribute toward a common project. This volume of my essays was created with the invaluable support of my staff at the Institute for Research in African-American Studies at Columbia University, New York City. Daria Oliver, my executive assistant, is invaluable in directing the office and responding to all of our daily problems and tasks. With her management skills and support, I had the sufficient space and time to write several new essays and to revise the others. Cheri McLeod-Pearcey, the Institute's secretary, helped to type and proofread the manuscript. My doctoral student and research assistant, Johanna Fernandez, discussed with me the themes and core arguments in the book's three major sections for over a period of one year. Johanna's own commitment to left and progressive politics as well as her diligence as a researcher created an environment for a lively exchange of viewpoints, greatly enhancing this work.

There are some passages in this book that no longer reflect my current political views and judgments. Although substantial editorial revisions were made, I tried to maintain the same basic arguments that appeared in my original texts. As I reread some of my essays, especially those on socialism and the Third World, I recalled a lengthy conversation I had with C.L.R. James less than two years before his death. I asked "Nello" whether he regretted any aspect of his political history or involvement in radical journalism. James pondered the question carefully and responded in a very soft voice. He regretted more than anything else the strident, polemical style of his earlier essays, lacking some of the complexity and irony that his later

work represents. Politics is more of an art than a science. To transform society requires the gift of speaking to a particular cultural reality, in a manner that can illuminate the problems of daily life for the oppressed. The
question of language is inextricably linked to the ability to speak truth to
power.

But my deepest debt of thanks belongs to three people. My parents,
James P. Marable Senior and June Morehead Marable, encouraged me to
study black history, supported my activities as a journalist even as a
teenager, and helped to shape my faith in our people. Leith Mullings was
central in helping me understand the contours of the recent political past,
related to my own sojourn. Although we are intellectual collaborators, we
have our own distinct political histories. There are a number of arguments
in this book that I am certain Leith finds objectionable. Occasionally we
disagree about politics, bringing our own theoretical insights and ideological tensions into an ongoing, intimate dialogue. I often learn more from our
disagreements, however, than from our numerous areas of political unity.
There are many paths in the effort to build a more democratic world, a society without exploitation. In her own way, from her own critical perspective, she uses the tools of the scholar to interpret and to reinforce the struggles of our people. Leith remains always my political confidant and
soulmate, guardian of my heart, and seeker of freedom.

Manning Marable
31 May 1996

Text Acknowledgments

The following essays in this collection have been previously published. I have also noted the dates and locations of specific speeches.

"The Tchula Seven: Harvest of Hate in the Mississippi Delta" first appeared in *WIN* magazine (October 15, 1982):18–22.

"The March on Washington, DC, 1983—What Next?" first appeared as "The March—What Next?" in a publication of the Democratic Socialists of America, *Third World Socialists* 1 (Fall 1983):4–6.

"The Paradox of Black Reform" first appeared in *Southern Exposure* 12 (February 1984):20–25.

"Harold Washington and the Politics of Race in Chicago" first appeared in *Black Scholar* 17, no. 6 (November-December 1986):14–23.

"Black Conservatives" was originally published as "Conservatives Gobble Up 'Oreo' Ideology" in *The Guardian* (July 18, 1990).

"Smoke and Mirrors: A City of Hope and Illusion" first appeared in *The Witness* 74, no. 10 (October 1991):14–16.

"Toward a Renaissance of Progressive Black Politics" was presented at a conference of black political organizers and activists, "Democracy and Its Discontents," Washington, DC, June 1992.

"Black America: Multicultural Democracy in the Age of Clarence Thomas, David Duke, and the Los Angeles Uprising" was originally a political speech I frequently gave throughout 1991 and 1992. It was first published as a pamphlet in 1992 and later appeared in Greg Ruggiero and Stuart Sahulka, eds., *Open Fire: The Open Magazine Pamphlet Series Anthology* (New York: New Press, 1993), pp. 244–264.

"The Challenge of Black Leadership: African-American Empowerment for the Twenty-first Century" was prepared as a discussion document at the NAACP-sponsored National African-American Leadership Summit, Baltimore, Maryland, June 12–14, 1994.

"Crossing Boundaries, Making Connections: The Politics of Race and Class in Urban America" was presented at the First National Conference on Urban Issues, "Crossing Boundaries: Collaborative Solutions to Urban Problems," sponsored by the State University of New York, College at Buffalo, and by the Buffalo Federation of Neighborhood Centers, Inc., Buffalo, New York, November 11, 1994.

An earlier version of "Violence, Resistance, and the Struggle for Black Empowerment" was published in *African Commentary: A Journal of People of African Descent* 2 (May 1990):16–21. That essay was published in Herb Boyd and Robert Allen, eds., *Brotherman: The Odyssey of Black Men in America* (New York: Ballantine Books, 1995), pp. 799–809.

"Louis Farrakhan and the Million Man March" was first published in *New Statesman and Society* (London), October 27, 1995.

"Zimbabwe and the Problematic of African Socialism" first appeared in *Contemporary Marxism*, no. 7 (Fall 1983):89–95.

"*Sin Libertad:* United Nations Appeal for Puerto Rican Independence" was originally published in *Third World Socialists* 1 (Fall 1983).

"Nuclear War and Black America" first appeared in *National Scene* 53 (January 1984):14, 18–19.

"Race and Democracy in Cuba" first appeared in *Black Scholar* 15 (May-June 1984):22–37.

"Free South Africa Movement: Black America's Protest Connections with South Africa" first appeared in *Colgate Political Review* 1 (Spring 1985):11–15.

"The Future of the Cold War" first appeared in Leon Wofsy, ed., *Before the Point of No Return: An Exchange of Views on the Cold War, the Reagan Doctrine, and What Is to Come* (New York: Monthly Review Press, 1986), pp. 120–125.

"The Bitter Fruits of War" first appeared in *The Witness* 74, no. 3 (March 1991):6–8.

"Toward a Pan-Africanist Manifesto for the Twenty-first Century" was an address delivered at the international conference, "Africa in the World, Fiftieth Anniversary Civic Celebration: The 1945 Pan-African Congress and Its Aftermath," Manchester, England, October 15, 1995.

"Why Black Americans Are Not Socialists" first appeared in Phyllis Jacobson and Julius Jacobson, eds., *Socialist Perspectives* (Princeton: Karzcohl, 1983), pp. 63–95.

"Black Politics and the Challenges of the Left" was originally published in *Monthly Review* 41, no. 11 (April 1990):22–31.

"Toward an American Socialism from Below: Beyond Stalinism and Social Democracy" first appeared in *Forward Motion* 19, no. 1 (March 1990):31–36.

"Remaking American Marxism" first appeared in *Monthly Review* 42, no. 8 (January 1991):40–53.

A version of "Toward a New American Socialism" was published under the title "A New American Socialism" in *The Progressive* 57, no. 2 (January 1993):20–25.

Introduction:
Toward an Autobiography of
the Politics of Race and Class

Blackness as an identity within American politics and society has always been imposed from without and constructed from within. African-American people are the product of historical forces and events which have given character and substance to their collective development and understanding of reality. Slavery, Jim Crow segregation, and ghettoization imposed structures of inequality and discrimination upon all black Americans. The institutional violence of race, which destroyed millions of black families over several centuries, was an integral aspect of an unjust social order. To be black was to be defined as unequal and inferior by the general standards of the white world. But blackness was also a symbol of hope, a means for asserting our cultural heritage and humanity. Under difficult conditions, African-Americans sought to overcome the burden of race, to redefine the boundaries of democracy, and thereby to reflect the multicultural spectrum of the total society. Thus black identity was inextricably bound to the values, traditions, and rituals of our people engaged in resistance and to the attainment of freedom.

My own particular identity as a black American can be traced to the year of our Lord 1854, when my great-grandfather, Morris Marable, was sold on an auction block, at age nine, for the sum of $500. The white man who sold Morris and profited from this exchange was his master, who was also his biological father. Kinship usually was not a factor which influenced whites' decisions about the purchase and sale of slaves. In the rituals of my family, in our collective memory, I still feel my great-grandfather's pain and anguish. I understand the courage it took to survive the harsh crucible of slavery. And from his and many others' sacrifices and struggles, the foundation was established for a new set of kinships and cultural networks affirming our heritage. African-American identity is part of that long memory which recalls being denied the right to vote, being forced to occupy seats at the back of the bus, being refused service at restaurants. We define ourselves as oppressed people largely by what we have endured. Through our survival, black people have kept faith with those who came before us, and nurture the spirit of freedom for the future.

This rich history of black struggle is an essential part of my own history and memory. I was born in 1950, only five years after the end of World War II. Millions of African-Americans from the rural South had become sojourners in the Great Migration north. As blacks settled in the cities, they found work in industries and manufacturing firms. For my parents' generation, there was a genuine sense of optimism for the future. The GI bill had opened doors to college education to thousands of African-Americans. Despite being largely confined to northern ghettoes, most black families experienced real wage increases and sharp improvements in their standards of living. In the previous decade, the establishment of the Congress of Racial Equality (CORE) marked the beginning of the strategy of nonviolent civil disobedience. A. Phillip Randolph's "Negro March on Washington Movement" had pressured Roosevelt to sign Executive Order 8802 outlawing racial discrimination in the employment policies of defense plants. The Supreme Court had already outlawed the "all-white primary" which kept millions of African-Americans from the ballot box across the South. African nations such as the Gold Coast and Kenya were in the midst of widespread anticolonial unrest, as the Third World began to achieve independence. There was a strong belief that the struggles of black people both at home and abroad were slowly but surely moving toward the goals of freedom and democracy.

But despite this background of hope, the politics of reaction, the "great fear" of McCarthyism and anticommunist hysteria, was in force. In the United States, more than 1 million workers who belonged to leftist trade unions were expelled from the AFL-CIO. Millions of Americans were fired from their jobs, harassed, and denied employment and even the right to travel because they fell under political suspicion as "Communists." State legislatures passed laws which made membership in the Communist Party a criminal act. Meanwhile, the NAACP, the largest civil rights organization, lurched to the right, firing one of its founders, W.E.B. Du Bois. Black America's greatest advocates for freedom, Du Bois and Paul Robeson, became virtual political prisoners in their own country. McCarthyism and mass anticommunism reinforced political conformity and severely compromised the prospects for liberal and progressive reforms. The campaign to desegregate the South was delayed for nearly a decade and would be revived only with the unexpected emergence of Rosa Parks and Martin Luther King, Jr. and the nonviolent movement in Montgomery, Alabama, in 1955–1956.

This was the world into which I was born. I was a child of first generation, middle-class black Americans; my father was a teacher and later a successful businessman, my mother an educator and subsequently a college professor. I did not know hunger or material hardship. I attended excellent public schools, which were usually racially integrated. Our home was filled with books, encyclopedias, music, and art. I was enrolled in art academy classes for a number of years during the weekends of my childhood; there I learned the magnificent gift of great art. I was trained to work hard, to be diligent in my studies, to compete aggressively, yet fairly in the classroom. Even before I was born, my mother had firmly decided that I would be trained to become a historian. In elementary school, I received history books as presents; I enjoyed memorizing details about American presidents and national elections. By the time I was in junior high school, I was frequently going to the public library to check out autobiographies and biographies of famous political personalities, regardless of their ideologies. During the summers, my mother would assign additional books to read; I would devour them eagerly and go back to the library for more.

This middle-class lifestyle was sustained by my parents only through great personal sacrifices. My father had worked the second shift at a factory for several years while attending college as a full-time student. Throughout the 1950s, he taught in a public high school during the day and worked in a factory at night. My father and his brothers built our family home in the suburbs by hand, working every day for several months to construct the house. My mother was first employed as an elementary school teacher and then returned to the university to obtain her doctorate in education. Like nearly all middle-class black people, working 70 or 80 hours each week was not unusual at all. Frequently, their effort to improve our material conditions, to create a positive environment for us, became almost overwhelming. One of the most vivid memories of my childhood was seeing my father collapse in a department store, falling into semiconsciousness. Overworked, overstressed, burdened with financial responsibilities, he still managed to recover. Yet whatever difficulties or hardships my family experienced were at best modest when compared to the normal lives of most working-class Negroes. We had at least escaped the repressive political and social environment of the Jim Crow South. We had some degree of economic security, and we believed that the "American Dream" could be achieved through sacrifice and hard work.

But as I grew up, I could never forget, not even for a single moment, that I was black. Regardless of our incomes, education, and material successes, despite our relatively privileged social status, we still lived in a world apart from whites. The barrier of race isolated us from opportunities in thousands of ways, even in a midwestern town where formal, legal segregation did not exist. My father attempted to obtain a mortgage to purchase a home and over a two-year period was denied credit at every bank in town. Negroes were confined largely to the city's ghetto on the west side; they were usually not allowed to purchase homes or even to rent apartments in many quarters of the city. Even as a child growing up in the 1950s, I could vividly comprehend that as Negroes we lived in a separate, unequal world. Yet within that world apart, we found joy and laughter; we found music and dignity within our souls. We prayed to the Lord in our own houses of worship; we celebrated our own heroes during "Black History Month" every February; when we sang our national anthem, it was James Weldon Johnson's "Lift Every Voice and Sing." We were the orphans of American democracy: part of the household, but never members of the family. The principles and policies of democracy, the core values and ideals in which Negroes deeply believed, were never fully extended to us. Our tenuous status as permanent outsiders gave us a peculiar insight into the nature and unequal reality of white power.

But beyond the veil of race stood another bastion of power and violence, which had definable features I could barely understand. Even as a boy, I gradually deciphered the burden of social inequality in its different manifestations: the unemployed who clustered along Fifth Street desperately seeking a day's wages, while affluent whites drove by, deciding which man would be hired; the factory workers living in our neighborhood who came home filthy and tired; the middle-aged black women standing at the bus stop, leaving their own children to travel across town to care for the children of well-to-do households. Traveling to the South, I watched in silence as our family automobile slowly passed a work gang along the side of a country road. The men wore black and white coarse garments and were roughly chained together at their ankles. Guards with guns supervised their labor. It was a shocking scene I never forgot. My family protected me from poverty and hunger; our middle-class status buffered to a considerable degree the harsh realities of inequality African-Americans experienced in the workplace, the courts, and throughout the social order. But I could also see white Appalachian families in our neighborhood who seemed poorer than nearly any Negroes I knew. There was something inherently wrong and unfair about the natural order of things, but I lacked the words or concepts to comprehend what that was.

The first real lessons in my political education occurred in the early 1960s with the eruption of the Civil Rights Movement, America's "Second Reconstruction." On television, I witnessed a series of moving, powerful confrontations: the "sit-in" movement which was initiated in February 1960 by a group of college students in North Carolina and which escalated in nonviolent protests across the South; the "Freedom Rides," led by CORE, which challenged segregation in public transportation throughout the heart of Dixie; the mobilization of thousands of men, women, and children in the streets of Birmingham during spring 1963, challenging the "Citadel of Segregation." We closely followed these events and were inspired to act in our own small community. There were demonstrations in white-owned department stores and businesses in our downtown demanding an end to racial segregation in hiring policies. Banks were pressured to extend credit and capital to blacks. The local newspapers and television stations, which had carefully ignored any coverage of the African-American community, gradually lifted the information blockade on blackness.

What I began to learn in the relatively idealistic days of the early 1960s was that the meaning and impact of "race" could be changed. As oppressed people mobilized themselves in nonviolent civil disobedience, as they registered new voters and organized Freedom Schools in shanties and churches across the rural South, the definition of what blackness could be was transformed. As the struggle for power grew intense, as Negroes asserted themselves as never before, white Americans were pressured and forced to reexamine their stereotypes and prejudices. Over time, many even began to modify their language, their public behavior, and their treatment of black people. I could observe the change in daily life from practical experiences. The schedules of public buses, which had never been routed through parts of the black suburban community on the extreme west side, were changed, permitting us to travel downtown. School curricula slowly began to reflect more multicultural themes and a new recognition of black history and culture. Blacks were hired in the police department and were elected to the city council. The Civil Rights Movement had permitted Negroes to perceive themselves as real actors in their own history. The boundaries of what whites had defined as blackness were radically reinterpreted and renegotiated. In short, race was not fixed, grounded in biological or genetic differences, or structured through "cultural deprivation"; it was the consequence of power, privilege, and violence. As Negroes challenged and overthrew the institutions of racial inequality, the actual relationship between black and white was sharply altered.

As a black teenager watching the great protests and demonstrations across the South, I felt an incredible sense of pride and empowerment. The youth group in our church became involved in civil rights activities. We initiated several joint discussions and cultural programs with Temple Beth Israel, the synagogue in the liberal Jewish community. I joined the youth divisions of the local chapter of the National Urban League and was elected vice president. As a high school student, I began contributing articles to the local African-American neighborhood newspaper, the *Dayton Express*. By the time I was 17, I was writing a weekly column largely devoted to politics, public issues, and race relations. I interviewed the city's black leaders, attended public meetings and local protests, and began to learn the craft of writing. If I had a coherent political ideology during these years, it would best be described as "inclusionism." With my family and the local Negro middle class to which we belonged, I believed in the goal of racial integration. I wanted black people to be assimilated into positions of authority

and power. Democracy could be achieved through the expansion of opportunities and resources to Negroes. To paraphrase our poet laureate
Langston Hughes, "We, too, were America."

All of these liberal beliefs and aspirations for reform came crashing down
with the rise of "Black Power." After the successful Selma-Montgomery desegregation march of 1965, King and the Southern Christian Leadership
Conference (SCLC) moved their efforts to Chicago, challenging northern
racism. But King encountered greater difficulties in the struggles to desegregation Chicago's suburbs than he had met in the South. Broad sectors of the
Civil Rights Movement, especially members of the Student Nonviolent Coordinating Committee (SNCC) and CORE, began to question the effective-
ness of nonviolence. As the US war in Southeast Asia escalated sharply in
1966, and as the numbers of African-Americans killed and wounded at the
front soared, the relationship between the Civil Rights Movement and the
white liberal corporate and political establishment soured. Young activists
began talking about "black consciousness" and the necessity to go beyond
integration as a strategy for social change.

In June 1966, civil rights activist James Meredith was shot while marching across Mississippi. Civil rights leaders quickly vowed to complete the
"Meredith March Against Fear" without him. But immediately, participants were polarized by the militant positions of SNCC's newly elected
chairperson, Stokely Carmichael. Carmichael insisted that the march
should "de-emphasize white participation" and advocate the need for independent black politics. When Martin Luther King, Jr. refused to denounce
Carmichael and SNCC, NAACP leader Roy Wilkins and National Urban
League director Whitney M. Young withdrew from the march. As the
march progressed through the Mississippi delta, the rallies of local, rural
blacks began to emphasize black consciousness and the need for black independent organizations. When Carmichael was briefly arrested in Green-
wood, Mississippi, the mood of the marchers turned militant. Speaking before 3,000 blacks after his release from jail, Carmichael declared: "The
only way we gonna stop them white men from whuppin us is to take over.
We been saying freedom for six years and we ain't got nothin. What we
gonna start saying now is BLACK POWER!" The crowd roared in response, "BLACK POWER!"

In the next year, Black Power polarized and fractured the Civil Rights
Movement. The NAACP and Urban League bitterly denounced Black
Power as divisive and antiwhite. SNCC and CORE expelled their white
members, moving to a program of black nationalism. In the 1967 book
Black Power, Carmichael and political scientist Charles V. Hamilton outlined the central parameters of the new black protest movement: establishment of an independent black politics challenging the two-party system; intense criticism of interracial coalitions and nonviolence; and the thesis of

"internal colonialism," which equated black America with other colonized Third World nations. Black Power was expressed within the poetry, prose, and theater of the Black Arts Movement; in music, James Brown captured the spirit of the times by chanting, "Say it Loud, I'm Black and I'm Proud."

Nevertheless, Black Power quickly came to mean very different things to different people. For the black entrepreneurs who manipulated blackness to sell goods and services in poor urban communities, Black Power was a demand to control black consumer markets. For young black automobile workers in Detroit, Black Power was expressed through the League of Revolutionary Black Workers. In Oakland, California, black revolutionary nationalism was led by Huey P. Newton, Bobby Seale, and the Black Panther Party. And in southern California, Maulana Karenga's US organization advocated "cultural nationalism," emphasizing the central role of culture in redefining black consciousness and reality. Beyond this rhetoric, the various formations inspired by the renaissance of black nationalism were frequently at odds, sometimes expressed through violent confrontations. Warfare between the Panthers and the cultural nationalists in California turned deadly. Ideologically and politically, Black Power could be interpreted to justify a range of policies, from Marxism-Leninism to conservative Republicanism. Significantly, the only presidential candidate in 1968 who openly endorsed Black Power was Richard M. Nixon.

American society seemed to be pulling apart at the seams. In Vietnam, 500,000 US troops were mired in a bloody conflict which was politically and morally unjustifiable. On February 8, 1968, three African-American youths were shot to death and 34 were wounded at South Carolina State College during a mass desegregation protest. Weeks later, the Kerner Commission on Civil Disorders issued its report, warning that the United States was "moving toward two societies, one black, one white—separate and unequal." Martin Luther King, Jr. was transformed by these turbulent events. He spoke out courageously against the Vietnam War, breaking with the Johnson administration. King called for a poor people's march on Washington, DC, bringing together the oppressed of all races and colors. Traveling to Memphis in support of that city's striking sanitation workers, the veteran civil rights leader was searching to define new goals and visions for black freedom. That search was tragically cut short on the afternoon of April 4 when Martin was assassinated as he stood on the second-floor balcony at the Lorraine Motel in Memphis. For much of black America, more than a "dream" had died. Nearly everyone I knew in my community was overwhelmed with grief and anger. In the following week, uprisings erupted in 125 cities across the country. Nationally, 46 people were killed, 2,600 were injured, and over 21,000 were arrested. Fifty-five thousand federal troops and National Guardsmen were deployed to quell civil unrest. Property damage was estimated at over $45 million. In Washington, DC, armed troops were stationed to protect the Capitol building for the first time since the Civil War.

My mother decided that I should attend King's funeral to witness a significant event in our people's history. The local black newspaper was eager to send a correspondent to provide coverage for its readers. So at the age of 17, I boarded an airplane for the first time and traveled directly to Atlanta, Georgia, the evening before King's funeral services were scheduled. I awoke the next day before dawn, walking by myself through the city's vacant streets on that cool spring morning. Guided by a small map, I eventually found Ebenezer Baptist Church at about 6:30 A.M., the very first person to arrive. Before long, a crowd gathered. Ralph Abernathy, Martin's longtime lieutenant, spoke to us briefly. Within several hours, tens of thousands of people had crowded tightly around the chapel. As the funeral procession slowly headed toward the Atlanta University–Morehouse College area, I marched along with thousands of others. In my own writing, I tried to convey my overpowering emotions at this mass event, which was both terrible and triumphant. With Martin's death, my childhood abruptly ended; my innocent faith in American democracy and freedom was forever shattered; my understanding of political change began a trajectory from reform to radicalism.

The years I spent in college and graduate school, between 1968 and 1976, were the high point of black nationalism and racial consciousness. As a freshman, I became involved in efforts to establish a statewide caucus of representatives from black student unions and organizations. I was elected president of our African-American student organization, which we named BLAC—Black Leadership Action Committee. I took part in demonstrations of all kinds, from teach-ins denouncing the Vietnam War, to rallies in defense of a young philosophy professor, Angela Davis, who had been unjustly fired for her Communist beliefs by California Governor Ronald Reagan.

My major political engagement, however, took the form of journalism. When I was 19, I obtained a third-class radio license and got a job at our campus radio station. For several hours each week, I hosted a radio program which featured jazz, rhythm and blues, political commentary, and interviews. I continued to write for my black hometown newspaper. I read virtually everything I could find on the topic of black liberation: *The Autobiography of Malcolm X;* James Baldwin's *The Fire Next Time;* Eldridge Cleaver's *Soul on Ice;* Stokely Carmichael and Charles Hamilton's *Black Power;* Sam Yette's *The Choice;* Robert Allen's *Black Awakening in Capitalist America;* Earl Ofari's *The Myth of Black Capitalism;* Oliver Cromwell Cox's *Caste, Class, and Race;* E. Franklin Frazier's *Black Bourgeoisie.* I fell in love with the poetry of Gwendolyn Brooks, Langston Hughes, and Sonia Sanchez. I was impressed with the sweeping historical analysis and polemics of Harold Cruse's controversial *Crisis of the Negro Intellectual*. But there were three black intellectuals whose works at this time had a profound and lasting impact upon my life. The first and foremost of these was Du Bois.

I was probably in junior high school when I first experienced *The Souls of Black Folk*. By the time I was in college, I knew passages of *Souls* by heart. I devoured *Black Reconstruction, The World and Africa, Darkwater,* and his other works. Du Bois represented for me the very model of committed scholarship and political advocacy on behalf of black folk. His writing resonated with passion and power; he fought racism with an unyielding will and a vision of a truly multicultural democracy. What was equally impressive were the contours of Du Bois's political biography, his shifts and turns, his constant search for truth. Du Bois was far more consistent ideologically than any of his critics. At a theoretical level, Du Bois attempted to construct a social philosophy which synthesized the essential duality of the African-American experience, the struggle of "warring souls" which are trapped between an identification with American culture and society, on one hand, and a commitment to black identity and the African Diaspora, on the other. It is this basic conflict which remains at the heart of the debate over the character of black consciousness today.

In summer 1969, I was employed in a warehouse, where I emptied railroad cars, moving refrigerators and other heavy appliances. During my breaks, I sat in the warehouse's furnace room reading and studying Frantz Fanon's *Wretched of the Earth*. Week after week, I committed large sections of Fanon's provocative thesis to memory. I was primarily struck by Fanon's definition of radicalism, which began with the reality of blackness but did not stop there. Embedded within Fanon's passionate, angry language was a rejection of reform and cooperation with the white power structure. I was even more profoundly influenced by Fanon's *Black Skin, White Masks,* a brilliant and soul-searching analysis of the psychological and cultural dependency of blacks within a white racist society. Fanon personified for me the ideal of the scholar-as-revolutionary.

The third black intellectual who shaped the direction of my intellectual and political life was Walter Rodney. I lived in Kenya and Tanzania in 1970–1971, at the time Rodney was teaching at the University of Dar es Salaam. Within months of publication by Bogle-L'Ouverture in England of Rodney's classic, *How Europe Underdeveloped Africa*, I had read it. With Du Bois as my theoretical foundation, Rodney brought home the role of European capitalism as the decisive historical force in the transatlantic slave trade and the colonial domination of the African continent. It was Rodney's writing on Africa, including his excellent history of the Upper Guinea Coast, which reinforced my decision to pursue the field of history. Taken together, the fundamental impact of Du Bois, Fanon, and Rodney largely shaped my understanding of history and politics. In overlapping spheres of political engagement and scholarly analysis, their works represent three great themes which defined protest movements and politics in the post–World War II world: the struggle against racism and for black empowerment, especially in the United States and South Africa; the struggle against colonialism and European domination, particularly in Africa and the Caribbean; and the various movements for "socialism," from Marxist-Leninist to social democracy, from Julius Nyerere's "Ujamaa" in Tanzania to Maurice Bishop's New Jewel Movement (NJM) in Grenada. These three central themes formed the basis of my entire intellectual work.

I completed my undergraduate education at a Quaker institution, Earlham College, in 1971. I received my M.A. degree at the University of Wisconsin the following year and finished my Ph.D. in history at the University of Maryland at College Park in 1976. It is difficult today to explain just how racist the university environment was for that first substantial group of African-Americans in graduate and professional schools in the 1960s and early 1970s. I remember vividly how one of my white professors informed me that I clearly possessed an inferior educational background, lacking the ability to compete with other students. I was recruited into the doctoral program in history at the University of Maryland—but no one informed me that no African-American had achieved a Ph.D. degree in history in that institution's history!

We had virtually no African-American professors or mentors and often experienced a profound sense of alienation and isolation. For some of us, politics provided an escape from the routine of the white environment of graduate school. Most of my engagement was at a distance—reading black intellectual journals like *Black Scholar* and Hoyt Fuller's *Black World* and *Presence Africaine;* following the intense ideological debates in the mid-1970s between black cultural nationalists and Marxists; attending African Liberation Day demonstrations in Washington, DC. As I was completing my dissertation, a biography of the founder and first president of the African National Congress (ANC), John Langalibalele Dube, I continued to write periodically for black publications. I wanted to apply the scholarly tools I had acquired to the political and social struggles of my people. I had become impatient and frustrated with graduate school and wanted to be actively engaged in the debates and controversies of the time.

Although I was employed for several years in the Afro-American Studies program at Smith College, my first real job was at Tuskegee Institute in 1976, one of the most famous black American colleges. This same year I began working with a group of progressive black scholars who had established a research center based in Atlanta, the Institute of the Black World (IBW). The day-to-day chief of staff was Howard Dodson, who would later become the director of Harlem's Schomburg Center. The scholars who were involved in the research projects and activities of the institute included political scientist William Strickland, Caribbean historian and Garvey biographer Robert Hill, and African-American historian Vincent Harding. IBW attracted scores of intellectuals from across the Black Diaspora, including West Indian Marxist scholar C.L.R. James and historian-activist Walter Rodney. For several years, I drove two hours each way between Tuskegee and Atlanta to participate in some modest way in the institute's programs. I was in many respects the "Benjamin" of the collective. It was through IBW that I met Rodney, who visited Atlanta periodically. On two occasions I took Walter to lunch or dinner on Martin Luther King, Jr. Street in the heart of Atlanta's black community. I saw in Walter the model of principled political engagement and historical scholarship which I wanted to emulate.

That same year, just before my relocation to Tuskegee, I became directly involved in national black activist politics. In March 1972 in Gary, Indiana, the largest political convention of African-Americans during the Black Power era was held. Led by Gary Mayor Richard Hatcher, Congressman Charles Diggs of Michigan, and then–cultural nationalist, poet, and activist Amiri Baraka, the Gary convention established a new formation, the National Black Political Assembly (NBPA). The NBPA was essentially a network of locally based black nationalists, community leaders, and elected officials who advocated a progressive political strategy of black empowerment both inside and outside the traditional two-party system. The Gary convention's primary document, "New Politics for Black People," articulated a radical critique of US politics and society: "The crises we face as black people are the crises of the entire society. They go deep to the very . . . essential nature of America's economic, political and cultural systems. They are the natural end-product of a society built on the twin foundations of white racism and white capitalism."

Although the militants usually dominated the NBPA's policy statements, the pragmatists and elected officials largely controlled the political activities of the formation, seeking alliances with white political interests. In the first four years of the NBPA, it went through a series of intense ideological conflicts and factional feuds. Diggs and many other African-American elected officials defected from the NBPA to build their influence inside the Democratic Party. As Baraka was breaking from cultural nationalism to adopt a rigid interpretation of "Marxism-Leninism–Mao Tse-tung Thought," many more moderate community-based and religious leaders were pulling away from the NBPA. In late 1975, Ron Daniels, a black nationalist activist with an impressive community base in Youngstown, Ohio, engineered the ouster of Baraka from his official position in the assembly, in effect purging the black Maoists from the organization. The NBPA then announced its plans for another national political convention, to be held in Cincinnati in March 1976. I decided that at whatever cost I wanted to be an integral participant in this process, to witness the convention, and to become part of the movement of black nationalism.

At the Cincinnati Black Convention, I met hundreds of black nationalists and community activists with rich histories of personal struggle from the Civil Rights Movement to Black Power. Like SNCC, the Black Panther Party, the early CORE, and other black activist organizations, the assembly was composed overwhelmingly of young black women and men. Over the next four years, I worked extensively with the NBPA, becoming personally close with Daniels. When Reverend Benjamin Chavis, a noted North Carolina activist and former political prisoner, later joined the assembly, we also became friends. At the NBPA's New Orleans convention in August 1980, I served as communications coordinator. The assembly was an invaluable education for me, although I would soon question and finally break with its essential ideological and political framework of black nationalism.

But the event which would have the greatest impact on my future political life occurred by accident in 1976. While teaching at Smith College and completing the final chapters of my dissertation, I had written several articles on politics for black student publications. After moving to Tuskegee, I was interviewed by the editor of the town's local newspaper. He informed me that he might be interested in publishing a political commentary column on a regular basis. So I began contributing articles to the *Tuskegee News,* commenting first on national and local politics and then on a range of social issues and public policy debates. Black-owned publications in nearby Jackson, Mississippi, and Panama City, Florida, began printing the column, then called "From the Grassroots." With my own very modest resources, I managed to print a brochure promoting the series and distributed it to dozens of black newspapers. My appeal was simple: the column was absolutely free of charge to any black-owned publication in the United States. I only requested as compensation a complimentary subscription to each newspaper. Within a few years, about 50 black publications were regularly publishing the column. Several large, well-established African-American newspapers, including the Sacramento *Observer,* the San Francisco *Sun-Reporter,* the Baltimore *Afro-American,* and the Chicago *Defender,* began to feature the series. It was through this newspaper series, by writing 40 to 50 short essays each year, year after year, that I discovered my own political voice. By commenting regularly on contemporary issues, I found the language to express my own ideological and political perspectives.

By the early 1980s, the column was regularly reaching more than 100 publications. I began receiving correspondence from readers all over the country, who both admired and criticized what I had written. I pulled together some of the better columns with several political essays I had written for such journals *Black Scholar* and *Review of Black Political Economy* into a volume, published by South End Press of Boston, called *From the Grassroots*. To sustain the series on a nonprofit basis, I tried to solicit lectures at academic institutions for a small honorarium. At first, I was extremely uncomfortable speaking before an audience of any size. I spoke in a scholarly tone, even and distinct; audiences usually seemed to appreciate my ideas but were bored beyond belief by my delivery and style. Finally, after hundreds of presentations before political groups, community organizations, and colleges, I slowly began to learn how to communicate my ideas to diverse audiences.

At Tuskegee, I began to study the major works of Marxism. I gradually became convinced that racism by itself could not account for the oppressed conditions of black people in America and, for that matter, across the globe. Capitalism as an economic system was based on an unequal exchange between the owners of capital and those who worked for a wage. Capitalism as a social system fostered class stratification, extreme concentrations of wealth, and poverty and promoted race hatred as a means to divide workers. This basic analysis seemed to make sense, based on my own experiences growing up inside the United States, in the context of racial discrimination and social inequality. I came to Marxism not out of some abstract love for the white American working class, or out of faith in the power of the international proletariat, or out of respect for the models of Soviet and Chinese communism, both of which I found equally problematic. I became a socialist because I believed in the struggles of black people, in their history and destiny, and because I believed that to eliminate racism and inequality decisively, a new democratic society would have to be constructed.

For a time, I tried to reconcile my respective commitments to black nationalism and socialism. I described my own political ideology as "left nationalism" or "revolutionary black nationalism." I argued with cultural nationalists that a class analysis was essential in understanding the dynamics of black exploitation; that coalitions with other oppressed people of color and progressive whites were necessary to challenge and transform the system. I criticized black elected officials who defended the conservative Democratic policies of the Carter administration, and I advocated the development of an independent, black political party. This was the essential political and theoretical orientation of my work between 1977 and 1981.

At the same time, my relationship with the white Left became much more extensive. I developed close contacts with the New American Movement (NAM), a group of socialist feminists largely drawn from the New Left movement of the previous decade. In 1979, I joined NAM as an "associate member" and participated in some of the organization's activities. Moving to Oakland, California, I quickly became a member of the editorial collective of *Socialist Review*. My newspaper series began to be published in the

democratic socialist newspaper *In These Times,* edited by James Weinstein.
When merger discussions developed between NAM and the Democratic Socialist Organizing Committee, headed by Michael Harrington, I strongly
supported this move. Although I still considered myself a black nationalist,
I believed that a united democratic Left based largely among white progressives could become a potential partner in a "common program" of radical
reform with African-Americans, Latinos, and other oppressed minorities.
The new organization which emerged from the two groups, the Democratic
Socialists of America (DSA), became the largest political formation espousing socialism in the United States. I was named one of the national vice
chairpersons of DSA, and I began to meet other young black and Latino
scholars and labor activists who had also been attracted to the organization. One of my closest and most productive friendships was with a brilliant young black professor at Union Theological Seminary, Cornel West.
Cornel and I worked jointly to create DSA's National and Racial Minorities
Commission, bringing together Asian-American, Latino, and African-
American democratic socialists.

My self-identification with black nationalism was rapidly coming to an
end. In retrospect, there were several important events in 1980–1982 which
pushed me away from black nationalism and toward Marxism. The first
was the Miami rebellion of May 1980, which occurred in the wake of the
acquittal of white police officers who had murdered a black man. When I
first learned about the Miami uprising, I immediately flew to the city, which
by then was under the civil control of the state's National Guard. My political column had been published for over one year in the local black newspaper the *Miami Times,* and this alone gave me the political credibility to
move freely and confidently inside the "riot zone." I went around National
Guardsmen to talk directly with black residents of Miami's Liberty City
and learned directly of their long-standing grievances against the local police and the criminal justice establishment. I saw large buildings being
torched and burning. After returning home, I wrote a passionate critique of
the uprising, which was promptly published in *Black Scholar.* "The Fire
This Time" captured the militancy of the movement.

The second event, coming only days after the Miami uprisings, was the
assassination of Walter Rodney in Guyana. Rodney had sacrificed his life to
the struggle for democracy against an authoritarian dictatorship. If his life
had any meaning, it was essential to extend his socialist analysis to the
struggles of black people throughout the world. So I began to write the
manuscript which eventually became *How Capitalism Underdeveloped
Black America.* Published by South End Press in early 1983, it became
something of a black Marxist manifesto, a thorough critique of the class
structure and competing political ideologies of black America. The language and style of *How Capitalism* broke sharply with the politics of reform and gradualism.

The third decisive event occurred in late 1980 when the NBPA organized the Philadelphia Black Political Convention, which launched the National Black Independent Political Party (NBIPP). NBIPP brought together cultural nationalists, revolutionary nationalists, Trotskyists, black Maoists in the Communist Workers' Party, and Pan-Africanist radicals behind the effort to construct an independent black political party. NBIPP claimed to be a "party of a new type," not merely an electoral formation attempting to elevate blacks into office. It called for a fundamental break from the two-party system. NBIPP brought together a collection of very talented and dedicated activists who had long histories in the black freedom movement: Ron Daniels; Ben Chavis; former Washington, DC, superintendent Barbara Sizemore; civil rights attorney Barbara Arnwine; and community organizer Hulbert James. At Philadelphia, I was elected to the national leadership of NBIPP, serving with Sizemore as regional representatives from the Northeast. But problems surfaced almost immediately, which led me to have serious reservations about the whole project. Much of our political literature and our public programs was stridently ideological, not designed to reach out to black working-class audiences.

It was becoming clearer to me that a black nationalist framework was inherently compromised because its theoretical premises were basically incorrect. A nationalist perspective generally minimized the importance of class stratification and income polarization among African-Americans. Race, however important, was not the fundamental issue which defined the nature of inequality and oppression within capitalism. Strategies for black empowerment and solidarity had to be grounded in something beyond skin color. A vision of progressive multiracial coalitions which advocated the democratic transformation of the US political economy and society was necessary to empower and liberate black people. Not for an instant did I ever question the continued importance of black self-organization or the crucial necessity to struggle against white racism. But now I recognized that the building of a viable democratic movement in the United States to challenge the establishment and two-party system would have to be based on a variety of constituencies and communities beyond the boundaries of black and white. I made the final transition from the politics of race to the politics of class.

Throughout most of the 1980s, I divided my political energies into three arenas: African-American empowerment and antiracism; Third World liberation efforts, especially in the Caribbean and southern Africa; and the movements for socialism throughout the world. I traveled far and wide internationally, speaking in new countries and widely diverse political contexts. *Speaking Truth to Power* documents my political sojourn during these years. The dominant political theme of the decade was, of course, "Reaganism." For much of white America, Reaganism meant lower taxes, anticommunism, relaxation of environmental protection laws, cutbacks in wasteful social spending, and deregulation of the economy. For black, brown, and poor America, Reaganism meant an escalation of racism and white prejudice, a retreat from the enforcement of civil rights laws, an aggressive assault to undermine labor unions and the right to strike, and an extreme consolidation of wealth and property in the hands of a privileged few at the cost of increased poverty for the many.

A group of middle-class African-Americans began to defect to the popular conservative trend in American politics. First, two of King's principal disciples, Ralph Abernathy and Hosea Williams, endorsed the election of Ronald Reagan for president in 1980. Then a small coterie of black political and academic apologists for Reaganism surfaced: ex-Marxist economist Thomas Sowell, who had become a devoted follower of conservative theorist Milton Friedman; economist Glen Loury; Robert Woodson, an advocate for privatized public housing in the black community; Clarence Pendleton, controversial chairman of the US Civil Rights Commission; and Clarence Thomas, Reagan's appointee as head of the Equal Employment Opportunities Commission and, a decade later, George Bush's nominee to the Supreme Court.

Nevertheless, Reagan's conservative agenda also created a new environment for resistance and black political activism. In rural Mississippi, I witnessed the struggle between black local activists and the traditional southern white power structure of businessmen, plantation owners, and political bosses. In Chicago, a coalition of blacks, Latinos, trade unionists, community activists, and white liberals defeated the entrenched Cook County Democratic machine by electing African-American Congressman Harold Washington as the city's mayor. The successful Washington candidacy and the unsuccessful but inspirational campaign of Mel King for mayor of Boston illustrated that an effective left-of-center public policy agenda could be achieved through the construction of a black-led progressive coalition including racial minorities, feminists, lesbians and gays, trade unionists, environmentalists, and other liberal constituencies. A revolt could be launched inside the Democratic Party's presidential primaries, advocating essentially a Left social democratic/progressive reform program, which could mobilize millions of African-Americans and others to resist the Reagan agenda.

This became the theoretical approach which formed the basis of the Jackson campaign of 1984 and, to a lesser extent, the subsequent Jackson mobilization in 1988. The twentieth anniversary March on Washington, DC, in late summer 1983 had catapulted Jackson into a position as the central figure of the anti-Reagan movement. And to his credit, Jackson proved to be an insightful, passionate leader, rapidly growing in his capacity to represent the political demands of racial minorities and various liberal and Left constituencies. The Jackson campaigns registered hundreds of thousands of new voters and illustrated for the first time in American history that a black person could actually compete seriously for the nation's highest office.

Internationally, I became extensively involved with Third World political parties and liberation movements. I wrote about the problems of postcolonial development in the newly independent African country of Zimbabwe; I spoke at a United Nations Commission on behalf of the movement for Puerto Rican independence and self-determination; I traveled to Cuba and reflected on the similarities and differences in our respective understandings of "race." In September 1983, I was asked to speak at the annual convention of the People's National Party (PNP) in Jamaica. During that brief first encounter and subsequent visits, I fell in love with Jamaica and became deeply interested in the politics of the Caribbean. A political and personal friendship developed with Jamaica's charismatic and complex leader, Prime Minister Michael Manley. I had interesting conversations with the leader of the PNP's pragmatic, moderate wing, P.J. Patterson, who would later become Manley's successor as Jamaica's Prime Minister. I developed a cordial and then close relationship with the Left intelligentsia of the country, prominently including Trevor Munroe, Rupert Lewis, and Don Robotham. Most significantly, at the 1983 PNP convention I had several lengthy and pleasant conversations with Vincent Noel, a trade unionist and representative of Grenada's New Jewel Movement government. Noel invited me to visit and speak at the NJM's fifth anniversary celebration of its revolution, planned for early 1984. Within one month, Noel would be murdered by his own comrades, along with Grenada Prime Minister Maurice Bishop, Jacqueline Creft, and other popular leaders of the NJM. This gave the Reagan administration the pretext for launching a massive military invasion of the small Caribbean nation. The Caribbean Left was shattered for years to come.

My major political and historical writings of this period were *Black American Politics* (1985), *W.E.B. Du Bois: Black Radical Democrat* (1986), and *African and Caribbean Politics: From Kwame Nkrumah to the Grenada Revolution* (1987). After working actively in DSA for several years, I quietly let my membership lapse in 1985. I was troubled by the essential direction of the organization. Michael Harrington's strategy to achieve democratic socialism in America rested with liberal reform and the Democratic Party. He was critical of independent politics to the left of the Democrats and was close politically to a number of white labor leaders who had less-than-progressive records in responding to blacks' interests. Harrington as an individual was an attractive and often courageous figure, motivated by a deep moral commitment to social justice and democracy. But his central strategy of working solely within the liberal wing of the Democratic Party could not build an effective movement for American socialism. When DSA refused to endorse Jesse Jackson's presidential candidacy in early 1984, my reservations about the organization's politics deepened. I had organized a national conference of DSA's leading members of color and edited a modest theoretical journal, *Third World Socialists,* featuring the contributions of DSA's national minorities. As a democratic socialist, I continue to agree with the basic social and economic insights of this tendency of the American Left. But as a black person, I had to find another political road to freedom which would more fully reflect the meaning and lessons of African-American struggle.

My main political "anchor" in these years was my newspaper column. Renamed "Along the Color Line" in 1983, the series expanded rapidly with the upsurgence of black political resistance moments in the decade. I attempted to apply my skills as a social scientist to an analysis of contemporary social problems, but in a style and language which were accessible to a black-working class audience. I tried to be more comprehensive in my coverage of events and issues of the day: the antiapartheid protests of 1984–1986 and the political campaign for divestment from South Africa; the Jackson presidential campaign of 1988 and the expansion of the Rainbow Coalition into a truly multiracial, progressive formation; the continuing burden of social inequality, health care, education, housing, and human services in America; the politics of the Black Diaspora, from the Caribbean to Capetown, from Lagos to Los Angeles. The series expanded to 250 publications worldwide, including political journals and newspapers in Belize, Canada, the United Kingdom, East Germany, and India. When I accepted an academic position at the University of Colorado in 1989, I explored the possibility of creating a radio version of "Along the Color Line." For several years, the radio version was regularly featured on over 80 radio stations in the United States, Canada, and Central America. The newspaper series continued to be free of charge, an educational service for black and progressive audiences. Although it was often difficult to financially sustain the commentary series, I was rewarded many times over by the hundreds of letters and communications I received from community activists, teachers, trade unionists, clerical workers, ministers—people from all vocations, representing all cultures and colors. It was through "Along the Color Line" that I "kept faith" with black people; I could not speak with meaning or authority over time to a predominantly black audience unless I was willing to speak truth to power.

The core political perspective which I had adhered to for nearly a decade was fundamentally challenged and transformed by the international and national events of 1989–1994. The Cold War between the United States and the USSR, which had dominated global politics for two generations, came to an abrupt end—first with Gorbachev's progressive political reforms within the Soviet Union, then the rapid collapse of the Soviet bloc in

Eastern Europe, with the dramatic fall of the Berlin Wall, and, finally, with the disintegration of Soviet communism itself. I had been throughout the Soviet Union in 1984, traveling as far as Tashkent, Uzbekistan, in Central Asia. I returned with a sense of a mighty multiethnic empire which at its roots was rapidly decaying and extremely inefficient; a massive structure of social welfare and universal employment combined with authoritarian political controls and censorship. The efforts in the late 1980s to democratize the Soviet system were, in retrospect, both too little and too late. The principal reason for the failure of the Soviet model was not Reaganism, the second Cold War, and the nuclear arms race: it was ultimately the fundamental schism between "socialism" and the ideals and practices of democracy. The massive crimes against humanity committed in the Soviet Union in the name of "socialism" could never be forgotten or forgiven. The destruction of Soviet communism, as well as the capitulation of Chinese communism to an economy dominated by private market capitalism, forced leftists throughout the world to rethink their own politics.

In the Caribbean, Africa, and elsewhere in the Third World, the collapse and disintegration of Soviet communism had a devastating political impact. For a half century, the geopolitical environment of the Third World had been defined by the competition between Western capitalism and Eastern communism. The nonaligned movement led by Nehru, Nasser, and Tito in the 1950s was an attempt to create a third bloc within international politics, tied to neither world power. To destabilize Western interests, the Soviets pursued an effective strategy supporting Third World liberation movements from Vietnam to southern Africa. Through a theory of "noncapitalist development," the Soviets profoundly influenced the internal politics and socioeconomic priorities of many radical Third World states. Consequently, with the disappearance of the Soviet Union, the entire pretext for political nonalignment and for a "Third World" also disappeared. The political reality of the "New World Order" was the fundamental demarcation between north and south, wealth and poverty, power and oppression. The Bush administration was able to marshal many European and Middle Eastern governments to send troops to invade Iraq in the most massive multinational military intervention since Vietnam. Governments in Ghana, Jamaica, and other countries capitulated to the strict fiscal demands of the International Monetary Fund and other Western interests, curtailing social expenditures and devaluing currencies. In South Africa, the brutal dictatorship of apartheid was finally toppled, and a progressive government led by former political prisoner Nelson Mandela came to power. But the ANC-led government pursued policies which were so "moderate" that the oppressed conditions and social exploitation of millions of South African black people were hardly touched. Many political parties in the Third World with long histories as "Marxist" and "revolutionary" sought new identities within moderate social democracy, neoliberalism, and even nationalism.

Inside the United States, the retreat from the political militancy of the mid-1980s was symbolized by the collapse of Jesse Jackson's Rainbow Coalition and the unexpected death of Harold Washington. In 1988, Jackson received over 7 million popular votes in the Democratic presidential primaries and became one of the country's most powerful leaders. But the Rainbow Coalition was sharply divided internally over what strategy to pursue after the elections. Jackson eventually discouraged the development of a Left-liberal politics outside the Democratic Party. Within two years, thousands of activists who had dedicated themselves to the Rainbow Coalition ceased their activities. The coalition became an empty husk, dominated by the overpowering personal presence of Jackson and little else.

In Chicago, Washington's untimely death in late 1987 destroyed his multiracial, progressive coalition. Blacks were bitterly divided between machine-oriented moderates and progressives; many Hispanics and liberal whites defected to the old Cook County Democratic organization. In 1991, the son of "Boss" Daley, Richard Daley, easily came to power as mayor. The local black electorate was demoralized and disillusioned. A decade of brilliant political struggle and triumph appeared to be completely reversed.

As the ideological basis for electoral politics tilted to the right, a new generation of African-American leaders began to emerge. Unlike black conservatives, they were not Republicans; they often supported many traditionally liberal public policies, such as affirmative action and universal health care. But in their approach to electoral politics, they frequently represented themselves not as "black politicians" but as politicians who happened to be black. They explicitly disavowed any specific obligation to the empowerment of African-Americans over and above white constituents' interests. These politicians prided themselves on their pragmatism and cooperative relationships with mainstream and conservative white Democrats and corporate interests. They had scant relationship with the insurgent movements for social protest which still simmered within America's ghettoes and barrios. I characterized this development as "postblack politics," or the deracialization of African-American electoral representation.

In the vacuum of effective leadership coming from the black middle class, the grievances and social anger of poor and working-class African-Americans were manifested in new and striking actions. The Los Angeles social uprising of April–May 1992 symbolized black collective outrage against the brutality of the police and the racism of the legal system, combined with the festering grievances of inferior schools, poor housing, second-class health care, and widespread unemployment. The cultural movement of Hip-Hop seized upon the historical figure of Malcolm X to articulate rage against the system's current ills. As racial polarization and reaction increased throughout white political society—as characterized by the emergence of racist politician David Duke in Louisiana, the national debate to outlaw affirmative action, and the decisive victory of white conservative Republicans in the 1994 congressional elections—African-Americans were forced to reevaluate sharply the traditionally inclusionist/integrationist strategies for interracial reform and gradual change. In 1993, the position of NAACP national secretary was narrowly won by Ben Chavis over Jesse Jackson. Chavis pursued a complex agenda: advocating liberal and progressive public policies and social programs; building strong black institutions and coalitions and establishing cooperative dialogues among all representatives of the black community, including Louis Farrakhan and the Nation of Islam; and encouraging productive contacts with the alienated Hip-Hop generation, urban black gangs, and young people inside the criminal justice system. This approach briefly won remarkable support from a broad spectrum of black activists, from cultural nationalists such as Maulana Karenga and Haki Madhubuti, to black socialists such as Angela Davis, Cornel West, and Charlene Mitchell. But within months, an effective campaign to oust Chavis was orchestrated in the media, supported quietly by more moderate, old-style Civil Rights leaders and many postblack elected officials. The political space which remained was quickly seized by Farrakhan and the Nation of Islam, advocating an agenda markedly to the right of both Jackson and Chavis: political chauvinism, petty entrepreneurial capitalism, patriarchy, and strict racial separatism. By the mid-1990s, for much of the Hip-Hop generation, the term "militancy" was symbolized by Farrakhan's conservative, black nationalist program.

We black progressives had failed, in part, because we had not articulated an effective, alternative political vision capturing the mind and mood of our people, recognizing the basic transformations in the political economy and social structure which had occurred inside black America since the Civil Rights Movement. We were still using old slogans and primitive theoretical tools to analyze a complex political culture dominated by high technology, cyberspace, and the information revolution. We urgently needed to question everything we had assumed previously; we had to find within ourselves the courage to admit our mistakes, to seek a politics which truly reinforced and reinvigorated ethical, democratic values. I frequently recalled the sound advice of African social theorist and revolutionary Amilcar Cabral: "Hide nothing from the masses of our people. Tell no lies. . . . Mask no difficulties, mistakes, failures. Claim no easy victories."

Theoretically, I began to rethink the whole history and political culture of black America, to reconstruct the past in order to comprehend the present and future. I tried to outline an alternative approach toward a new African-American politics, and I prepared a discussion document on black leadership for the National African-American Leadership Summit sponsored by the NAACP and held in Baltimore, Maryland, in June 1994. Chavis had inspired a movement to foster political dialogues across ideological and organizational boundaries within the black community. The summit represented to a limited extent something of a nascent black united front, with many representatives from cultural nationalist formations, black professional associations, civic groups, sororities and fraternities, the Nation of Islam, and black Christian denominations. Unfortunately, Chavis's financial mismanagement of the NAACP and his personal errors of judgment, combined with a relentless media and political attack against his initiatives, led to his downfall.

Simultaneously, I was working to create a new democratic dialogue within the US Left or, at least, what remained of it. Many American radicals interpreted the collapse of the Berlin Wall metaphorically as the failure of the socialist vision. Some retreated into political liberalism, middle-class feminism, environmentalism, or other less radical political trends within the white mainstream. I attempted to restate the necessity for a class analysis to understand the problems of social inequality, but also to point out that American socialists had to create a more effective means of democratic political intervention. I interpreted the term "Marxism" essentially as the method of historical materialism, a social theory which helps interpret the contours and contradictions within any society—not a rigid dogma or economic determinism.

But this "beginning" did not go far enough, theoretically or conceptually. Years earlier, I had attempted to explain the various factors contributing to the inability of the Left to gain the support of African-American poor and working-class people. Now I made a sharp distinction between authoritarian Marxism and elitist social democracy as forms of socialism from above and the radical democratic politics of socialism from below. But perhaps the problem was that "socialism" had remained for years something of an alien ideology, which didn't adequately ground itself in the distinct radical struggles for democracy within the textured patterns of American social history. What was truly radical and egalitarian about the various people's movements for freedom and human dignity within our common history? By what language, by which cultural representations, and by what ethics could a new progressive politics emerge? These questions motivated me to travel extensively across America during the 1990s. I spoke at more than 300 events over a four-year period at churches, synagogues, labor union halls, colleges, and community centers; before audiences which were African-American, Latino, Asian-American, Pacific Islander, feminist, gay and lesbian, environmentalist, liberal Democratic, and nearly everything else in between. But I listened much more than I spoke. I wanted to rediscover what organic patterns of democratic resistance, what models for community mobilization and social transformation currently existed and could be created. We had to recover an American voice and democratic vision grounded in a commitment to human equality and possessing a compassionate openness to multicultural diversity, dialogue, and cooperation.

In lectures (published herein) I spoke to this deep yearning for freedom among the oppressed, the struggle for equality which must be at the heart of our democratic politics. In a basic political address I delivered more than one dozen times in various versions across the country, I discussed the politics of multicultural democracy, and I invoked the strategy of "speaking truth to power." Speaking truth to power means, for me, a commitment to human equality, a vision of democratic empowerment and reform from below which builds upon the incredibly rich history of American radicalism, of Paul Robeson and Fannie Lou Hamer, Ida B. Wells and W.E.B. Du Bois, Cesar Chávez, and John Brown. I continued to be actively and proudly identified as a democratic socialist. In 1993, a broad representation of socialist and radical democratic groups came together to establish the Committees of Correspondence (CoC). It was never designed to become "the party" of the Left; the CoC is a transitional formation, part of the inevitable political realignment of progressive social forces in the organizational Left and well beyond, among our constituencies in labor union halls, schools, churches, and community centers.

But no single group on the American Left today possesses the program, strategy, or even political language necessary to generate a renaissance of the broader progressive movement. That democratic language must be constructed; that strategy must be appropriate to the actual processes of the US political system, with demands which go beyond reform and empower the oppressed to seek even greater social changes. Central to this strategy must be the targeting of one collective group above all others: the emerging American majority of Latinos, Asian-Americans, Native Americans, African-Americans, Arab-Americans, and other people of color, especially in our central cities. That is *not* to say that there aren't many serious and even fundamental differences between and among these constituencies— there are. And it is not to build political unity on the simplistic basis of "identity," racial, ethnic, or gender based. But the entire history of this country illustrates that the actual experiences of oppression, the materiality of daily life and the collective efforts for resistance and spiritual transcendence, created a political culture consciousness and protest traditions largely defined by black Americans and many other people of color, which may construct a new progressive politics in the United States.

For all of us, these are difficult times: a resurgent political Right represented by Newt Gingrich and the "Contract with America"; the retreat from affirmative action and the enforcement of civil rights provisions; the Supreme Court's restrictions of majority-minority legislative districts; the failure to pass a comprehensive national health care system; the massive expansion of the US prison system, which today includes 1.5 million Americans, and the reinstatement of chain gangs in Alabama; the US government's virtual abandonment of our central cities, with their infrastructures collapsing and decaying before our eyes, their streets and neighborhoods plagued by poverty, homelessness, violence, and fear. As progressives, we must remind ourselves, as Frederick Douglass suggested, that "power concedes nothing without a demand." We need to engage in the full range of democratic methods of political change: mass demonstrations, civil disobedience, economic boycotts, changes in voting procedures and election laws, independent political parties, and direct electoral involvement, among others. We must encourage a national discourse on the democratic values and dimensions of US civil society, that vast social space between the family and the state, between the intimate and the fully public arenas of decisionmaking. What do we have a right to expect of each other in an increasingly diverse, multicultural, class-divided society? What should be the new parameters of the "social contract" between the majority of Americans and the government?

We are currently in a battle for the "political soul of America." The ideologues of reaction and conservatism, the William Bennetts and William Kristols, completely understand this. We are challenged to find the appropriate democratic strategy and language for resistance and empowerment, leading to social transformation. And with the faith of my black foremothers and forefathers, in the great traditions of African-American activism for freedom and equality, I remain confident that we shall overcome.

PART 1

Black Liberation
in America

1

The Tchula Seven:
Harvest of Hate
in the Mississippi Delta

For millions of blacks living in the rural counties and small towns of the "New South," the terrors of Jim Crow and racial exploitation which sparked the civil rights movement of the 1950s still exist. Nowhere is this more vivid than in the sovereign state of Mississippi.

The roots of black poverty and political powerlessness in Mississippi are found in the economics of racism. In 1949, black farmers owned 80,842 commercial cotton-producing farms in Mississippi's black belt region, about 66 percent of all cotton farms in the state. During the 1950s and 1960s, "agribusiness"—corporations which went into agricultural production aggressively pushed thousands of these small rural farmers out of business. By 1964, the number of black-owned cotton farms declined to 21,939 statewide. Five years later, the figure dropped to only 1,000. Since the civil rights movement, the number of black farm residences has fallen still further, both in Mississippi and across the country.

Part of the reason for this process is the extreme difficulty which black farmers have in obtaining capital. According to a 1982 Civil Rights Commission report, "Many insurance companies, which finance the bulk of farm loans, require loans to be at least $100,000. While commercial banks lend lesser amounts, they often require payment within five years, a term too short for the average black landowner. Federal land banks tend to require amounts of collateral that are too great for blacks to qualify."

The federal government has done little to reverse the decline in black farming. For example, the Farmers' Home Administration (FmHA), which is the principal public lending agency for farmers, lent $6.3 billion in fiscal year 1980 and almost $7 billion in fiscal year 1981 to farmers nationwide. Loans to blacks were so few, however, that in March 1981, black Mississippi farmers helped stage a 21-day sit-in at one FmHA county office to protest discrimination. In Mississippi alone, the number of black FmHA committee members declined 53 percent from 1979 to 1980. Between 1980 and 1981, not surprisingly, the number of farm ownership loans to blacks in Mississippi also fell—from 101 to 30. Under intense criticism, the Carter administration authorized the FmHA in 1980 to initiate a project especially "geared to reach small farm enterprises with gross annual incomes as low as $3000" in Mississippi and six other Southern states. However, no loans were ever made under the project, and few black potential borrowers ever learned about the project's existence. Under Reagan the FmHA discontinued the program.

Economically, rigid racial segregation was always a curse and a blessing. The South's version of apartheid was never confined to social and civil separation of the races. It provoked the rise of white vigilante groups such as the Ku Klux Klan, and justified the lynching, castration, and mutilation of literally thousands of blacks throughout the South. In Mississippi alone, between 1882 and 1927, 517 black men and women were lynched—the highest state total in the country.

Desegregation—and Dispossession

Despite these brutalities, however, segregation was also paradoxically a barrier which permitted the development of small black businesses. In 1887, for example, a former slave, Isaiah T. Montgomery, established an all-black town, Mound Bayou, Mississippi. In less than 10 years, Mound Bayou had several banks and real estate firms, a technical school, one newspaper, a sawmill, and a power and light company—all owned and operated by blacks.

Desegregation in the 1960s and early 1970s was, of course, supported by the overwhelming majority of blacks as a necessary and progressive reform. But in the process, as white-owned banks, insurance companies, laundries, groceries, and restaurants began to accommodate black customers, the market for black entrepreneurs was seriously eroded.

Losing their land, many rural black merchants and potential businesspersons tried to establish themselves in Jackson, Greenville, and smaller Mississippi cities. With rare exceptions, they were unable to compete with larger, white-owned firms and quickly went out of business. In Greenville, for instance, a middle-sized city with about 38,000 residents in 1977, 179 of the town's 247 black-owned firms do not possess a single paid employee. The five black-owned real estate firms in the city have average gross receipts of $5,000. The 68 black shops without employees collected an average gross of only $11,320 in 1977. This process of underdevelopment, therefore, afflicts urban blacks as well as farmers, and their collective economic plight has actually become worse with desegregation.

The current economic conditions of rural Mississippi blacks are symbolized, again, by Mount Bayou. By 1979, the all-black town was over $133,000 in debt. When the town lost a civil lawsuit judgment that year, which totaled an additional $59,000, bankruptcy seemed imminent. Banks froze the city's accounts, and the 19 acres of city property, including a park, the city's public swimming pool, and its only municipal building, were sold at auction. Southern Bell cut off the city's telephones because of an unpaid $1,700 bill, and Mississippi Power and Light threatened to halt city services. In April 1982, a Memphis radio station helped to raise $120,000 to pay off some of Mound Bayou's bills. But without adequate state or federal assistance, the status of this town's 2,900 people seems bleak.

Racist Terror Upsurge

The general economic decline for most Mississippi blacks since the 1960s has been accompanied by the resurrection of white racist terrorism and political violence. In May 1981, the *Jackson Advocate* reported that in Mississippi alone there have been 12 murders "in as many months which are suspected by blacks of being [racially motivated]." The tortured body of one unidentified black man was found floating down the river in Cleveland, Mississippi. The man's sex organs had been hacked off and the coroner later reported finding his penis in his stomach.

On January 11, 1981, the body of 45-year-old Lloyd Douglas Gray was found hanging from a tree in Tallahatchie County, Mississippi. Tallahatchie coroner A.W. Hulett pronounced Gray's death a suicide, and no autopsy was performed. A month later, the body of 32-year-old Roy Washington was found in Cypress Creek, in Holmes County, Mississippi. Washington had been "badly beaten in the head and face," his hands bound behind him, and then shot in the head at point-blank range. The corpse was weighed down with a car jack and wrapped by barbed wire. Scars around his neck indicated that he had also been lynched. Local white newspapers were silent on the murder.

Holmes County police did not aggressively pursue leads in the case, and even followed a black reporter around while he conducted his own investigation. The majority of the other black men who have been found beaten or hanging in Mississippi have also been officially labeled suicides. Familiar with the pattern of racial violence, one black resident of Tallahatchie County declared, "If they say it was suicide, it was probably a lynching."

What kind of human beings can commit such hideous crimes? To understand contemporary Mississippi race relations, one must invariably return to the past. Consider William Alexander Percy's classic, *Lanterns on the Levee,* first published in 1941. Percy explains that the nightmare of white supremacy ushered into the public arena a series of "vain demagogues" who competed with each other in denouncing blacks' rights.

The most successful practitioner of race-baiting was Theodore G. Bilbo of Pearl River County. From 1907 until 1946, Bilbo was elected state senator, lieutenant governor, governor, and US Senator. To describe Bilbo as an obscene racist would be too modest; he was also an outrageous anti-Semite. Before one congressional committee during World War II, he "defended himself against charges of racial and religious intolerance [by stating] that he was for 'every damn Jew from Jesus Christ on down.'" He campaigned vigorously for repeal of the Fifteenth Amendment to the Constitution, and voiced support for plans to transport all blacks "back to Africa."

But if the wealthy planters of the Mississippi River delta, the sons and grandsons of slaveholders, could agree with Bilbo on the necessity to disfranchise the Negro, they found Bilbo and his extremist colleagues repulsive. Percy explains that

[Bilbo] was a pert little monster, glib and shameless, with that sort of cunning common to criminals which passes for intelligence. The people loved him. They loved him not because they were deceived in him, but because they understood him thoroughly; they said of him proudly, "He's a slick little bastard." He was one of them and he had risen from obscurity to the fame of glittering infamy—it was as if they themselves had crashed the headlines.

And what of the white voters who repeatedly put Bilbo into public office? Percy captured their mind and mood in his description of a typical white Mississippi crowd during an electoral campaign:

I looked over the ill-dressed, surly audience, unintelligent and slinking. They were the sort of people that lynch Negroes, that mistake hoodlumism for wit, and cunning for intelligence, that attend revivals and fight and fornicate in the bushes afterwards. They were undiluted Anglo-Saxons. They were the sovereign voter. It was so horrible it seemed unreal.

Unquestionably, the white population of Mississippi was the South's vanguard in the "Massive Resistance" campaign to preserve white supremacy in the 1950s and 1960s. Upon Bilbo's death in 1947, John C. Stennis, a racist politician by all accounts, was elected to replace him in the Senate. He is still there today.

When Paul B. Johnson, Jr. was elected governor in 1963, he denounced integration in messianic terms: "Evil days are upon the land. We must fight fire with fire." Yet Johnson had been defeated in a previous gubernatorial race in part for being "too soft" on the "Negro Question"! This is a state where George Wallace polled 63 percent of the presidential popular vote in 1968; where NAACP state chairperson Aaron Henry was illegally banned from speaking at the University of Mississippi for years; where lynchings are still not uncommon occurrences.

White Mississippi politicians frequently describe their state as the most "progressive" in the nation today as far as electing black officials. Superficially, this assertion appears to be true. As of July 1977, Mississippi had 295 black elected officials, the highest number in the US. But a detailed analysis of this figure, more than double the total number of black officials in the entire country in 1965, reveals some incongruities.

Only four of Mississippi's 98 state representatives and state senators are black. Virtually all of the other black officials are mayors or city councilpersons in small, rural, majority-black towns, law enforcement officers, or serve on municipal school boards. None are congressional representatives.

Furthermore, the black percentage of Mississippi's statewide population, at 35.9 percent in 1975, is significantly higher than in Illinois, Michigan, and Arkansas. Yet, proportionately, these states have elected a much larger number of black officials—Illinois, 281; Michigan, 251; Arkansas, 218.

Moreover, many black elected officials in Mississippi took no leading roles locally in the desegregation struggle of the 1960s. According to Charles Tisdale, the editor of the *Jackson Advocate*, at least three-fourths of these 295 black "public servants" are on the "payroll" of former segregationists, corporate interests, and local white political machines. Independent black politicians who criticize the state's power structure are few and far between.

The Case of Eddie Carthan

Eddie Carthan understands Mississippi—its heritage of segregation, racial brutalities, and economic exploitation of the black working class and rural poor. As a youngster he attended the "Freedom Schools" conducted by idealistic activists in the Student Nonviolent Coordinating Committee. He witnessed the political intimidation of black farmers who tried to register to vote. In his hometown of Tchula, the population is 85 percent black. Thirty percent of the town's adults are unemployed; 66 percent are on welfare; 81 percent of all Tchula's housing units are classified as "deteriorating."

As the first black mayor of a Mississippi delta town, elected on a reform platform in 1977, Carthan thought that "I could represent those who had come through slavery, knowing nothing about voting, about going to a motel, sitting in the front of a bus or eating in a restaurant." But Carthan's election was an intolerable threat to the racist power structure of Holmes County and, indirectly, of the entire state.

Carthan recognized that the county, which is statistically the tenth poorest in the US, could not develop without massive federal assistance. The mayor obtained CETA funds to weatherize and remodel Tchula's homes. A nutrition project was established to provide meals to senior citizens and the handicapped. A federal grant was solicited for the projected construction of a public library. A child care program was begun specifically for mothers who worked or who lived on AFDC payments. A public health clinic was started in Tchula, and plans were made for a cable TV system, door-to-door mail service, and the construction of public basketball and tennis courts. In less than three years, Carthan obtained $3 million in federal and private support for the town, and created 80 new jobs.

But change in a repressive society does not come about without opposition. Upon Carthan's election, a political representative of the "four most powerful men in the state—more powerful even than the governor," offered the mayor a $10,000 bribe if he agreed to do things "the way they have always been done." When Carthan refused the bribe, the forces of reaction began to move.

Two "loyal" blacks on the town council sided with the lone white alderman, John Edgar Hayes, to undermine Carthan's progressive program. In 1979 they forced the black city clerk to resign, replacing her with a local white; forced the black water supervisor to resign, replacing him with the sister-in-law of the white county supervisor; and refused to pay costs for the city's telephone and light bill. Carthan's salary was lowered from $600 to $60 per month.

When local black supporters of Carthan protested, the aldermen voted to increase their property taxes. For two months, they refused to pay city employees. To intimidate Carthan, they locked city hall for eight weeks and placed white police chief Sharkey Ford at the front door. Shotgun in hand, Ford was ordered to "shoot anyone who tries to enter." Carthan's family began to receive threatening phone calls and racist letters.

The situation worsened in 1980. In April 1980, Ford finally resigned. Carthan appointed a black officer, Johnny Dale, as temporary police chief. At a special meeting of the City Council called specifically to hire a permanent police chief, Carthan's opponents left the session before a vote could occur. Walking to a local convenience store, they immediately phoned Jim Andrews, the white whom Carthan had defeated for mayor in the previous election. Andrews was told to "take over as police chief." Without taking an oath or being bonded, Andrews put on his "old uniform," picked up his service revolver, and took over the police department.

When Mayor Carthan learned about Andrews' actions, he located two regular police officers and several auxiliary policemen. Carthan and his police officers confronted Andrews at city hall. Andrews refused to leave, and pulled his gun when Carthan informed him that he would be arrested if he didn't leave. Andrews was finally disarmed nonviolently. Subsequently, both Carthan and Andrews filed charges against each other, but only Andrews' charges were acted upon. On April 12, 1981, Carthan and six co-defendants were convicted on charges of simple assault of a "law enforcement officer." The co-defendants received three year suspended sentences and fines. Eddie Carthan was ordered to spend three years in the Mississippi State Penitentiary.

But Carthan's legal troubles were not over. A local white businessman claimed that he had paid Carthan a bribe for signing papers for a bank loan, which federal authorities say was fraudulently obtained. Although the federal government's attorney conceded that Carthan's signature on the documents presented to the bank for a loan was "forged," the mayor was convicted. Carthan's bond was revoked on August 30, and he is in jail pending appeals as of this writing. But even with the destruction of Carthan's political influence, the Old Guard of white supremacy fears any open discussion of the cases. When the *Jackson Advocate* published information favorable to Carthan last December, the newspaper's office was fire-bombed. Organizing efforts still continue to free Carthan and the "Tchula Seven." On October 11, a national march will begin at Tchula, culminating in the state capital on October 16. A broad coalition of civil rights activists, church leaders, legal aid agencies, and civil liberties groups have endorsed the march.

Three decades ago, V.O. Key asserted that "the beginning and the end of Mississippi politics is the Negro." Despite desegregation and the election of black officeholders, this statement is still true today. The battle for civil rights, black economic development, and simple justice has not ended in Mississippi. It has hardly begun.

2

The March on Washington, DC, 1983: What Next?

Those of us who attended the magnificent March on Washington, DC, this August will never forget the event.

Between 250,000 and 300,000 women, men, and children of all races, nationalities, classes, and religious affiliations were at the Lincoln Memorial that blistering August afternoon. Thousands endured day-long bus rides or sleepless nights on trains, but on Saturday morning, they were there. An astonishing array of political forces were present—black nationalists and NAACP members, feminists and labor leaders, environmentalists and Latinos, peace activists and elected officials, gay men and lesbians, Marxists and liberal Republicans.

It was the coalition of the oppressed which comprises a majority of American society—the same bloc of social and political forces which made the basis for Harold Washington's mayoral victory in Chicago earlier this year. The call for "Jobs, Peace, and Freedom," despite the general theoretical fuzziness of March Convenors Coretta Scott King and Joe Lowery of SCLC, can become the foundation for developing a progressive multi-class, multiracial program. This new agenda can attack the domination of the corporations over the lives of working and poor Americans, challenge the Reagan war machine and its policies which promote nuclear confrontation and Third World intervention, and create across the grassroots communities of America the realization of a need for a more advanced definition of democracy and human equality.

What was the political base for this "Coalition of Conscience"? Some observers have suggested that the current policies of this administration are solely responsible for the unprecedented unity among Center-to-Left forces. As the saying goes, "Ronald Reagan is the best political organizer for the Left since Eugene V. Debs." Today's unity, however, is more accurately a progressive reaction to the political trend toward inequality, escalating racism, and conservatism over the past decade.

A Response to Reaction

Although the basis for contemporary conservatism and Reaganism is the structural crisis of monopoly capitalism, various aspects of the trend toward reaction have been evident throughout American political and civil society. Since the *Bakke* decision, for example, the number of black, Latino, and Native American students recruited and admitted into many professional schools dropped sharply. The logic of *Bakke* was applied to electoral politics in the Supreme Court decision *City of Mobile v. Bolden*, which upheld an electoral arrangement which diluted the voting strength of blacks. Associate Justice Potter Stewart argued in this case that the Fifteenth Amendment did not include the "right to have black candidates elected."

Simultaneously, a wave of random racist attacks against civil right leaders, community organizers, and Third World citizens swept the country after the mid-1970s. After the 1980 shooting of Urban League head Vernon Jordan and the brutal murders of black males in Buffalo and Atlanta in 1980–1981, many blacks concluded that a pattern of racial genocide existed.

Fears of a new type of American authoritarianism—or in Bertram Gross' terms, "friendly fascism"—assumed a concrete form in August 1982 when new and dangerous CIA guidelines for covert operations inside the US were approved by Attorney General William French Smith. Last December, President Reagan issued Executive Order 12333, which calls for sweeping "police state–type" authority for the FBI. In 1983, Smith announced a plan to implement Executive Order 12333 which would target all groups advocating "political or social change through the use of violence." Reagan's and Smith's idea of a "dangerous, violent person" came close to being anyone who opposed the Reagan military budget, who favored peace over nuclear war, or who was opposed to racism. As journalist Nat Hentoff observed, the FBI "will now be able to investigate persons or groups advocating criminal activity," as well as those who are actually conspiring to carry out specific acts. The FBI will "clip and file articles, letters to the editor and ads" of anyone they consider suspicious. Undercover agents can infiltrate any group, from a black neighborhood group concerned about police brutality to a coalition opposing the nuclear arms race. The FBI's budget for fiscal 1984 exceeded $1 billion. And some liberal members of Congress were too frightened of the agency to halt the drive toward legal terrorism. As California Representative Donald Edwards stated, "The FBI is more powerful than we are when there's something it wants."

Against this background of political conservatism and racist violence, the Reagan administration attempted to solidify and institutionalize right wing dogma as official state policy. In two and one half years, Reagan purged the US Commission on Civil Rights of his critics; ordered the Office of Federal Contracts Compliance Programs to halt enforcement activities; severely reduced the legal activities of the Civil Right Division of the Justice Department; passed reactionary budgets which purged millions of poor, African-American, and Latino families from public welfare; seriously reduced food stamps and public health care benefits; and stopped construction on new public housing units.

Politically, the Black Movement was thus confronted with a qualitatively new and dangerous situation. Reformers had become accustomed to making appeals to the executive branch of government to enforce civil rights policy; now lifelong reactionaries were ensconced in the Office for Federal Contracts Compliance Programs and the Justice Department's Civil Rights Division. Civil rights leaders and members of the Congressional Black Caucus (CBC) were aware that they had to find allies to halt the Reagan program and that, more than ever before, the social economic agenda for black reforms had to reestablish definable linkages with concomitant progressive forces—the women's movement, the nuclear freeze campaign, environmentalists, and liberals from organized labor. Initially, this effort to build programmatic linkages took the form of the CBC "Alternative Budget" of May 1982, which called for massive cuts of both conventional and nuclear weapons expenditures and restorations of federal funds for human needs. The bill was trounced in the Democratic controlled House by a vote of 86 yes, 322 no, and 24 not voting.

The left wing of the CBC advanced even more progressive proposals. Ronald V. Dellums introduced an alternative Appropriations Bill (HR-6696) which would have reduced by more than $50 billion the Reagan war budget. HR-6696 was also crushed in the House, receiving only 55 votes in favor. Several months later, Brooklyn Representative Major R. Owens introduced a constitutional amendment which "guarantees" the "right to employment" for "each person in the United States." What is striking about Owens' amendment was its "transitional" character. That is, it could not be achieved without a fundamental transformation of the capitalist political economy, yet it was at face value a "reasonable" legal demand which had the potential of winning majoritarian support among black, Latino, and white voters. Strategically, Owens, Dellums, John Conyers, and other black progressive elected officials increasingly used their positions in the state apparatus to link the issue of employment, the necessity for defense spending cuts, US nonintervention in Central America, and for greater civil rights advances. In short, the CBC called for "jobs," "peace," and "freedom."

When Lowery and Coretta King decided independently in mid-1982 to issue a call for another March on Washington, the "agenda" of the new mobilization had essentially been set by these major social forces, and by the realization common to black reformers that the key to defeat Reaganism, racism, and economic reaction was through the creation of the broadest possible front of Third World, liberal, moderate, and progressive constituencies. Programmatically, the linkage of "jobs, peace, and freedom" was the axis around which such a front could be organized.

National Minority–Labor Unity

What comes next? Ideally, a permanent popular front, an anticorporate bloc of these social forces organized to fight racist violence, Reaganomics, and nuclear arms proliferation must emerge. The basis of such an ongoing coalition must begin from a principled unity between those groups most affected by Reaganism. A prime example would be national minorities and labor.

The experience of the August 27th March illustrates that such unity is possible. Early this year, AFL-CIO leader Lane Kirkland attempted to force the March organizers to drop the "peace" demand from their agenda, without success. Subsequently the labor leader, in a cynical maneuver, called for the unions to place their energies into local Labor Day marches, one week after August 27. This not-so-subtle attempt by the Cold Warriors of labor was largely ignored by progressive and centrist elements within the unions.

Representatives of labor on the March's National Planning Council included Howard Samuel, President of the Industrial Union Department, AFL-CIO; Willie Felder of the United Auto Workers; Robert White, President of the National Alliance of Postal and Federal Employees; and Cleveland Robinson, Vice President of the Coalition of Black Trade Unionists. Locally, union activists and leaders independently took the initiative to build toward August 27. On June 13, a major press conference for Coretta King was staged at the New York headquarters of District 65, UAW. Also attending the gathering were leaders of District 1199 of the hospital workers union; DC 37, the American Federation of State, County, and Municipal Employees; and the Amalgamated Clothing and Textile Workers. Henry Nicholas, the President of 1199—National Union of Hospital and Health

Care Employees, donated $10,000 to the March, and pledged that his union would "charter and fill 150 buses." The union also promised to appoint staff in fifteen cities to assist the campaign.

By the end of June, progressive unionists were actively building support for the March at the grassroots level. One of hundreds of examples was the individual action of Earl Keihl, District 4 Director of the United Furniture Workers of America. The York, Pennsylvania, labor leader sent leaflets for plant bulletin boards, urging members to sign up for buses and carpools. Keihl stated: "The struggle for JOBS requires little explanation. There are millions of workers who through no fault of their own, have been thrown out on the street. . . . The fight for PEACE is the ultimate struggle, for without peace, we will continue to suffer the social cuts and finally, we will perish in nuclear ashes. . . . The fight for FREEDOM is as necessary today, if not more so than it was 20 years ago. Black unemployment is more than twice that of whites."

The Communication Workers of America endorsed the March at its June convention in Los Angeles; the General Executive Board of the United Electrical Workers (UE) called for "the biggest possible UE participation in the march." Leon Lynch, Vice President for Human Affairs for the United Steelworkers of America, also urged members to participate. Lynch stated in a widely distributed memo: "We are still in search of a discrimination-free society. Now more than ever we need jobs. The callous policies of the Reagan Administration have had a devastating impact on workers, minorities and poor people."

On the day of the March, organized labor had generated more buses than all of the civil rights groups combined; at least one third of the participants came in labor groups. The recent actions of labor indicate that the basis for independent, progressive, and antiracist policies exists within the working class. The hard task of political organizers is to develop a mechanism of accountability which can direct the electoral and grassroots political activities of these constituencies. The immediate goal is to defeat the Reaganites in both political parties. But over the long term, we must create an apparatus for power appropriate to the unique social and political terrain of this country. Perhaps, in retrospect, the latest March on Washington will have assisted in this larger and much more ambitious project.

ON NOVEMBER 2ⁿᵈ THE WORLD WILL CHANGE... **But How?**

DEMOCRACY NOW!

INDEPENDENT UNEMBEDDED NEWS
RADIO • TV • INTERNET

STAKES ARE HIGH IN 2004. November's elections are widely viewed as some of the most important in the history of US politics.

In these critical times, we need independent media more than ever. Tune in to the show that dares to ask the questions the corporate media won't.

THE EXCEPTION TO THE RULERS.

KGNU 1390 AM 88.5 FM | **Denver** Community TV Ch. 57, 59

7-8 am M-F

www.democracynow.org

The Paradox
of Black Reform

Since 1964, the number of black elected officials in the US has increased from 104 to about 5,500. Major Southern cities—Atlanta, New Orleans, Birmingham—which vigorously maintained Jim Crow have had black mayors for years. In the decade between 1960 and 1970, the estimated percentage of blacks in the total number of registered voters soared: in Alabama, from 7.1 to 19.2 percent; in South Carolina, from 10.7 to 24.5 percent; in Mississippi, from less than 1 percent to 30.5 percent. The black electorate is such a decisive factor in state and local elections that even former arch-segregationist George C. Wallace aggressively courted black voters in his successful 1982 gubernatorial campaign in Alabama. Socially, racial segregation still exists, but its crudest manifestations have largely disappeared.

The basic and bitter irony is that the structural or institutional basis for racism remains, and in some respects has become worse in recent years. Thousands of black-owned small farms go bankrupt every year across the South, as the rural poor flock to urban areas of employment. Despite the growth of new industries and human service–oriented businesses, black joblessness rates in many Southern towns now rival those in Harlem and Chicago's South Side. Politically, dozens of black elected officials, such as former Tchula, Mississippi, Mayor Eddie Carthan, are the victims of harassment and legal indictment. The number of blacks imprisoned in Southern penitentiaries has increased dramatically and almost 1 million of the region's 14.5 million blacks are arrested every year. Local patterns of political repression and extralegal racist violence are reinforced by the Reagan administration's vocal opposition to civil rights.

Thus the root causes of racial discrimination, poverty, and unemployment, remain permanently in place, while the illusion of black equality is perpetuated within the public discourse. Qualitatively, the paradox of reform confronts the Black Freedom Movement with new political and economic challenges for which the rhetoric and tactics of the "We Shall Overcome" period are inadequate.

The acceleration of systematic attacks against blacks has produced a variety of suggestions for the future of black political activism. In general, black political debate in the 1980s is characterized by its focus on three theoretical and strategic points.

First, what future directions should black economic policy take, for the South and the nation? It is premature to discuss a democratic socialist option, or is a "neo–Booker T. Washington" approach of black capitalism more appropriate in the age of Reaganomics?

Second, how can we best relate our concerns about ethnicity and social organization to public policy? Is a black nationalist approach, which eschews biracial coalitions, meaningless in a post–civil rights period?

Third, these two concerns merge into an infinitely more complex set of questions about the utility of electoral politics itself. Is there an "electoral road" to black liberation in the United States? Can a strategy based within the liberal wing of the Democratic Party successfully consolidate the civil rights gains of the '60s, and provide the basis for a more radical socioeconomic agenda for the future? Or, to restate a question Malcolm X posed in a Detroit speech in April 1964: Is there really a choice between "the ballot or the bullet" in the struggle for black freedom?

Owen Brooks, the Director of the Delta Ministry of Greenville, Mississippi, represents one current of black contemporary protest thought. A veteran of the 1966 Meredith March, Brooks has organized black poor and working class people in the impoverished Delta counties for almost two decades. Brooks's basic political position can be characterized as "radical" (i.e., anti-corporate), "black nationalist," and "nonelectoral." Since his involvement in the 1948 presidential campaign of Henry Wallace, Brooks has been a critic of corporate capitalism. With the economic recession of 1982–83, he predicted, "More whites will fall from the upper echelons of society into the ranks of the poor; as will many more middle-class blacks." Brooks suggests, however, that the bulk of white society will not support any fundamental change in the capitalist political economy. Therefore blacks must create their own self-sustained economic institutions which will generate the means of group subsistence. Staunchly critical of desegregation's effects, he argues that biracial coalitions are not possible over the long run within a racist culture and society.

Brooks bluntly condemns the notion of an electoral road to black liberation. "Our people get dragged into a series of disappointments via electoral politics," Brooks protests. "There are two schools of thought" on black political change. "One is that you can change the system from the inside . . . that you have to elect a pretty, three-piece-suit nigger with four years of schooling, and get him inside." Brooks complains, however, that this tactic always fails "because there is no mechanism within the black community that he is accountable to. We don't have the time and resources within the black community to engage in fruitless kinds of political endeavors."

When asked for an alternative approach, Brooks predicts that "black people are going to vote in ever diminishing numbers." A non-electoral "black political instrument," he argues, could emerge as an "ongoing, living mechanism that attends to all of the aspects of black life." This nontraditional organization would concentrate on developing consumer and producer cooperatives to house and feed thousands of low-income people and to advance "independent political thought" within the black community.

Predictably, Brooks views any active relationship with the Democratic Party as antithetical to blacks' interests. He argues that black Mississippi "leaders such as Aaron Henry and Charles Evers have used the movement to advance their own political careers. They've led the black community down the wrong road—into the Democratic Party." Ironically, Brooks himself ran unsuccessfully for a seat on Greenville's City Council four years ago. The Delta Ministry's staff participates in voter registration efforts, and repeatedly uses traditional political forums to express the interests of their clients. Even for Brooks, a complete divorce from the electoral system is apparently neither possible nor desirable.

Another political strategy, which draws from a curious mixture of black nationalism, liberal corporatism, and electoral activism, is that of Jesse Jackson, leader of Operation PUSH (People United to Serve Humanity). Like the black nationalists, Jackson accuses the Democratic Party of "taking the black vote for granted," while the Republican Party writes blacks off. "For Democrats," he continues, "race is increasingly becoming a litmus test and the central threat to the viability of the Party."

Instead, Jackson's black nationalistic rhetoric eventually culminates into a two-pronged "assault" on the system. First, he argues, black consumers must unite to force corporate concessions to the fragile black entrepreneurial class. "Corporate economic rape," to use Jackson's term, can be curtailed by forcing "joint trade agreements: between civil rights agencies and big businesses." Typical of Jackson's efforts was the four-year "covenant" signed between Operation PUSH and the Burger King Corporation on April 18, 1983. Worth an estimated $450 million, the food chain, which owns 3,400 restaurants worldwide, promised to increase the number of black employees, upgrade existing minority-owned restaurants, and significantly increase the number of black franchises.

Jackson himself quite candidly admits that the goal of these agreements is not socialism but an integrated private market economy. "Blacks and other minorities in this country need trade, not aid. The way to achieve equality is to allow minorities the opportunity to share in the trade with the whole community—to allow them to partake of the benefits." Jackson does not ask whether several black Horatio Algers and the creation of a select group of black entrepreneurs will provide employment for millions of jobless women and men. Operation PUSH is a sophisticated attempt to reinforce the capitalist spirit among those whom the system has most brutally exploited.

The second and more dramatic aspect of Jackson's effort revolves on the concept of a black presidential campaign. In a strategy similar to his corporate covenants, the self-proclaimed "Country Preacher" is currently attempting to revive black hopes in the Democratic Party through a "semi-revolt." Jackson asserts that a black candidate would be able to "advance the issues of concern to Hispanics, women, the poor, and whites who are interested in social justice . . . as well as blacks. A black should run because bargainers without bases are beggars not brokers. . . . We cannot ride to freedom in Pharaoh's chariot. . . . All of Santa's other reindeer have had their chance to pull and lead the sleigh and present their gifts to the American people. Now it may be time for Rudolph, who has consistently pulled more weight, to have his turn." In short, Jackson suggests that blacks' issues cannot be "put in the stomach of any of the present Trojan horses and expect them to come out once they are inside the White House fence."

More concretely, Jackson's purpose is to maximize black voter leverage within the Democratic Party, and simultaneously establish Operation PUSH as the pre-eminent civil rights agency in the nation. The principal focus of this strategy is based in the South. In May 1983, at Jackson's request, the North Carolina Black Leadership Caucus invited him to the state to initiate a "Southern crusade." The announced goals of the crusade are "to focus on the lack of enforcement of the 1965 Voting Rights Act," to register an additional 2 million black Southern voters by November 1984, and "to pressure state party organizations who are accepting integrated voting but practicing segregated slatemaking [by] always putting whites at the top of the ticket." Crusade activists staged local rallies and meetings in Raleigh, Rock Mount, Greensboro, Charlotte, and in other cities.

The black community is currently deeply divided over the viability of Jackson's strategy. Mary F. Berry, a former US Civil Rights Commissioner, argues that the mere threat of a black presidential candidate forces every white aspirant to speak favorably to traditional black concerns. Berry feels that any criticism of Jackson's questionable career is moot, given that none of the "more qualified" black politicians—Julian Bond, Congressman Walter Fauntroy, former Atlanta Mayor Maynard Jackson, and others—had seized the "opportunity" to ride the crest of the black electoral wave so evident in the Chicago and Philadelphia mayoral races in 1983.

Randall Robinson, Director of the influential lobbying group Transafrica, asserts that white Democratic candidates did not address US relations with the South African apartheid regime "until Jesse Jackson began to emerge as a potential candidate." Robinson emphasized the distinction between a "black presidential option" for 1984 and the particular merits and/or contradictions inherent in Jackson's own candidacy.

Even black nationalists who have traditionally stood outside of electoral politics voice support for this aspect of Jackson's strategy. Maulana Karenga, founder of the "Kwanzaa" celebration and a leading black nationalist theorist, states that an independent challenge inside the Democratic Party is absolutely essential. "The political timidity of the Democratic Party in the face of the Rightist tendency in the US makes it imperative that blacks play their traditional role of raising the radical and progressive banner around which others can rally," Karenga argues. Only a black candidate "can produce a spirit of mobilization and organizational formations which can be used after the campaign in other projects." Jackson's campaign will "increase voter registration levels," despite the fact that "one should have no illusions of a black candidate winning."

Karenga's analysis is reinforced by the views of a black former aide to George Bush, Thaddeus Garret. The White House is convinced that Jackson's campaign would weaken former Vice President Walter Mondale's chances of winning the nomination, thus giving the Democratic Party's mantle to conservative Senator John Glenn. Garret claims that Reagan's advisers are convinced that the President can defeat Mondale, but that they would lose against the former astronaut. On the other hand, in late August federal auditors announced that Operation PUSH and a subsidiary misappropriated over $1.7 million in government contracts and ordered Jackson to return the money. Education Secretary T.H. Bell declared in a press conference that this was simply "a routine audit," but added that "the reason there is all this publicity is the Reverend Jesse Jackson is considering running for President."

Similarly, in early 1983, when aides to Congressman Ronald V. Dellums held discussions with several activists concerning a Dellums presidential campaign, the black socialist and his staff were charged with drug use. Perhaps this is merely coincidental, but it is clear that the leaders of both major parties, for different reasons, wish to discourage any black candidacy. As Congressman John Conyers notes, white opposition to the strategy "seeks to head off the democratizing trends of the presidential selection process."

The third, and certainly the most conventional approach to black politics is represented by the NAACP, the agency of the black upper middle class. Joseph Madison, the NAACP Director of voter education, argues that any black presidential candidacy would be "a hoax" that would drain black

support away from liberal white candidates—particularly Mondale. "Anyone with any deal of sense knows that the chance of a black being elected—
we're not talking about running, but being elected—is extremely remote."

Madison outlines the problem by pointing to figures indicating that a
maximum of 778 delegates out of more than 3,900 to the Democratic National Convention in 1984 will be African-Americans. Over two-thirds of
these black delegates will already be pledged to white candidates, "meaning
that the maximum of delegate votes that a black candidate should depend
on would be 250." Madison simply recommends that civil rights groups
concentrate on registering an additional 7 million voters by November
1984—enough to shift the balance of power significantly in a national election. Implicit in this approach to black politics is the assumption that a
black presidential candidate could not obtain enough support among other
constituencies—feminists, liberals, progressive labor unions, Latinos, and
the Left—to win. It defines "politics" in purely electoral terms, despite the
fact that many of the meaningful gains registered by the desegregation
movement two decades ago occurred in the streets, through nonviolent
demonstrations, marches, pickets, and other protest actions. It also implies
a type of "proxy" politics, wherein blacks' interests would have to be represented by white politicians.

What is particularly striking about all of these strategies is their profound pessimism. Brooks and other radical black nationalists assume that
most whites are irredeemably racist, that authoritarian or conservative politics will define the social terrain for some time to come, and that the electoral apparatus is alien to blacks' interests. Jackson's challenge to the Democratic Party's leadership has not yet advanced a program of radical
social reform which qualitatively departs from that articulated by his un-
charismatic white counterparts, the "Sominex Seven." The NAACP's bland
emphasis on voter registration implies an acceptance of the liberal status
quo, a resignation about serving as a loyal component of a fragmented
New Deal/Great Society coalition which is increasingly irrelevant to the
1980s.

Each of the positions is a reaction to the contemporary crisis, rather than
a qualitative advance in strategy. In any effort to find political answers in
this period of rapid and confusing social change, we must first ask the right
questions. Where should we begin?

The first and most essential question in understanding the paradox of reform concerns the contradictory nature of the Democratic Party and its relationship to black people. During most of the electoral experience of
blacks, the party which claimed our allegiance was the Republican Party.
Few blacks voted for a Democratic presidential candidate until 1940. More
than 40 percent of all black voters supported Dwight Eisenhower in 1956.
Democratic Party officials and officeholders worked hand in hand with

white vigilantes when I was a teenager to keep my family members from voting. White Mississippi Democrats did virtually nothing to elect a black state senator, Robert Clark, to the House of Representatives in November 1982, despite blacks' support for their old arch-enemy, John Stennis. Unquestionably, the Democratic Party contains some of the most racist, pro-corporate, and sexist politicians this nation can produce. Yet this same party includes a progressive, antiracist, and democratic bloc which represents an American version of "social democracy."

This "party-within-the-party" articulates the material interests and political demands of blacks, as well as those of Latinos, feminists, gays and lesbians, labor, and peace organizations. Because no massive socialist presence in the US national politics has existed since 1920, most black elected officials are "invisible social democrats," for all practical purposes. They do not consciously identify with European social democracy, and their own history is grounded in a pragmatic and often eclectic practice which is devoid of socialist, much less Marxian, theory. Nevertheless, the public policies they propose—from Dellums's extensive national health care bill to Major Owens's extensive national health care bill to Major Owens's recent constitutional amendment calling for a guaranteed job for all American workers—directly parallel legislative reforms enacted by labor and socialist parties throughout the world.

Of course, distinctions must be made here: Dellums in the British political context would be Tony Benn, and Andrew Young would be Roy Jenkins—but they are acting in the very real world of American political culture, where Marxism is usually equated with Soviet or Chinese communism. The democratic Left inside the black community does not need specifically to identify itself with "socialism" per se to exercise influence among black voters. Most blacks run as Democrats because, given the history of black folk since the New Deal, it makes "common sense" to do so. They operate as a democratic and antiracist political current within an admittedly undemocratic and often racist political formation. But when circumstances dictate that the interests of blacks will be better served by a third-party candidate, an independent, or even a liberal Republican, black voters and their representatives often revolt against their party.

Numerous incidents from the past several years illustrate this pattern of revolt. In a Mississippi election in 1978, for example, over 80 percent of the state's black electorate voted for an independent black candidate, Charles Evers, for the US Senate, splitting the Democratic vote. As a result, a white conservative Republican, Thad Cochran, was elected. Black voters had concluded that there was no meaningful difference between the two candidates, and that an unsuccessful black challenge in the general election would do more to advance their interests in the long run than their becoming "yellow dog Democrats" in this particular election. This is not to suggest that the majority of black voters is ready to form either an all-black or a multiracial liberal-Left political party; the avenues for meaningful reform within the existing two-party system have not yet been exhausted.

It is clear, however, that the actual political behavior of black workers and the poor in general implies a far greater sophistication than that exhibited by the NAACP leadership and others who cling to the idealistic notion that loyalty to white Democratic Party leaders transcends black electoral independence. When properly mobilized, the black electorate will turn out in massive numbers to support any candidates who advance their economic, social, and political interests, and will block those Democrats and Republicans alike who betray those interests.

Given the actual class status of blacks as a group, this independence means in practice that blacks form a decisive bloc for a uniquely American version of social democracy—without being called "socialism" by name. Moreover, for most black workers, voting is and will remain for the foreseeable future the central essence of "politics." Despite the chimeras of black nationalism, the hard-won democratic rights of blacks are deeply cherished within the African-American community, and the battle against Reaganism and institutional racism will continue to manifest itself as essentially a struggle within the existing political system. The fight for democracy thus becomes a battle against the racists and conservatives of both major parties.

We are now witnessing a fundamental and long overdue shift in the American political system. There have been others. The 1896 election contest between William Jennings Bryan and William McKinley established the Republicans as the dominant party for the next 35 years, buried Southern and Western populism, and created the basis for the solid Democratic South and Jim Crow. The elections of 1932 and 1936 created the New Deal coalition, which in turn coincided with the long and difficult process of creating a black voice in national public policy.

Despite initial appearances, 1980 was no watershed electoral year (though 1984 may well be). Nevertheless, there were some interesting and perhaps ominous developments in the Carter-Reagan race. Over 90 percent of all black voters supported Carter, while only 35 *percent* of all whites supported him. Fifty-six percent of all whites voted in proportions of nearly two to one for the California Republican. Beyond the election of 1984, if the current mobilization of black voter registration continues, the weight of the black electorate will have a major position in the viability of the Democratic Party, and within the public policies of the national government. The black voter will be the central component in transcending the limitations of New Deal liberalism.

To resolve the paradox of reform, black political activists (and progressive whites) must advance an "inside-outside" strategy for social reform.

We must actively campaign for those progressives advocating programs which go beyond the old liberalism, both inside the Democratic Party primaries (against Democratic centrists and conservatives) and in general elections (against most Republicans). We must build a powerful, multiracial coalition of labor, women, and other potential allies *inside* the progressive party-in-the-party. Yet we cannot transform the system by working on the inside alone. *Outside* challenges must raise the issues of racism, sexism, poverty, and powerlessness and must occur simultaneously with electoral work—teach-ins, demonstrations, neighborhood organizing, civil disobedience, and every form of nonelectoral protest. Both aspects of inside-outside work should be guided by a vision of human equality and greater democracy—guaranteed health care, full employment, universal education, decent public housing, workplace democracy, a non-sexist and antiracist society— along with massive reductions in national spending for the mechanisms of war, foreign intervention, and US corporate domination of the Third World.

Much of the viability of the "inside-outside" theory rests with the Left's ability to maximize voter turnouts at every election and to expand the national electorate through extensive voter registration and education campaigns. Poor people and national minorities often do not vote because they cannot see that it will produce any meaningful changes in their lives or in their communities. In Chicago, for example, black voter turnouts in South Side wards ranged from 40 to 22 percent until the late 1970s. Every political observer in Chicago knew that former Congressman Harold Washington did not want to run in the mayoral election as of mid-1982. What convinced Washington to run was the registration of an additional 150,000 black and Hispanic voters. Their mobilization, culminating in a nearly 80 percent turnout in the elections, shifted both Washington's campaign and the dynamics of Chicago politics to the left.

Conversely, any decline in grassroots mobilization creates the possibility of a restoration of conservative power. Fifteen years ago, Carl Stokes was elected mayor of Cleveland on the basis of an 81.7 percent black voter turnout. When Stokes betrayed his constituents' program, confidence in electoral political work declined, neighborhood groups began to bicker with each other, and finally a white Republican was elected mayor in 1971. By 1978, black voter turnouts in Cleveland had dropped to 30.8 percent.

The examples of Chicago and Cleveland indicate that black activists and the Left should create independent political structures which can do three things: educate the oppressed to constantly demand their rights, promote massive electoral participation, and maintain pressure on elected officials to carry out progressive programs. Independent grassroots structures must never be tied to the Democratic Party, but they can use the party's primary process to get their agendas into the public discourse, and to elect their own people. Occasionally, independent races for elective office will be viable at local levels outside of the Democratic Party. The question of working "within" the Democratic Party is fundamentally a tactical one; our principles will not be compromised by such activity so long as the goal of human equality and social transformation guides our practice, and our programs articulate the interests of the oppressed.

The year 1984 confronts the democratic Left with a series of problems. Much of the focus will be placed on the presidential arena. Despite a black candidacy—which despite its flaws merits at least critical support—in November 1984 we will be faced with a choice between Reagan and Mondale or Glenn. It's certain that the overwhelming majority of black people will repudiate Reaganism, and that any third party candidacy will be viewed as irrelevant or sectarian. Thus the energies of activists must be focused at the municipal and state level, building wherever possible upon the "Coalition of Conscience" constituencies which were mobilized by the August 1983 March on Washington. Independent candidates must be run in non-partisan races, in Democratic Party primaries, and/or occasionally outside both parties, depending primarily upon local conditions and the prior establishment of progressive political structures and multiracial/multiclass coalitions. Sometimes we will have no alternative except to embrace the "lesser evil." The classic case here is provided by North Carolina, where Governor James B. Hunt is undeniably a poor alternative, but Helms's pivotal role as the leading national ideologue for racism and reaction may well induce progressives to support Hunt. This must not rule out, however, a progressive challenge against Hunt inside the Democratic Party's primary.

Our ability to overturn the historical limitations of our political consciousness and assert our optimism in the capacity of blacks, poor people, women, and labor to mobilize themselves—both within the electoral system and outside of it—may determine the future course of American politics and society. Our capacity to transcend the structural limits of reform depends in part upon our active intervention inside the system. Our opportunity to create a unique American form of democratic socialism and the basis for human equality rests with our efforts both to challenge and to transform the Democratic Party and also to create a permanent grassroots protest movement divorced from electoral politics.

4

Harold Washington and the Politics of Race in Chicago

When Sékou Touré and the Guinean people were offered membership within a French commonwealth in lieu of complete independence in 1958, 95 percent of the population voted, "No." Toure's famous challenge to Charles de Gaulle was, "We prefer poverty in freedom to riches in slavery." France responded by withdrawing all its personnel, equipment, and facilities from Guinea. Even the telephones were "pulled out of the walls and taken away to France."

A quarter century later, in another political confrontation highly charged by white racism, the overwhelming majority of Chicago's black population rejected its domination by the corrupt Democratic Party Machine and elected Harold Washington mayor of the city. Washington's reform administration was immediately confronted with a $121 million long-term deficit left by defeated Democratic Mayor Jane Byrne, as well as gross bureaucratic inefficiency and corruption.

But most striking to the new mayor was the petty vindictiveness of the old regime. On the first morning in the mayor's office, Washington discovered that virtually all crucial administrative files had vanished. Other items which also had disappeared included a "television, typewriters, and Oriental rug and a complete video camera setup." The only item left in the white former mayor's desk drawer was one paper clip.

It is not an exaggeration to draw political parallels between Harold Washington and the first generation of African nationalists who achieved independence, frequently through the mass mobilizations of African peasants and workers against the racist and colonial-capitalist states imposed

49

upon them. Since 1910, black Chicagoans were controlled by corrupt political machines—first the Republican organization of William Hale Thompson, and subsequently the Democratic organization of Edward J. Kelly and
Richard Daley.

Legacy of White Domination

The long-term oppressive legacy of this domination is outlined in the
Chicago Urban League's recent socio-economic survey of black Chicago.
Comparing all US urban areas with populations above 2.5 million, the report affirms that social and economic "disparities between blacks and
whites are far greater in Chicago than in any other major metropolitan area
in this country." Chicago's black population ranks lowest in median family
income, the labor force participation rate, and the percentage of persons
below the poverty level. It was also a close second from the bottom in the
percent of adult high school graduates, and owner-occupied housing statistics.

Breaking out of a two generation–long pattern of electoral apathy and
repression, 73 percent of all African-American voters turned out on April
12, 1983, giving Congressman Harold Washington over 514,000 votes.
Combined with other key constituencies—79 percent of the Puerto Rican
vote, 68 percent from Mexican-Americans, 52 percent from Cuban-Ameri-
cans, and 38 percent from Jewish voters—Washington obtained a total of
668,176 votes, defeating heretofore obscure Republican candidate Bernard
Epton.

In the next four years, Washington would attempt to reform the city's
Byzantine-style government while providing new initiatives to address
urban poverty, homelessness, public health, police brutality, and other daily
problems largely confined to black and Latino neighborhoods.

Immediately following Washington's dramatic victory, the boss of Cook
County's Democratic Party Machine, Alderman E.R. "Fast Eddie" Vrdolyak, hatched a clever scheme to deprive the mayor of any real authority.
Controlling 29 aldermen out of 50, Vrdolyak changed the City Council's
rules to require a two-thirds majority to take bills away from committees
that refused to act on them and permit the whole council to vote on them.
"Regular" Democrats tied on the Machine were left in powerful committee
chairmanships.

"Bloc of 29" Fights Washington

Despite Washington's initial offers of compromise, the "bloc of 29" did
everything it could to disrupt the normal procedures of government. Washington's administrative appointees were blocked from office; council ses-
sions turned into shouting matches. Vrdolyak even began wearing a new

bullet-proof vest at council meetings. Chicago journalist David Moberg suggests that the "council wars" produced a "two party" system. "Chicago has become like Mississippi in 1964, when the Freedom Democratic Party challenged the segregationist regulars," Moberg notes. The Vrdolyak bloc was essentially a "white Conservative Party . . . that is in practice hostile to blacks and to any reform that lessens its own power."

Superficially, Chicago's council wars appeared to be motivated solely by race. Vrdolyak, a lawyer by profession, first made his mark in the late sixties as leader of an anti-busing organization. During the 1983 contest, Vrdolyak rallied white supporters of the incumbent mayor by race-baiting: "It's a racial thing. Don't kid yourself. . . . We're fighting to keep the city the way it is." But Washington's election did not create a massive white exodus from the city into the suburbs, as some observers predicted. Since the 1970s, the average annual population loss of Chicago whites has declined by nearly one half.

The fundamental issues behind the council wars are patronage and power, not race. Vrdolyak and his allies "are concerned about loss of power and patronage and opportunities to engage in illicit lucrative opportunities," observed Edwin C. Berry, former Director of the Chicago Urban League. "If Harold Washington were as white as the driven snow and he took away those privileges, they would be equally against him."

One prime example was the "personal fiefdom" of Democratic Machine leader Edmund Kelly, who served as superintendent of the Chicago Park District for many years. A 1982 survey of Kelly's agency illustrated that out of "400 top-paid employees, almost 90 percent were white and all were male. With only one quarter the park acreage of New York City's park system, the Chicago Park District had twice as many administrators." Park employees "had no protection against arbitrary firing and demotion and thus were required to do political work to keep their jobs."

Fiscal Reorganization

Any mayor's chief difficulty is managing the budget, finding new sources of revenue, and providing services to core constituents. Washington's task was complicated for three years by his inability to control his own City Council. Moreover, during these years the amount of federal community development funds to the city dropped from $140 million to $85 million in 1985. But Washington believed that most Chicago residents would support additional user fees and taxes, if the budgetary process was honest and aboveboard, and if the financial alternatives were clearly spelled out.

According to Moberg, by late 1983 Washington had moved the city toward collective bargaining with all employees and elimination of inequities that came with the old "handshake" agreements for a few. He introduced new cost controls, efficient management, and personnel cuts in departments that have been patronage havens. He quickly shifted $13.5 million in Federal Community Development Block Grant funds out of administrative salaries and into a variety of neighborhood and service improvements.

The Washington administration initiated a series of new tax hikes: $11.2 million in increased tax for vehicle sticker fees, $17.5 million in water rates, $8 million in the city's sales tax, $10 million tacked on to city parking fees, and an additional $29.1 million from the employer's head tax.

In all, Washington increased all city taxes by $312 million over a three-year period. The city's overall payroll was cut by 3,000 workers. Consequently, Washington was able to reduce the city's long-term debt by $27.5 million. But many efforts to locate additional sources of revenue were blocked by the City Council. Proposals to tax health clubs and boat moorings were tabled by the council's Finance Committee, and a plan for a $79 million commercial lease tax on corporations was also halted in court litigation.

Dismantling the Patronage System

Some of this additional revenue was allocated for garbage collection, gutter-curb repair, and for other street services. About 160 foremen were removed from the Streets and Sanitation Department payroll, and overall expenditures were cut from $257 million in 1982 to $249 million three years later. Garbage truck crews were ordered to shift from four-man to three-man crews, and the number of overtime hours was sharply cut back.

But these austerity moves didn't compromise public sanitation in most areas. In many black neighborhoods, citizens reported cleaner conditions and fewer abandoned automobiles. The pounds of garbage per laborer-hour collected increased from 785 in 1984 to 1,123 in 1986.

In public administration, Washington reduced the number of patronage employees from over 40,000 to barely 800. A lottery was established to select applications for new city jobs. Consequently, the racial hiring pattern of the City of Chicago began to change significantly. In 1981–1982, under Mayor Byrne, 64 percent of all new employees were white, 28 percent were African-Americans, 6 percent were Latinos, 1 percent were Asians, and 26 percent were females. Under Washington's administration in 1985–1986, the overall percentages were: blacks, 55 percent; whites, 30 percent; Hispanics, 12 percent; Asians, 2 percent; and women, 41 percent.

The "bloc of 29" insisted that Washington's new lottery system was actually a "wily form of patronage" which institutionalized reverse discrimination against white victims. Anti-Washington leader Roman Pucinski complained: "[Washington] told his followers to register for these jobs. Once he had a big backlog registered, they had a lottery to select workers. But since they are all his people, they got picked. His worst enemies have to admit he is clever."

Desegregation of Private Sector

One central element of Washington's reform agenda focused on the increased desegregation of Chicago's private sector, and more specifically, the encouragement of local black and Latino entrepreneurship through public sector intervention. The Chicago Urban League estimated that only 0.5 percent of all policy-making positions in white-owned non-financial corporations in the city were held by African-Americans in 1977. In the banking industry, there were only 21 black administrators and policy-making officers (0.7 percent) out of a total of 2,943 positions; in the white-owned insurance companies, there was not a single black executive out of 592 policy-making positions.

During his campaign, Washington pledged to give at least 20 percent of all city contracts to women, black, Latino, and other national minority-owned firms. In 1984, the mayor established a contract review board to check all public bids above $50,000. That year, roughly $64 million in city contracts went to national minorities and women, the largest amount in Chicago's history. Through political pressure, corporations began to make some important concessions. At the United Airlines' $350 million terminal project at O'Hare Airport, for instance, $67 million have been set aside for women and national minority contractors. One $3 million contract has already been given to three black-owned painting firms.

In the area of human services, a mixed record of success and failure emerges. The problems of homeless people and the shortage of decent public housing remain. The Chicago Coalition for the Homeless estimated in 1983 that the number of homeless people and the shortage of decent public housing remain. The problems of decent public housing remain. The Chicago Coalition for the Homeless estimated in 1983 that the number of homeless people in the city was between 12,000 and 25,000. Most are black and Latino males in their 20s and 30s, but a growing number are black women with small children. In 1979 about one dozen homeless people actually froze to death in Chicago's alleys and streets. The Byrne administration authorized $200,000 to aid street people in 1982, but its officials "carefully shied away from assuming wholesale responsibility for the problem."

Housing: Problems and Progress

One contributing factor to homelessness is the destruction of urban residential dwellings in black and Latino neighborhoods. Under Byrne's administration, the city destroyed 16,177 dwelling units, while building only 12,811 units. In 1982, Byrne also reduced the Housing Department's Home Acquisition Program by $2.8 million, despite strong support expressed for it by black, Hispanic, and low-income people. In Washington's initial two years, the city built 9,596 residential units and destroyed 8,131.

Washington's housing staff was reduced by one fourth, but it rehabilitated more than twice the number of homes than under Byrne. The Housing Department also has given emergency grants to nonprofit organizations which are renovating low-income houses. Despite these gains, the projected cutbacks in state and especially federal funding for low- to moderate-income shelter will undermine nearly all of these efforts.

The status of public health programs are similarly mixed. Under Washington, the city's infant mortality rate dropped from 18.6 per 1,000 live births to 16.4. However, this rate is still 55 percent higher than the national average. In several black communities in Chicago, the infant mortality rate was between 24 and 30 deaths per 1,000 live births.

The city has only 37 public health field nurses who make house calls-but, according to minimal federal government guidelines, at least 150 field nurses are needed. Even in the late 1960s, the city employed more than 200 nurses. The Health Department budget has been reduced by inflation, and the number of staff and professional workers has been cut from 2,234 to 1,962. This fiscally strapped department alone runs six large health care centers, numerous small clinics, and serves as "the basic health care provider for 230,000 Chicagoans a year."

Difficulties with Health Care Expenditures

Tragically, some of the scarce health care funds from the federal government have been returned because they were not spent in the required period of time. In fiscal year 1984, $11,792 allocated for the Women, Infants, and Children (WIC) Program was given back to the federal government, approximately 7.2 percent of Chicago's WIC budget for the year. The Maternal Child Health Program, which focuses on infant care, also returned $50,000 in fiscal year 1984. Bureaucratic errors and poor planning were to blame. The *Chicago Reporter* also notes:

> The [Health] Department's inability to comply with federal guidelines also forced it to spend about $500,000 originally intended to hire health personnel on office equipment, accounting reports and furniture. . . . As a result the city missed a chance to spend the money to hire about 70 public health nurses at a time when Chicago faces a critical shortage of nurses.

Washington's administration has been more successful in the area of public safety. During the 1983 campaign, Police Chief Richard J. Brezczek openly supported Byrne. White policemen aggressively worked for Epton and distributed the Republican candidate's literature while on the job. Flyers were circulated warning that "white women will be raped" if "Mr. Baboon" was elected and that the city's Police Department emblem would be changed to "Chicagoans Po-Lease."

The Chicago police force's 11,000 white officers—out of a total corps of 12,500—had a well-deserved reputation for brutality throughout black and Latino communities. For 12 years, police recruits were not even given psychological testing. Officers were ordered to shoot all unarmed suspects involved in crimes against private property. Not surprisingly, police shootings of civilians were commonplace—84 persons were shot by police in 1979.

Public Safety Policies

Washington initiated psychological tests and more strict narcotics checks for all personnel, and pushed for the hiring and promotions of national minorities. By 1986, the Police Department was 21 percent black, 4 percent female, and 8 percent Latino. Similarly, the city's Fire Department's force is 16 percent black and 4 percent Hispanic. Police shootings of civilians declined by more than 60 percent in three years. But many white officers still refuse to accept black supervisors and vigorously undermine official policies. Several months ago, 13 white policemen successfully sued the city for $4.29 million in damages, by claiming that their job transfers constituted reverse discrimination.

Chicago currently spends more than half of its total budget for police and fire protection. Yet the deteriorating social and economic conditions for young people of color continue to create the context for rampant street crime and drug trafficking. About 13,000 Chicago teenagers are "hard core" members of urban gangs, and perhaps another 50,000 or more are peripherally associated with gangs. Murders by street gangs numbered 70 in 1984 and 55 in 1985. Washington allocated $4.2 million to create a new youth anti-violence program, the Crisis Intervention Network.

But despite this latest initiative, youth gang crimes, prostitution, and drug involvement are increasing. Network director Roberto Rivera states: "The underground economy associated with gangs is the distribution of drugs and has led to a lot of violence. The disaster in many of our communities has taken generations to emerge. This is the first administration that admits to having problems with it."

Machine Losses in Ward Elections

The turning point of Washington's first term occurred in early 1986 when a federal court ordered special elections in seven city wards that had been gerrymandered to protect pro-Machine aldermen. The Democratic Machine took three seats to Washington's two seats in the March 18, 1986, election. Two wards, which would determine the control of the City Council, were forced to hold runoff elections on April 29, 1986.

Incumbent Alderman Frank Grady, a "long-time machine stalwart," faced Marlene C. Carter, a black clerical worker and neighborhood leader closely associated with Washington. With the strong support of the mayor, Jesse Jackson, and Congressman Gus Savage, Carter trounced Grady, winning 10,463 votes (65.4 percent) to 5,525 votes (34.6 percent).

More crucial was the hotly contested race in the heavily Latino Twenty-sixth Ward, which matched pro-Machine hack Manuel A. Torres versus progressive Puerto Rican activist Luis Gutierrez. Torres was endorsed by both Byrne and Vrdolyak, and he attempted to smear Gutierrez as an apolitical leftist and radical "bomb-thrower." Such tactics worked against the Machine's favor, as 62 percent of all eligible voters turned out for the runoff election. Gutierrez received 7,429 votes (53.1 percent) versus Torres's 6,549 votes (46.9 percent).

With Gutierrez's election, both the mayor and Vrdolyak each controlled 25 votes on the council. However, the mayor was legally empowered to break all ties. Bitterly, Vrdolyak admitted that Washington now had "achieved his goal in the Council." More candidly, Vrdolyak lieutenant Richard Mell stated: "After tonight Harold Washington is the odds-on favorite for re-election."

Board Appointments by Washington Majority

Washington's fragile majority of "25 plus 1" promptly moved to secure the appointments of 67 nominees to various public boards. Several nominations had been delayed by Vrdolyak since December 1983. A few members of the Machine's bloc recognized the new political situation, and with characteristic opportunism announced to the press their newfound "independence." In July 1986, Park District head Edmund Kelly was forced to resign, and was replaced with Jesse Madison, "one of the first of the city's black political leaders to espouse independence from the Democratic Machine." Madison immediately gave civil service ranking to most of the Park District's 6,000 employees, and ended the policy of political patronage.

Washington secured the appointment of black banker Walter Clark to head the board of the Chicago Transit Authority (CTA). Former CTA boss James Cardilli had been intimately tied to the Machine. Another new CTA board member, disabled rights activist James Charlton, states that Cardilli "hired hundreds of people, mostly in administration but throughout the system, who knew absolutely nothing about what they're supposed to do."

On September 24, Washington pushed his 1986 city budget and a hefty property tax increase through the City Council by a 26–24 margin. Increasingly the mayor dictated the city's legislative and public policy agenda.

The Machine has not given up. It continues to resort to the demagogical politics of race-baiting in its desperate attempts to mobilize the white working class electorate. Vrdolyak has organized a "Save Chicago" task force, which repeatedly charges that the mayor blunts critics by calling them racists. Vrdolyak has described Washington as dishonest, untrustworthy, "dumb and stupid. . . . [He has] never been an effective legislator, and he has great difficulty with basic arithmetic. . . . If he were white, with the same record, how many votes would he have gotten?"

Racial Politics

One of Vrdolyak's aides on the council privately explains the coarse utility of crude racism: "There has always been racial politics in Chicago, but a black has never been in a 'money' position of real power. . . . In the bungalow wards, the wards where people may have already moved once or twice to get away from blacks, you're going to find real racism among people and among their leaders."

Machine politicians deliberately cultivate antiblack and anti-Latino sentiment for their own economic motives as well. Thirteenth ward Alderman John S. Madrzyk, a powerful Vrdolyak supporter, has used his influence inside the council to dezone about 100 businesses in his own ward to a more restrictive zoning category. Many of the small business owners are told that more restrictive zonings will keep "black shoppers and residents out of the predominately white 13th Ward."

But several critics suggests that this strategy is designed to force small business people to provide financial contributions to white politicians. One disgruntled merchant relates: "What this means is that we have to kiss Madrzyk's [behind] if we want to operate in this ward."

Although Vrdolyak has been jailed previously for assault with intent to commit murder (but legally cleared), he and his closest associates are careful not to embrace racial vigilantism. Vrdolyak has "learned how far he could go, and he learned not to step over the line into anything that would lead to prosecution." Instead, the Machine's rhetoric creates a local political culture of bigotry which provokes others to engage in racially motivated random violence.

Racial Violence

Since 1983, there have been a series of racist firebombings, assaults, and murders in Chicago's suburbs and mostly white urban neighborhoods. Klansmen worked for several of the Machine's candidates in the March 1986 special ward elections. On June 28, 1986, the Ku Klux Klan held a "White Pride Rally" at Marquette Park, which initially attracted between

300 and 500 white residents. When a small number of black and progressive white counter-demonstrators led by the International Committee Against Racism attempted to march into the park, several hundred whites physically attacked them, and while shouting taunts, pushed them out of the neighborhood. Several police officers were injured trying to protect black marchers. After the confrontation, nearly 1,000 enthusiastic whites, mostly young men, came out to join the racist rally.

In subsequent weeks, other less publicized incidents occurred. In Dolton, a white mob verbally assaulted and stoned a black marching corps during a July 4 parade; in the white suburb of Lynwood, a black family found racist graffiti defacing their home; another black household was firebombed. These random acts of terror are not committed or planned by the Democratic Machine, but they serve its purposes. If working class and poor whites can be manipulated to attack blacks and Latinos, a mass anti-Washington coalition may be built.

Washington Electoral Coalition

The Washington electoral coalition of 1983 drew its deepest strength from black civic reformists, black nationalists, and labor unions. Along with these core constituencies, Washington's candidacy was also favored by most black entrepreneurs, a majority of progressive Latino activists, and a minority of black clergy and white liberals. Each group embraced Harold Washington for different reasons.

The mayor's current staff and key advisors reflect this social class and ideological diversity. The "Mayor's Policy Advisory Cabinet," the top administrative body, includes 10 blacks, one Latino, and five whites. Four black women serve as senior lieutenants: Jacqueline Grimshaw, political strategist for intergovernmental affairs; Lucille Dobbins, a former banker who represents the mayor's interests in the Law, Personnel, and Budget Departments; Sharon Gist Gilliam, who directs the city's $2 billion budget; and Brenda J. Gaines, who serves as deputy chief of staff.

Some of Washington's top advisors come directly from civil rights organizations and community organizing; several have Black Power–era backgrounds. These include Al Raby, former desegregation leader who currently directs the Human Relations Commission, and Reault Robinson, former leader of the African-American Police League, who now chairs the Chicago Housing Authority. Other advisors, especially those in Washington's unofficial kitchen cabinet, are drawn largely from the private sector, such as Cadillac dealer Al Johnson, banker Jacoby Dickens, hair-product makers Edward Gardner and George Johnson, and publicist June Rosner.

As a result, depending upon the particular issue, the Washington administration may take a variety of policy positions which are not always in harmony with the objective interests of low-income black and Latino voters.

These internal conflicts generally have not surfaced, in part due to the Democratic Machine's fierce opposition. A makeshift political solidarity is imposed on most of the anti-racist and democratic reform forces. Black criticism of the Washington administration, even when it is deserved, is also somewhat muted precisely because no one wishes to aid Vrdolyak indirectly.

Electoral Politics: Democratic or Independent?

A number of Washington's nationalist-oriented followers would favor a clean break with the Democratic Party, lock, stock, and barrel. The creation of a black electoral political party would give the mayor an alternative if he wanted to seek office outside of the Democrats' ranks. Black journalist and community leader Lu Palmer states: "Many of us feel that there is little difference between the Democratic and Republican parties. Neither has demonstrated an interest in solving the problems of the black community." Other endorsers of an independent black electoral slate include pro-Washington Alderman Danny Davis, Alderwoman Marlene Carter, and State Senator Emil Jones.

More moderate supporters of Washington have consistently urged him to follow the strategy of Detroit Mayor Coleman Young by collaborating with the national Democratic Party's hierarchy. Thus in mid-1983, Washington publicly denounced the prospective presidential candidacy of Jesse Jackson, warning: "We do not have the luxury to be in any campaign behind a black candidate who can't win and re-elect Ronald Reagan." After Vrdolyak endorsed Democratic leader Walter Mondale for the presidency, however, Washington gave his unofficial support to Jackson. But in the summer of 1986, when the Reverend Charles Koen, an Illinois civil rights activist and former President of the National Association of Neighborhoods, attempted to organize a statewide black party for the elections, Washington did virtually nothing.

Dissension in Washington's ranks also was displayed over the issue of apartheid divestment. As of 1985, the City of Chicago held investments in numerous banks and financial institutions which did business with South Africa or through apartheid-linked subsidiaries: First Chicago Corporation, Drexel Burnham Lamb, Bache, Citicorp, Kleinworth, Continental Illinois Bank, Dean Witter, Merrill Lynch, Unibank, as well as others. The Chicago Teacher's Retirement System had invested $623 million in South Africa–related companies, 30 percent of its total assets.

Controversy over Divestment Bill

Alderman Danny Davis introduced strict divestment legislation into the City Council in March 1985. Davis's original proposal included a total ban on the investment of public money inside South Africa; the divestiture of public funds from "any bank, savings and loan association, investment house or corporation doing business with South Africa"; the prohibition of "new or renewed city contracts with companies doing business with South Africa"; and a total ban on any city contracts with apartheid-linked firms.

Black local businessmen quickly caucused with Washington and warned that if Davis's ordinance was approved, many large companies would no longer be permitted to do business with the city. Several of these firms, most prominently Matra and Westinghouse, had already promised to give substantial subcontracts to black entrepreneurs in the O'Hare Airport project.

Prexy Nesbitt, a leader of the Coalition for Illinois Divestment from South Africa, was informed by administration officials that "the bill was such that it could not be signed by the mayor because it was too strong." Davis was pressured to submit a "softer" version of his bill, which would protect the subcontracts of minority entrepreneurs. As Nesbitt later related, "There are black business interests in Chicago . . . [that believe] if you divest, some of the crumbs from city contracts will be lost."

Inside every electoral coalition, ethnic, ideological, and social class tensions exist which may escalate into permanent political schisms. In the last campaign, Washington made several political overtures to the white lesbian and gay community. However, they generally supported Byrne in the Democratic primary. Since then, Washington has become more responsive to gay issues, and has taken a more aggressive stand against homophobia. In late June 1986, the mayor and over 30,000 Chicagoans attended the city's "Gay-Lesbian Pride Parade" on the north side. But some of Washington's black and Latino supporters, especially those who have yet to come to terms with their own homophobia, undoubtedly question this alliance.

Relations Between Blacks and Latinos

Another potential issue is the political relations between blacks and the Latino community. The only Latino inside the Mayor's Policy Advisory Cabinet, Benjamin Reyes, directed the successful Twenty-sixth Ward campaign. However, "there is no Hispanic in his kitchen cabinet," notes Armando Triana, Director of the Center for Research on Hispanics at De Paul University. "He listens to some things we say, but not enough."

As of the 1980 Census, there were 310,400 Mexican-Americans and 116,600 Puerto Ricans residing in Chicago. The Puerto Rican family median household annual income, $1,959, was more then $300 *lower* than that for the median black family. Thirty-two percent of all Puerto Rican households and 18 percent of all Mexican-American households in Chicago are below the federal poverty level. Black leaders and administrators who seriously intend to build local Rainbow Coalitions must extend a much greater role to Latinos at all policy-making levels and address the special concerns of their community. Neither Washington nor any other black mayoral candidate can ever win without active Latino support.

Not even Washington's staunchest supporters would claim that his administration has made no mistakes. But something fundamental separates a Harold Washington from many other black mayors, who are often manipulated to blunt the potential political militancy of the African-American community—Philadelphia's Wilson Goode is a notable example. Washington is the culmination of a rich black reform tradition in Chicago, which can be traced through Ida B. Wells, Earl Dickerson, and Jesse Jackson. His re-election campaign should be a democratic protest movement of oppressed national minority groups and exploited social classes. Undoubtedly, it will be dominated by the liberal and progressive petty bourgeoisie; it will make mistakes, errors, and blunders; yet standing on the broad shoulders of the 1983 victory, it has the potential to attain greater heights.

Black Conservatives

1990

The ideas that have catapulted black neoconservative Shelby Steele to prominence are nothing new. The San Jose State University English professor has made the highly publicized argument that affirmative action hurts black people. The media and many whites—both conservative and liberal—have seized on Steele as if he were cracking a monolith of African-American thought. But throughout the twentieth century, the system has frequently relied on black conservative politicians and intellectuals to justify patterns of race and class inequality.

A century ago, black educator Booker T. Washington called for "separate but equal" race relations throughout the South, justifying political disfranchisement and segregated public accommodations. Washington was intensely popular among northern capitalists and Republicans because he urged blacks to work as strikebreakers undermining labor unions, and he urged African-Americans not to agitate publicly for civil rights.

During the civil rights movement of the 1960s there were conservative blacks who attempted to undermine Martin Luther King, Jr. and the struggle against racism. Some were privately financed by white conservatives; others genuinely believed that social change should occur through gradual reform efforts in established channels, rather than through civil disobedience or economic boycotts.

Corporate America has always recognized political and class diversity within the African-American community, especially the tendency of the black petty bourgeoisie to support policies that promoted capital formation and ownership. At the 1968 Black Power Conference in Philadelphia, for example, the head of the Clairol corporation endorsed the gathering, declaring that the demand for Black Power really meant "equity, empowerment . . . the ownership of apartments, ownership of homes [and] ownership of businesses" for the African-American elite.

A decade later, when Gulf Oil Corporation was being boycotted by African-Americans activists for its financial support of the repressive Portuguese colonialist government, the multinational responded by attempting to co-opt influential blacks. The corporation funneled $50,000 to the Rev. Ralph Abernathy, former assistant to King and head of the Southern Christian Leadership Conference; $55,000 to the Rev. Leon Sullivan's Opportunities Industrialization Centers; and hundreds of thousands of additional dollars to other black cultural groups and civic leaders.

In 1980, the Republicans cultivated several groups of conservative middle-class blacks in an effort to expand the party's political base inside the African-American community. A group of civil rights leaders, including Abernathy and Georgia state legislator Hosea Williams, publicly endorsed Ronald Reagan's election bid. NAACP head Benjamin Hooks, a closet Republican and former Nixon appointee, was invited to speak to the Republican convention on prime time, and he used this opportunity to extol the virtues of black capitalism.

More influential was a small group of black academics with personal ambitions who were amenable to the Republican Party's policies.

The first important gathering of this group occurred in late 1980 under the auspices of the Institute of Contemporary Studies, a reactionary think tank. The key sponsors were two conservative black economists: Thomas Sowell of the Hoover Institution and Walter Williams, currently a professor at George Mason University. Guests and participants included journalist/entrepreneur Tony Brown, Republican newspaper columnist and former Black Power advocate Chuck Stone, *Black Power* co-author Charles Hamilton, and former Manhattan borough president and businessman Percy Sutton. Sowell established the tone of the gathering by taking positions against affirmative action, liberal social welfare programs, and the minimum wage.

Throughout the 1980s, the black neoconservative current expanded significantly, nurtured by the Reagan administration's desire to counter charges that it policies were racist. Joining Sowell and Williams as principal ideologues were Glenn Loury, professor at Harvard's Kennedy School of Government; J.A.Y. Parker, President of the Lincoln Institute for Research and Education; Robert Woodson, President of the National Association of Neighborhood Enterprises; and Joseph Perkins, editorial writer for the *Wall Street Journal*.

In government, the top black Reaganites were Clarence Pendleton, controversial head of the US Civil Rights Commission, and Clarence Thomas, chair of the Equal Employment Opportunity Commission.

Both Sowell and Loury suffered from reputations for arrogance and abrasive political styles designed to win few converts. Moreover, both were somewhat tainted by their earlier political and ideological commitments. Loury had been a liberal Democrat only a decade before, and Sowell had claimed to be a Marxist into the late 1960s.

With the election of George Bush, a tactical shift occurred. The Republicans initiated a "kinder, gentler" approach toward the "Negro Question." Unlike Reagan, who seldom failed to display his contempt for the African-American community, Bush was properly coached in the liberal discourse of the civil rights movement.

During his eight years in office, Reagan met briefly with representatives of the black community a total of eight times. By comparison, Bush has conferred with leaders from the Congressional Black Caucus, civil rights organizations, and black neoconservatives at least 40 times since early 1989. Bush has praised Nelson Mandela's courageous struggle against apartheid and rhetorically embraced the legacy of Martin Luther King.

These efforts have not been lost on the majority of African-Americans. Public opinion polls find Bush's approval ratings among blacks at record levels for any Republican president. Considering the undisguised racism of his predecessor in the Oval Office, Bush's rather modest response to blacks' interests has appeared unduly magnified, almost liberal and enlightened.

But style does not reveal substance. Bush continues the repressive policies of Reagan toward black-oriented policy questions.

Bush's foreign policy treats Third World societies with scarcely veiled disregard. For example, Poland and Hungary were slated for $900 million in US foreign aid; newly independent Namibia was allocated $500,000. The administration actually cut Jamaica's aid by $18 million to provide greater assistance for the restoration of capitalism in Eastern Europe.

On the domestic front, Bush proposes little to nothing to address widespread African-American unemployment, cutbacks in public transportation, and inadequately funded public housing and education programs.

Civil rights enforcement also continues to be curtailed. The Education Department's Office for Civil Rights, for example, recently stopped staff members from traveling to conduct compliance investigations or to review universities that had already been caught violating civil rights laws.

And Bush apparently will attempt to further erode the Supreme Court's already crumbling protection of civil rights. The President nominated Clarence Thomas for a seat on the US Court of Appeals for the District of Columbia, a move widely viewed as positioning the black conservative to replace elderly liberal Justice Thurgood Marshall on the High Court.

But the most important element of Bush's offensive against civil rights is the administration's continued hostility and opposition to affirmative action programs. Bush's position was strengthened by the Supreme Court's recent *Wards Cove Packing* v. *Antonio* decision, which declared that the underrepresentation of blacks and other minorities in the workplace could not be used as proof of racism in hiring. To prove discrimination, one must now show that the criteria employed in the selection of workers were clearly biased, with the intent of excluding minorities.

Shelby Steele is the most recent neoconservative star to appear on the political horizon. In a series of public statements, articles, television appearances, and in excerpts from his soon-to-be-published book *The Content of Our Character,* Steele advances a more sophisticated version of the Sowell-Loury thesis, attacking affirmative action and the current legislative and legal agenda of civil rights advocates.

Steele's first criticism of affirmative action programs is historical. He observed in a recent *New York Times Magazine* article that the "1964 civil-rights bill was passed on the understanding that equal opportunity would not mean racial preference. But in the late '60s and early '70s, affirmative action underwent a remarkable escalation of its mission from simple anti-discrimination enforcement to social engineering by means of quotas, goals, timetables, set-asides and other forms of preferential treatment."

Steele's basic insight is partially correct. The majority of civil rights leaders were racial integrationists, at least initially. They believed in the goal of a "color-blind" society, a social order in which racial identity would become irrelevant. The Supreme Court's 1954 *Brown* v. *Board of Education* decision, which outlawed the segregation of public schools, argued that any form of racial separatism was de facto evidence of discrimination. The ruling declared: "To separate Negro children solely because of their race generates a feeling of inferiority as to their status in the community that might affect their hearts and minds in a way unlikely ever to be undone."

The legal profession adopted and reinterpreted this color-blind ideology as a theory of race neutrality, disconnecting race from social relations or economic conditions.

King helped establish this interpretation of race in his most famous address, delivered at the 1963 March on Washington: "I have a dream that my four little children will one day live in a nation where they will not be judged by the color of their skin but by the content of their character." Using this quotation in his book title, Steele, unlike Sowell and other black conservatives, attempts to position himself as an ideological comrade of King and an opponent of so-called racism within the white and black communities alike.

Steele, in his attempt to claim the legacy of the civil rights movement, completely ignores the fact that there has always been another tendency in the movement counterposed to integrationism. Adherents of this different approach, represented by W.E.B. Du Bois and others, have insisted that the goal was not color-blindness, but cultural pluralism within a democratic and humane social order. To uproot racism, Du Bois argued, race-conscious remedies were necessary.

In fact, this perspective gradually won out, even among the reformist integrationists within the NAACP and Urban League, who recognized by the early 1970s that it was not enough to dismantle the structures of formal segregation. Measures had to be taken to ensure that blacks, Latinos, women, and others who had experienced systematic discrimination received compensatory justice.

Steele insists that the imposition of affirmative action goals and timetables creates a false sense of pluralism and equality inside campuses. "Racial preferences allow society to leapfrog over the difficult problem of developing blacks to parity with whites and into a cosmetic diversity that covers the blemish of disparity," Steele asserts. In short, most African-Americans are not culturally or intellectually prepared to compete with whites on an equal basis.

Here Steele unthinkingly draws from an older ideological tradition of black conservatism, the rhetoric of Booker T. Washington. The architect of black capitalism and accommodation to lynching called his compatriots "ignorant and inexperienced" and unfit to begin "at the top instead of at the bottom" during the Reconstruction period. Washington was incensed "that a seat in Congress or the state legislature was more sought than real estate or industrial skill."

White Liberals Retreat

Steele, like Washington, implies that blacks are not intellectually or socially ready to assume their rightful share of power. In the meantime, he similarly carves out for himself the role of broker between the "undeveloped" black masses and the white capitalist power structure.

Finally, Steele resorts to a social psychological argument against affirmative action. Racial quotas that discriminate against "innocent whites" create two destructive social dynamics, Steele argues. Whites draw the conclusion that all blacks, regardless of their abilities, achieve position or status solely due to their racial category. And blacks "feel a stab of horror," Steele maintains, because they detest being viewed in this manner.

"The effect of preferential treatment—the lowering of normal standards to increase black representation—puts blacks at war with an expanded realm of debilitating doubt," Steele claims, "so that the doubt itself becomes an unrecognized preoccupation that undermines their ability to perform, especially in integrated situations."

This critique has been early seized upon both by white conservatives, who had always opposed affirmative action anyway, and by weary white liberals, who have retreated from the problems of the ghetto. Journalist Charles Krauthammer, writing in the *Washington Post*, for example, praises "Steele's view on this terrible psychic toll of affirmative action." "Affirmative action," he concludes, "costs more than it is worth. . . . It dispenses unequal justice. It balkanizes communities. It distorts the merit system. . . . And now, it attaches a question mark to every real black achievement."

There are several ways to illustrate the intellectual bankruptcy of Steele's arguments. For example, one could focus solely on the slippery concept of "merit." The leadership of a given institution and its dominant ideology largely set the criteria for determining merit. If women and people of color are systematically denied positions of authority within a particular field, or if their intellectual contributions to the subject are ignored, the field becomes biased in its methodology and criteria for excellence.

Another argument against Steele's imaginary meritocracy is provided by black radical theologian Cornel West in his 1986 essay "Assessing Black Neoconservatism." The false debate of "merit versus race" obscures the fact that "job hiring choices are both meritorious and personal choices," West observes. "And this personal dimension often is influenced by racist perceptions. Within the practical world of US employment practices, the new black conservative rhetoric about race-free meritorious criteria does no more than justify actual practices of racial discrimination against blacks."

Perhaps the most telling criticism of Steele's thesis is that he fails to correctly define or describe institutional racism. For Steele, racial discrimination is an irrational relic of the past, an archaic form of behavior linked to segregation. This ignores the rising tide of racist incidents and harassment experienced by black college students and the violent racism manifested in the streets against African-Americans and other people of color.

Racism is not irrational. It is part of a political and economic system of domination, structurally linked to capitalism, and perpetuated in the power and privileges which a small minority of Americans exercises over the vast majority of people.

Steele symbolized a real turning point in the facade of institutional racism in American life. The old system of Jim Crow no longer serves the goals of capitalism. Demographically, American society is becoming increasingly multiethnic; within 30 years about one-half of the adult labor force between the ages of 25 and 54 will be nonwhite.

A new system of domination is emerging which employs the discourse of equal opportunity within the framework of capitalism. Increasingly, elements of the Latino, Asian-American, and black petty bourgeoisie are being absorbed and assimilated into the secondary ranks of the corporate, educational, and political establishments.

The ideology of affirmative action is potentially threatening because it speaks to the specific grievances and historical claims for material equality and social justice of various exploited groups. As these constituencies gain in numbers and potential power, their capacity to challenge the prevailing ideology of individualism, materialism, and Eurocentrism also increases. To fragment the ranks of the opposition, "the system" brings ideologues like Steele to the forefront, to preach of a meritocracy which has never actually existed, even for white, property-owning males.

So long as racial discrimination and class exploitation exist, we should anticipate a series of Shelby Steeles to arise, one after the other, in defense of the status quo. Our task is to recognize always that just behind such ideologues, "partially hidden by their rhetoric," exists a powerful political and economic apparatus, motivated by profit and perpetuated by racism, hatred, and fear.

6

Smoke and Mirrors:
City of Hope and Illusion

1991

Detroit has always been for me a state of mind, a mixture of hope and lost opportunities, of dirt and despair, of shiny new automobiles and unimaginably long unemployment lines. As a boy, I regularly visited the city. My favorite aunt and a large, extended family lived in the suburban community of Inkster. When summer rolled around, we trekked north to the mecca of Motown.

Hundreds of thousands of African-American families from Tennessee, Alabama, and Mississippi had flooded into the city during the 1940s and 1950s, searching to escape rigid segregation and the penury of sharecropping. Detroit seemed an ideal place for black opportunities. There was by the end of World War II a small but growing black entrepreneurial and professional class. Black enterprises such as Barry Gordy's Motown were influential. By the sixties, it was no longer unusual to see African-Americans in some positions of importance in the school system, government, and, in smaller numbers, inside white businesses.

But a rigid system of racial apartheid and police violence permeated the entire community. At the city's northern boundary, Eight Mile Road represented a racial version of the Berlin Wall. White realtors in the suburbs, as a rule, refused to sell homes to blacks, regardless of their income, education, or credit. The city's police force was brutal in its harassment and victimization of black citizens.

In the automobile plants, the system of racial exploitation for blacks was commonly called "niggermation." At Dodge Main plant, for example, 99 percent of the general foremen were white, 100 percent of the plant superintendents were white, and 90 percent of all skilled tradesmen and apprentices were white. Blacks received the worst jobs at the lowest levels of pay; my cousins and their friends were always assigned to the very worst and dirtiest jobs—in the engine assembly area, the body shop, and the foundry. It was unusual to find a black autoworker with more than 15 years of experience who had not already suffered some crippling accident, such as the loss of a finger or an eye.

The urban uprising of 1967 pushed thousands of middle-income whites out of the city, fearful of their lives and property. Large corporations began a pattern of "milking" their industries inside the city limits, reallocating their profits from local consumers to new firms based in the all-white suburbs or in the sunbelt. Economic decay overtook Detroit by the 1970s. Schools declined as the tax base fell. A drop in jobs meant that low-income people had to rely on the underground economy of hustling, illegal drugs, prostitution, and other forms of illegal activity simply to survive. Rapidly, Detroit's central core became unlivable for the black middle class, which began to relocate to neighborhoods adjacent to the city in the 1970s and 1980s.

Other people of color began to move into the city searching for the same opportunities which African-Americans had never really found. The largest group consisted of Arab-Americans. First the Lebanese and Syrians, and later the Palestinians, Iraqis, and Saudis, established an economic and cultural infrastructure. By 1990, nearly 200,000 Arab-Americans lived in the greater Detroit-Dearborn area. Unfortunately, despite many common economic and political interests, working class and poor people of different ethnic communities rarely come together. The elderly are afraid to go out at night to attend civil meetings or cultural events because they fear being mugged and robbed; the poor have ceased to look for jobs, because the corporations have relocated their offices beyond the reach of public transportation.

The challenge of rebuilding and resurrecting Detroit, it seems to me, should be the cornerstone of a new, national policy of urban reconstruction for the twenty-first century. Because if we could turn around the problems of this crucial city, attacking and uprooting widespread poverty, generating new jobs and new hopes, we might be able to see progress in every other city.

Part of this strategy must be economic. Religious groups and foundations could help finance community-controlled corporations which provide investment capital, technical advice, and business expertise to community cooperatives and minority small entrepreneurs. We need to restructure welfare programs to reward, rather than punish, unmarried women with children with initiative to go back to school and obtain job skills. We must employ federal government resources to expand and to strengthen the so-called safety net, providing a decent living wage to those who cannot work, and an expanded housing program to address the problems of the homeless.

Part of the solution must also be educational. For decades, many black educators have argued that the violence and socially destructive behavior which one witnesses in our inner cities demand a new approach toward the education of young people. The chaos outside the boundaries of our schools, the drugs and crime destroy the self-esteem and constructive social values which help to give any community a sense of itself. Young black males, especially in single, female-headed households, lack black male adult role models in their lives.

Clifford Watson, an elementary school principal in Detroit, has advanced a proposal which attempts to address these problems. The original plan envisioned the creation of three grade schools, involving a total of 560 inner-city youths. The schools' proposed names—Malcolm X Academy, Marcus Garvey Academy, and Paul Robeson Academy—were designed to reinforce a sense of "Afrocentrism"—racial pride, historical and cultural consciousness—within African and African-American traditions. Special Saturday classes and tutorials were planned in specific areas, such as mathematics and the sciences. Anchoring this program would be the presence of articulate and culturally aware black male educators, serving as mentors, instructors, and disciplinarians. In the proposal, the Robeson Academy was to be all-male, with the other schools making this transition over a period of time. Last February, the Detroit School Board reviewed the controversial proposal, and approved it by a vote of 10 to one.

Opposition surfaced from several quarters. The American Civil Liberties Union and the National Organization for Women Legal Defense Fund went to Federal district court this August to successfully block the implementation of the plan, fundamentally on the grounds that it discriminated against black female students. The Michigan branch of the ACLU's executive director, Howard Simon, argued: "These schools may open up a whole new world for these boys. That world should be open to girls too."

Watson countered in television interviews that the particular manifestations of this urban crisis were particularly devastating to young black males, who comprise the overwhelming majority of those engaged in criminal activity and violence in the city, and 90 percent of all students expelled from the school system. Black feminists and others aligned with NOW's Legal Defense Fund and the ACLU were characterized as "Uncle Toms" or the active agents of white supremacy.

Where some Afrocentric educators such as Watson err is their argument that a system of instruction which specifically excludes black females will contribute constructively to an environment in which young black males can be saved. A co-educational setting could accomplish even more, all things being equal. Young black males could be challenged to interact with their sisters not from the basis of male chauvinism but with respect. They could begin to acquire the values essential in a responsible approach to social relations, including sexuality and child raising. By dividing their project on the basis of sex, they indirectly contribute to the tensions and contradictions which already fuel problems between black males and females—which is directly against the interests of the African-American community as a whole.

The struggle to save Detroit, and other cities like it, cannot be viewed in narrow political, economic, or educational terms. The larger question we must confront is our attitude toward human beings of different ethnic identities, cultures, religions, and lifestyles than ourselves. Is there a moral and ethical responsibility which links those living in the comfortable confines of the suburbs with families struggling to survive the rats, roaches, and crack dealers on their local street corners? One cannot embrace the pain of the poor from a distance; one cannot understand the outrage of young black and Latino teenagers who desperately are searching for work and self-respect, just by voting for liberals at election time. Detroit is a symbol for the vast class and racial chasm which cuts across our country. Our ability to remove the barriers of inequality which still plague millions of poor, unemployed, and minority people is simultaneously a test of our political resolve and spirituality.

Toward a Renaissance of Progressive Black Politics

The Los Angeles racial uprising of April–May 1992 illustrated the current crisis of African-American political leadership in this country. With relatively few exceptions, such as Congresswoman Maxine Waters, the vast majority of middle-class black leaders did little to justify or to explain critically the factors behind the rage among young African-Americans. The bulk of black leadership less than one year ago displayed the same absence of political courage and integrity during the national debate generated by the Anita Hill–Clarence Thomas conflict. Throughout black America, there is a sense that a newer, more progressive voice on politics and public policy must be articulated. We need to bring about the rebirth of a more aggressive, principled black activism which speaks to the new Hip-Hop generation and taps the talents and experience of those who were politicized during the Civil Rights and Black Power Movements. The political, economic, and ideological context for black politics has fundamentally changed during the past decade, yet African-American leadership has failed to recognize this transformation and the necessity to advance a new strategic vision and tactical actions in challenging the system of white racism and corporate power.

One factor which has radically changed the context of African-American politics is the post–Cold War international conjecture and the collapse of Third World revolutions. The defeat of the Grenada revolution less than a decade ago spelled the end of the possibility of radical black alternatives in the Caribbean, at least for decades to come. The collapse of the Soviet Union, the demise of the Soviet model in Eastern Europe, and the decay

73

and decline of Third World socialist systems as represented by Ethiopia, Mozambique, Afghanistan, Cambodia, and other countries utterly change the international environment. Most "leftist" or "radical" alternatives in politics, even those not identified with Soviet-style Communism, have been discredited. The recent electoral loss of the Labour Party in the United Kingdom, for example, represents only one of a series of defeats suffered by liberal and left parties. Where social democratic parties are in power, they have consciously moved sharply to the right to accommodate the new authority and power of Western imperialism. The best example in the Caribbean is provided by the People's National Party government of former Prime Minister Michael Manley. In the 1970s, Manley represented a bold challenge to US power in its historic "backyard"; today, he defines "democratic socialism" as "market economics with a commitment to social justice." Many socialists have become liberals, and liberals have become conservatives.

The old division of "East versus West" has been replaced by a new geopolitical and economic alignment of "North versus South." An increasingly unified Europe, dominated by Germany, Japan, and the United States, now largely dictates the entire world's economy and access to technology. With the decline of the left, the conditions for eroding the rights of trade unions, reducing the social wage, and fostering ethnic tensions have increased. Throughout Europe in the past five years, there has been a sharp rise in racist and ethnic violence against Third World emigrants. This spring, the fascist political party of Jean-Marie Le Pen received 14 percent of the national vote in France. Fascist parties are developing in Germany and Italy, and England is taking repressive legislative measures against its black population.

These international factors are important because they profoundly influence what happens inside our own system. The first impact of the post–Cold War period is the collapse of the bipartisan consensus in electoral politics. For decades, the Democrats and Republicans operated within a coalition government: the Republicans controlled the federal executive and judicial branches, and the Democrats usually dominated the legislature. The external "threat" of world communism and the commitment to the political economy of militarism (what some refer to as the "permanent war economy" or "military Keynesianism") cemented the two major parties together for all practical purposes. There was no fundamental difference on economic, fiscal, or foreign policies, for example, between Nixon and Kennedy in 1960 or Carter and Ford in 1976. But with the breakdown of the Cold War, the external pressure which forged the bipartisan consensus domestically began to evaporate. The space for new challenges to the bipartisan coalition form of government was greatly increased, leading to challenges from the left, right, and center. Such challenges were prefigured

12 years ago by the liberal campaign of Edward Kennedy against Carter in the 1980 Democratic presidential primaries and by Republican moderate John Anderson's independent race in the general election. The Jackson assault of the Rainbow Coalition in 1984 and 1988 also eroded the connection of the Democratic Party with the Republicans by pushing a progressive agenda. Finally, in 1992 the fragmentation erupted on the far right as conservative journalist Patrick Buchanan ran a largely symbolic campaign against incumbent President George Bush in the Republican primaries. More effective was the challenge by eccentric billionaire Ross Perot, who launched an independent campaign in the general election. All of these independent-style challenges indicate what political scientists term a "crisis of legitimacy," when people question whether the entire electoral process is relevant to their daily lives. The rationales for both major parties seem to most Americans ineffectual and anachronistic.

The termination of the Cold War also revealed the massive destruction to the US domestic economy caused by the policies of militarism. Much has been written about the defeat of the Soviet Union by the United States, but in truth both sides truly "lost" the Cold War. The real beneficiaries and "victors" were the economies of Japan and Germany. The trillions of dollars invested in nuclear and conventional weapons in the decades of Cold War confrontation should have been spent on hospitals and neighborhood health clinics, roads, and schools, on the upgrading of factory equipment and the improving of technology. Americans may have had the best tactical nuclear missiles in the world, but one cannot ride a missile to work or to school. Because of a absence of national industrial policies, hundreds of automobile, tire, and steel plants shut down. The entire industrial infrastructure of major cities such as Cleveland and Chicago nearly disappeared in a generation. By the 1990s, 37 million Americans were without any medical insurance, and 61 million were without health care at some point in a typical two-year period. The number of homeless doubled in the 1980s as government investment into public housing sharply declined. Real incomes for young workers dropped by one-fifth between 1970 to 1990. Public transportation systems in many cities deteriorated, making it nearly impossible for inner-city workers to compete for the new jobs being generated in the suburbs.

As the "Communist menace" receded, the US right was forced to redefine itself by creating a new public "enemy." In the wake of the post–Cold War, the new ideological glue became opposition to a variety of trends loosely termed "political correctness." On college campuses and in public school systems, the new rallying cry of conservatives and the Bush administration was to undermine "multiculturalism," "Afrocentrism," "feminism," "affirmative action," and any limits on "free speech" (with the exceptions of flag burning and the suppression of rap music) and to halt "reverse racism" by people of color against "innocent" white victims. Vice President Dan Quayle's recent rhetorical tirades against the "cultural elite" symbolize the far right's shifting focus from economic to cultural/social/ideological issues. This is due partially to the fact that the Democrats agree with most of the key economic assumptions about capitalism long held by mainstream Republicans. Both parties support capitalism, oppose extensive state intervention for the purposes of social justice and equitable redistribution of wealth, and reject government policies to effectively uproot systemic racial discrimination. As in Europe, the new focus on cultural and social issues permits the rearticulation of racism in the political arena. Thus, the emergence of David Duke in Louisiana, winning more than 55 percent of the whites' votes in that state's gubernatorial election in 1991, and the rise of the racist and anti-Semitic Buchanan are not isolated phenomena. "Willie Horton" advertisements and the popularity of David Duke are paralleled by the racism in Western European politics.

All of these factors have directly contributed to a crisis within the state of black American politics. The "strategic vision" of the mainstream African-American leadership today can be described as "liberal integrationism." Liberal integrationism, in brief, is a strategy of political action which calls for the deconstruction of institutional racism by liberal reforms within the government and the assimilation of blacks as individuals within all levels of the workforce, culture, and society. At root, this approach to political change is based on what I term "symbolic representation"—that is, a belief that if an African-American receives a prominent appointment to government, the private sector, or the media, then black people as a group are symbolically empowered. This was essentially the argument by many black liberals who defended the nomination of Republican conservative Clarence Thomas to the Supreme Court. Despite his reactionary ideology, it was argued, Thomas is nevertheless racially "black"; he shares our experiences of oppression and will "sympathize with our concerns once he's appointed to a lifetime job."

This thesis was largely true during the era of Jim Crow segregation. Black professionals were connected with black working-class and poor people by innumerable linkages. Black doctors depended upon black patients; black college professors taught in historically black colleges; black lawyers usually had black clients, maintained their offices in black neighborhoods, and lived next to other black people. The police didn't inquire about an African-American's socioeconomic background or level of educational attainment if she or he was in violation of Jim Crown laws. But in the post–Civil Rights era, the structures of accountability on the black professional middle class began to erode. A new type of African-American leadership emerged inside the public and private sectors, which lived outside the black community and had little personal contacts with African-

Americans. Symbolic representation no longer works with bureaucrats and politicians like Clarence Thomas, who feel no sense of allegiance to the black freedom struggle.

Liberal integrationism's chief economic assumptions were those of expansive, liberal capitalism and Keynesianism. Two generations ago, when the NAACP and the black liberal political leadership were integrated into the New Deal coalition as junior partners, the economic basis of unity was liberal capitalism—the belief that the economic "pie" could expand indefinitely. Today's black leadership in the Democratic Party holds many of the same economic assumptions, despite the radical transformation, deindustrialization, and destruction of the US political economy in the past 30 years. The dire economic conditions of African-Americans cannot be addressed by liberal reforms tinkering at the margins of a system in the midst of structural crisis. Poverty in the black community won't be reduced significantly by minority economic set-asides, urban "enterprise zones," or neo–Booker T. Washington–style black capitalism.

Since the 1960s, the vast majority of black liberal integrationist leaders have defined "politics" almost solely as "electoralism." Electing more African-Americans to Congress, state legislatures, and city councils is perceived as increasing the political power of blacks as a group. There are at least two major problems with this notion of politics. As previously mentioned, symbolic representation works in empowering a constituency only when there exist institutions of structural accountability, the power to reward and to punish, between leaders and those whom they supposedly represent. Moreover, African-American leaders currently minimize tactics which a generation ago were at the heart of the black freedom movement—sit-ins, teach-ins, selective buying campaigns or boycotts, civil disobedience, strikes, and demonstrations of all types. It is significant to note that Martin Luther King, Jr., Malcolm X, Paul Robeson, Fannie Lou Hamer, and A. Philip Randolph were *not* elected officials, nor did they draw their political authority from the electoral arena. King's chief political practice was going to jail to assert his political and moral beliefs. Somehow, black leadership today has forgotten the tactics and lessons of the past and has invested heavily in an electoral process which was never really designed to articulate black grievances or demands.

Finally, liberal integrationism has at its core a blind loyalty to the Democratic Party. Since the Walter White regime at the NAACP 50 years ago, the bulk of the national black leadership has perceived itself as an essential part of the political coalition behind national Democratic Party candidates for the presidency and Congress. Even Jackson's break from this mainstream position, challenging Walter Mondale and Michael Dukakis inside the Democratic presidential primaries in the 1980s, was in retrospect a maneuver to articulate black grievances inside the framework of the existing system.

It is always difficult, if not perilous, to read Jesse Jackson's mind—but I believe that the Country Preacher never really intended to break with the Democratic Party and to launch in Perot-style, independent, liberal-left challenge to the two-party system. Mentally, emotionally, and ideologically, most black leaders are committed to the Democratic Party—even if their constituents increasingly are not. It's a sad commentary on the state of black leadership when a conservative Texas billionaire has a more "independent" and provocative approach to the national political system than those who speak for the African-American community.

How do we revive the sense of militancy, activism, and independence within African-American politics as we enter the twenty-first century? What is required is not a full-blown ideology or a political dogma but a creative, flexible approach and a critical perspective on politics based on contemporary realities and the new conditions confronting African-Americans today. Organizationally, we need several new kinds of institutions which can help rebuild the black freedom movement. First, and perhaps foremost, we need a new "SNCC" (Student Nonviolent Coordinating Committee), a youth-oriented formation which taps the energies and abilities of the Hip-Hop generation. A militant black youth movement, directed and led by young people themselves, could target the issues of black-on-black violence in a more effective manner. It could help develop leadership skills among young people, acquainting them with the whole range of political interventions and tactics, such as economic boycotts and civil disobedience.

We need a progressive political forum or activist/theoretical center bringing together progressive intellectuals, legislative aides, and community organizers to articulate a public policy agenda which is progressive and breaks from the strategy of traditional liberal integrationism. This center must serve as a creative vehicle for debate and dialogue, constructing the public policies and tactics which can foster a new spirit of activism. It could serve as a pressure group on public policy, creating the influence necessary for greater accountability among traditional black leaders. Such a center could hold regular public forums covered by C-SPAN and the national media on crucial economic, social, and political issues, or it could respond to crises as they erupt.

If such a center existed, several recent political events could have had very different outcomes. In winter 1989, for example, Jesse made a deliberate decision to demobilize the Rainbow and then cut off any avenues toward independent politics at the local level. This decision demoralized thousands of young activists throughout the country. If a progressive black policy center had existed, with real connections with dozens of grassroots, labor, women's, and youth organizations across the country, pressure could have been exerted against Jackson to reverse his decision. In fall 1991, there was no coherent, collective black progressive voice which was heard nationally on the Anita Hill–Clarence Thomas debate. Without such pressure from black progressives, African-American formations such as the Southern Christian Leadership Conference and the Urban League either endorsed Thomas or equivocated in their public stance. Nine months later, the Los Angeles uprising erupted, forcing a debate on the failure of national urban and racial policies. But where was the collective voice of African-American progressives in this discourse? In November 1992, there could be a major Constitutional crisis generated by the presidential election, with no one winning a majority of electoral votes. How should blacks in Congress vote in such a situation? Should African-Americans cast their ballots for the candidate (Clinton, Perot, or Bush) who won their districts, for the plurality victor of their state, or for their party's presidential candidate regardless of the votes cast? Black progressives need a center or structure to articulate their own perspective on this potential Constitutional crisis, influencing African-American political opinion and perhaps even national discourse on the election.

I propose the creation of a collective framework to maximize the progressive African-American voice and vision on politics, economics, and public policy. I am not calling for a political party or an electoral movement; a mass-based, social protest movement; or a rival oppositional group which has as its primary agenda the criticism of existing black organizations. Instead, what we need now is a new kind of activist/intellectual formation which in many respects would parallel the historic role of the Niagara Movement of 1905–1909, which challenged Jim Crow segregation and white political reaction at the dawn of this century. Niagara was essentially an annual forum which brought together progressive black voices without the imposition of arbitrary political or ideological conformity, but with the goal of advancing a black progressive agenda. It distinguished itself from Washington's "Tuskegee Machine" by calling for open, legislative, and judicial challenges to segregation and by opposing the racist violence against, lynching of, and disfranchisement of black people. It established the foundations for a new type of African-American politics, crystallizing in the formation of the NAACP.

How should we define the term "progressive" at the end of the twentieth century and in the context of the African-American struggle for freedom? What I favor is a critical approach to political action informed by points of agreement or consensus. To initiate the discussion, I would suggest six themes which constitute some of the elements of a progressive black politics. The first element would be a criticism of corporate capitalism—that is, for us to address the contemporary urban crisis, the problems of health care, housing, unemployment, and hunger, we must restructure fundamentally the American economic system. We need a massive national investment policy to rebuild the economic and social infrastructure, establishing initiatives for cooperatives and small entrepreneurs in the central cities. Our vision of economics for black liberation must include the principle of a job or guaranteed income as a basic human right. We need to go beyond the flawed limitations of Keynesian economics and the illusions of black capitalism.

Second, black progressivism should mean a strong commitment to the principle of democracy. We must make African-American leadership more responsive and responsible to the black community. Fighting to expand the options and electoral choices for African-American people is a central part of political democracy. But democracy is also an approach toward leadership and our relationships with each other. We need to nurture a style of politics which is nonauthoritarian and antihierarchical. Politics which encourages wide participation and decisionmaking should be favored over charismatic and sexist leadership behaviors and organizations.

Third, no definition of progressivism is possible without a commitment to struggle against gender oppression, in theory and practice, and for the empowerment of African-American women. Black political formations should reflect greater gender balance and the full representation of women at the top leadership levels of all groups. We must place greater specific emphasis on issues which speak to the oppression of African-American women: violence against black women such as rape and partner/spouse abuse, sexist discrimination at places of employment, legal restrictions on the right of choice, and so forth.

Fourth, a progressive black agenda should be explicitly "antiracist." That is, it should emphasize the necessity to dismantle the institutions of white racism throughout the United States and the world. We must be in the forefront of the antiapartheid struggle and make the linkages between our movement and the black formations arising today in England and elsewhere in Europe. An antiracist perspective includes challenging the criminal justice system for its perpetuation of institutional racism, fighting against the racist death penalty, and advocating the expansion of civil rights laws and affirmative action.

Fifth, a progressive black perspective must be internationalist. The end of the Cold War revalidates W.E.B. Du Bois's prediction of 1900—that the "problem of the twentieth century is the problem of the color line." We are inevitably part of the new configuration of the North-South struggle. We need a progressive black voice to challenge Bush's New World Order and to pressure Jackson and other African-American leaders to pursue a more consistently progressive position on foreign policy issues. We need to make direct linkages to democratic protest movements throughout Africa, Brazil, the Caribbean, and the entire black world.

Sixth, progressive black politics should explicitly reject the simplistic strategy of a long-term alliance with the national Democratic Party in favor of a more flexible, "inside-outside" response, maximizing independence by exploring tactics which transform the two-party system. We need to advocate reforms in the electoral system such as a "None of the Above" voter option in certain races, which would permit voters to express their lack of support for candidates by selecting a "None of the Above" line; fairer ballot access for independent parties and third-party candidates, eliminating unreasonable restrictions such as excessive signature requirements and ballot maintenance rules; and cross-endorsement or fusion, which would permit candidates to run simultaneously on the Democratic line while also contesting election on a third-party line. Other measures meriting our support are increased efforts for African-American voter education and registration, bringing into the electoral process millions of new voters. The American electoral system reflects a race/gender/class bias which is perpetuated by the fact that the typical voter profile doesn't reflect the actual population of the nation. In the presidential election of 1984, for example, about 61 percent of all registered white voters cast ballots, compared to 50.5 percent of African-American voters and barely 30 percent of all Hispanic voters. The unemployed versus the employed electorates voted in 1984 at rates of 41.7 percent versus 61.8 percent. People with personal incomes above $25,000 annually voted that year at the rate of 73.8 percent, compared to a voter participation rate of 39.4 percent for income earners with less than $5,000 per year. College graduates voted at 84.3 percent, compared to barely 50 percent for high school graduates. Millions of people, disproportionately black, Latino, blue collar working class, unemployed, and undereducated are outside the electoral process. And unless we reach and mobilize that constituency, in both electoral and nonelectoral politics, black empowerment will be a dream deferred.

Concretely, a New Niagara Movement could hold a series of public forums on major policy issues; perhaps this could take the form of a year-end "State of African-American Politics" review, summarizing the major events, controversies, and elections and suggesting the major issues for the next year. Such an annual political review might be televised on C-SPAN and featured on public radio stations, creating a greater awareness of a progressive black political agenda. An annual meeting or conference could be held in the summer, bringing together community-based activists with scholars and legislative aides into a creative dialogue on strategy and tactics. A New Niagara Movement could identify progressive black elected officials, working with them and their staffs to promote progressive agendas.

But perhaps the greatest challenge which we have to confront in politics is the failure of historical imagination or vision which seems to plague our current caste of leaders. Historically, African-American politics has been characterized by its ability to challenge and to expand the democratic contours of American society as a whole, pushing the boundaries of participa-

tion forward for every oppressed group. It is up to us, the generation of activists who were created by the Civil Rights and Black Power Movements,
whose politics were shaped by struggles of labor and women's groups, community organizations and black nationalist formations, socialist and Rainbow activism, to construct a new strategy of politics. We must rethink our
old assumption about politics and dare to articulate bold and creative agendas for a fundamental restructuring of society.

8

Black America:
Multicultural Democracy in
the Age of Clarence Thomas,
David Duke, and the
Los Angeles Uprisings

Uprising in Los Angeles

The recent racial uprising in Los Angeles revealed a fundamental division which separates two Americas along a race and class fault line. The responses to the violence on the "white" side of this race/class division help to illustrate why more urban unrest is inevitable.

In a shameful display of political cowardice, President George Bush's initial instinct was to attribute blame for the Los Angeles revolt on the liberal "Great Society" programs of Lyndon Johnson, a quarter century ago. But when pressed for specific programs which contributed to the racial crisis of today, White House press secretary Marlin Fitzwater could only mumble, "I don't have a list with me."

Did Bush mean the 1964 Civil Rights Act, which had outlawed racial discrimination in public accommodations? Was the president blaming the National Housing Act of 1968, which established the National Housing Partnership to promote the construction of houses for low- to middle-income people? Or maybe the reason blacks rioted was due to the 1965 Voting Rights Act, which had established the principle of "one person, one vote" a century after the abolition of slavery. Bush's pathetic effort to rewrite history, to blame the victim, was yet another example of his Willie Horton racial politics. The current agony of our inner cities is a direct and deliberate consequence of Reagan-Bush policies, and no amount of historical distortion can erase that fact.

On different sides of the race/class fault, each group tends to perceive issues in radically different ways. The vast majority of all Americans—black, Latino, Asian-American, and white—believed that the innocent verdict in the King case was wrong. But according to one poll in *USA Today*, 81 percent of all African-Americans stated that the criminal justice system was clearly "biased against black people." Sixty percent of all blacks agreed that there was "very much" police brutality against people of color, and another 33 percent believed that such violence was "considerable." Conversely, only 36 percent of all whites responded that the justice system was racially biased. Only 17 percent of whites stated that there was excessive police brutality against minorities. The unanticipated eruption of rage stripped away the facade of black progress in the central cities, boiling with the problems of poverty, drugs, gang violence, unemployment, poor schools, and deteriorating public housing. The white media tried desperately to turn attention away from these issues, in part by arguing that the Los Angeles uprising was merely a "riot" which was opposed by most African-Americans. This ignores the historical evidence about the dynamics of all civil unrest. After the Watts racial rebellion of 1965, for example, sociologists later determined that only 15 percent of all black ghetto residents had actually participated in the arson and violence. However, between one-third to one-half of all residents later expressed support for those who had destroyed white-owned property and attacked symbols of white authority. About two-thirds later agreed that "the targets of the rebellion got what they deserved." So although the majority of African Americans in South Central L.A. didn't take to the streets, that doesn't mean that they aren't alienated and outraged by race and class oppression.

The same race/class fault line which trembled and shook across impoverished South Central Los Angeles also runs directly beneath the affluent white suburbs as well. This time, young black and Latino rebels weren't content to destroy the symbols of ghetto economic exploitation. Violence and arson unexpectedly struck against white-owned property across Los Angeles County. The Bloods and Crips street gangs established a fragile peace pact, announcing to the media that the current street violence was a "slave rebellion, like other slave rebellions in black history." One local Samoan rap group declared that the rebellion was "great," but that the violence against property should have been directed not against the Korean stores, but at the "rich people in Beverly Hills." For the black middle-class professionals, many of whom had come to believe the mythology about racial progress under the Reagan-Bush era, the King verdict was like a "firebell in the night." They were jolted into the realization that they, like Rodney King, could be halted by the police, brutalized, kicked, and possibly killed—and that their assailants in police uniforms would probably walk away free. They were awakened by the haunting fear that their college-bound sons and daughters could be stopped for minor traffic violations, and later be found dead or dying in the city streets. This is what Representative Floyd Flake of Brooklyn meant when he explained why the hopes of millions of African-Americans in the inherent fairness oft he legal system were shattered: "When Rodney King was on the ground getting beat, we were all on the ground getting beat."

But if we listen carefully to young African-Americans in the streets, this generation is telling us more than just its dissatisfaction with the King verdict. The violence was not directly generated by reactions to courtroom decisions. What our young people painfully realize is that the entire "system"—the government and its politicians, the courts and the police, the corporations and the media—has written them off. They recognize that Bush had virtually no coherent policies addressing urban problems, until he was confronted by massive street violence. They feel instinctively that American businesses have no intention of hiring them at real "living wages," that the courts refuse to treat them as human beings, and that the politicians take their votes and ignore their needs. By taking to the streets, they are crying out to a society: "We will be heard! We will not be ignored, and we will not go away quietly. And if the system and society refuse to listen to us, we intend to burn it to the ground." That is the meaning of Los Angeles.

This Is Democracy?

One of the most striking things about the 1980s and 1990s is how the nature of racism has transmuted and transformed. In the 1950s and 1960s, the struggle against racial discrimination was very clear to everyone. Racism was embodied in the reality of "white" and "colored" signs that relegated African-Americans to go into second-class positions, whether in lunchrooms, schools, toilets, or hotels. Racism was simply a form of legal segregation—Jim Crow. The racist renaissance of the 1980s and 1990s has ushered in a transformation in the character and essence of institutional bigotry. Think back—in the wake of the civil rights movement, it was no longer possible or viable for white elected officials, administrators, or corporate executives to attack African-Americans as "niggers." At least not openly. The Ku Klux Klan and other violent racist groups still existed, but they did not represent a mass movement among white Americans. But over the past 10 years a neo-racist presence has emerged that attributes the source of all racial tensions to the actions of people of color themselves.

Consider the presence of David Duke. According to voter surveys, about 55 percent of all Louisiana whites supported Duke over three-term former Governor Edwin Edwards. Duke's greatest concentration of support was registered among whites who had suffered most in the state's economic recession. Sixty-eight percent of all whites with a high school education or less voted for Duke; 69 percent of the white "born-again Christians" and 63 percent of all whites with incomes between $15,000 to $30,000 favored Duke. Conversely, only 30 percent of whites who earn more than $75,000 annually voted for the former Klansman. This illustrates that race can be highly effective in mobilizing white working class discontent.

Both the Democrats and the Republicans are aware that race will be the crucial factor in determining the 1992 election. The Democratic candidates go into the election as distinct long shots for several reasons. First, despite Bush's decline in popularity, incumbent presidents of either party rarely lose. The only incumbent presidents who were defeated seeking reelection since World War I were Hoover, Ford, and Carter, the victims of the Great Depression, Watergate, and the oil/hostage crisis.

Second, Republicans have received a majority of whites' votes in every presidential election except one since 1948. No matter who the Democrats nominate for the presidency, any candidate will have the same difficult task: pulling together northern white ethnics and many white workers from the South while courting African-American and Latino voters. The only recent Democratic candidate who achieved such a coalition was Jimmy Carter back in 1976. But even Carter failed to gain a majority of the white vote nationally.

The Republicans and Bush have already begun to respond by playing the "race card," the deliberate manipulation of racial prejudices for partisan political purposes. By first vetoing and later signing a weakened civil rights bill, Bush postured in the shadow of Duke. Bush's counsel, C. Boyden Gray, attempted to force the president to sign a policy statement which would have ended the use of racial preferences in federal government hiring policies. Although Gray's statement was repudiated, the controversy it provoked among civil rights and congressional leaders illustrated once again that Bush has absolutely no principles or commitment to the fight against discrimination.

Bush knows that if 66 percent of all white Americans support him in 1992—exactly the same percentage of whites who backed Reagan eight years before—that he would win the White House without a single black or Latino vote. By pandering to white racism, Bush solidifies his support among fearful, frustrated whites. Millions of jobless, discouraged whites are searching for simplistic answers to explain their poverty and economic marginality.

But all speculation concerning the demise of Duke as a national presence due to his recent electoral loss in Louisiana is highly exaggerated. Duke flourishes because Bush has prepared the ideological and cultural terrain by his own pandering to racism. In political terms, Duke is Bush's "illegitimate son" and heir. Duke is the child whom the president desperately desires to disown, but his political features of hatred and hostility to civil rights bear too striking a resemblance to those of his "father."

The "race card" will continue to be decisive in American politics, so long as white Americans vote according to their perceived racial interests, and not in concert with their basic material interests. Millions of white Americans are unemployed, just like Latinos and African-Americans. Millions of white women do not receive equal pay for equal work, and experience discrimination on the job like minorities. If a Democratic presidential candidate had the courage and vision to attack the lies behind the "race card," and carried an aggressive message of social justice, the Republicans could be defeated.

Racism and Stereotypes

What is racism? How does the system of racial discrimination that people of color experience today differ from the type of discrimination that existed in the period of Jim Crow, or legal racial segregation? How is the rich spectrum of cultural groups affected by practices of discrimination within American's so-called "democratic society" today? What parallels can be drawn between sexism, racism, and other types of intolerance, such as anti-Semitism, anti-Arabism, homophobia, and handicappism? What kinds of national and international strategies are needed for a multicultural democracy in the whole of American society and throughout the Western world? And finally, what do we need to do to not just see beyond our differences, but to realize our commonalties and deepen one another's efforts to seize our full freedom and transform the nature of society?

Let's begin with point one: Racism is the system of ignorance, exploitation, and power used to oppress African-Americans, Latinos, Asians, Pacific-Americans, Native Americans and other people on the basis of ethnicity, culture, mannerisms, and color. Point two: When we try to articulate an agenda of multicultural democracy, we run immediately into the stumbling block of stereotypes—the device at the heart of every form of racism today. Stereotypes are at work when people are not viewed as individuals with unique cultural and social backgrounds, with different religious traditions and ethnic identities, but as two-dimensional characters bred from the preconceived attitudes, half-truths, ignorance, and fear of closed minds. When seen through a stereotype, a person isn't viewed as a bona fide human being, but as an object onto which myths and half-truths are projected. There are many ways that we see stereotypes degrade people, but perhaps the most insidious way is the manner in which stereotypes deny people their own history. In a racist society like our own, people of color are not viewed as having their own history or culture. Everything must conform to the so-called standards of white bourgeois society. Nothing generated by people of color is accepted as historically original, dynamic, or creative. This even applies to the way in which people of color are miseducated about their own history. Indeed, the most insidious element of stereotypes is how people who are oppressed themselves begin to lose touch with their own traditions of history, community, love, celebration, struggle, and change.

If we don't have a sense of where we've been and what we've experienced, how do we know where we want to go? This is crucially important, and one can see this as a form of political crippling, a type of historical amnesia that exists for a whole generation of young Americans who did not individually participate in the national ordeal to demolish Jim Crow, who did not participate in the social struggles in the streets against the war in Vietnam or for black empowerment, who did not participate in the mighty democratic movements of the 1960s. Many of us have a type of historical amnesia whereby we perpetuate the stereotypes, internalize them, and project them upon others within our community.

If we don't have a sense of those who have contributed to democratic struggles and how those struggles relate to us now, how can we deepen the patterns of social change and continue to create greater vistas of democracy for our children and for their children? My grandmother, who never went to college or high school, who never finished elementary school, is far more articulate than I am. She used to say, "Manning, if you don't know where you're going, any road will get you there." So we need to understand the road that we're traveling. Where we're going is a function of where we've been.

The Racism of Reagan and Bush

The Ronald Reagan/Bush administration was unquestionably the fountainhead of much of the new racist upsurge. Remember: When Reagan won the Republican Party's presidential nomination, the very first place he chose to speak was a small town named Philadelphia, Mississippi. The day Reagan arrived the people of this town were holding a county fair, and Reagan got up before a crowd of several thousand white people who were waving Confederate flags and he said, "I have always been for states' rights." Question one: Why Philadelphia, Mississippi? Question two: What does the phrase "states' rights" mean in the context of Mississippi? It means white supremacy. The crowd understood that. The president's speechwriters understood that. Even though Ronald Reagan had an IQ lower than a rock, even he understood that.

Question three: What happened in Mississippi in the town of Philadelphia in 1964? Remember: Three civil rights workers were brutally murdered: two whites, one black. The crowd knew that instinctively. It was red meat for them. Of course Reagan's speechwriters knew it too. It was an incredulous kind of posthumous affirmation of the hatred and violence of the murderers, and a nauseating attack against the democracy and freedom for which the three slain men were struggling. We have to understand that there is a correlation between racism and the absence of democracy in all this. That's really the thesis guiding my research and much of my whole political life. To understand the absence of democracy in this country, to understand the absence of equality and a decent life for millions of Americans, we must begin by understanding the odious structures of institutional racism. Racism will not answer all of our questions, but it does put us on the path to understanding why we have not achieved the reality of democracy in this country.

In the 1980s we saw a proliferation of racist violence, most disturbingly on college campuses. Several years ago at Purdue University a cross was actually burned in front of a black cultural center. A short time later someone carved into a black employee's door: "Death to you, nigger." At the University of Texas, Austin, there was the formation of the Aryan Collegiates, who have the goal of the elimination of "all outspoken minorities" from the campus. There have been a whole series of racist incidents over a three- or four-year period at the University of Michigan at Ann Arbor. At Columbia University in the spring of 1988 there was an assault against several African-American students by a group of whites, prompting an anti-racist rally of over 1,000 students denouncing racism on campus. There are only a few of countless incidents occurring across the nation.

Why the upsurgence of racism? Why was it occurring in the 1980s, and why does this disease continue to spread into the 1990s? How is it complicit with other systemic crises that we now face within the political, economic, and social structures of our society?

First we need to be clear about how we recognize racism. Racism is never accidental within a social structure or institution. It is the systematic exploitation of people of color in the process of production and labor, the attempt to subordinate our cultural, social, educational, and political life. The key concepts here are subordinate and systemic. The dynamics of racism attempt to inflict a subordinate position for people of color—Latinos, Native Americans, Arabs, Asians, African-Americans, and other people of color within the society.

The people and policies working for Bush and Reagan have consolidated the process of inequality in the legal system, because the real legacy of Reagan is not what occurred in the White House over an eight-year period. Along with leaving us an insurmountable national debt and an obese military arsenal, the real legacy of Reagan, I believe, is going to be the 425 judges that he appointed to federal district courts and circuit courts of appeals. Through these appointments he ensured that the discrimination of Reaganism would continue long after his presidency had ended. The average age of the judges Reagan appointed to the federal level is only 46 years. Reagan ensured that his ideology would permeate the legal apparatus, and this ideology bears definite racist dimensions. Remember: During Reagan's first term in office, the percentage of black appointments to the federal district court and the US Circuit Court of Appeals fell below 1 percent. By comparison, Jimmy Carter made 56 appointments to the US Circuit Court of Appeals from 1977 to 1981. These included 11 women, 10 African-Americans, two Latinos, and one Asian-American. Reagan's appointments were slightly different: one woman, one black, one Hispanic, and probably all the same person.

The Reagan/Bush administration was openly contemptuous of African-American rights; it nominated virtually no people of color to the federal courts, and it openly supported the apartheid regime in South Africa through Reagan's policy of "constructive engagement." George Bush pursued the presidency in 1988 by employing Reagan's racial strategy. His campaign cited the infamous example of black convict Willie Horton as an example of the Democrats' "softness on crime." Even without openly appealing to white supremacy, Bush nevertheless benefited from a racist backlash against the gains achieved by racial minorities since the 1960s. As president, Bush continues to pursue a racist agenda while employing a public style and discourse of racial harmony. He openly courts black middle-class leaders. He invites them to the White House for lunch. He said, "O.K., Thurgood Marshall, the only African-American on the Supreme Court, is leaving the court, but I believe in racial equality. I'm going to give you another black justice." So he produces a black justice who's against women's right of choice. It's a black justice, Clarence Thomas, who clearly is antithetical and hostile toward the civil rights agenda. This is a black justice who is opposed to affirmative action, opposed to workers' rights and trade union rights, a so-called black justice who has carried out in his personal and public life an attitude of contempt for women and particularly for African-American women! But that's the one Bush has given us. This is a kind of "slick" racism, as one of my students once put it. In fact, Malcolm X developed a term for it: he called it *tricknology*. It gives us something without giving us anything—an appearance that diverts attention away from the real and malignant social impact.

Racism in the 1990s means lower pay for equal work. It means a process that sustains inequality within the income structure of this country. Institutional racism in America's economic system today means that the rhetoric of equal opportunity in the marketplace remains, in effect, a hoax for most people of color. Between 1973 and 1986 the real average earning for black males between the ages of 20 and 29 actually fell 50 percent. When thousands of African-American families struggle to save enough for home mortgages and loans to start small businesses, they are frequently denied these loans from banks. There was a recent study in the *Rocky Mountain News* and other newspapers over the last several months, commissioned by the Federal Reserve Bank of Boston, indicating that the percentage of loans made to predominately black communities is substantially lower than those granted to white neighborhoods. From 1982 to 1988 mortgages were issued on 7 percent of properties in white areas and only 2.5 percent in areas that were virtually black. When banks unfairly deny African-Americans credit, the process of urban gentrification accelerates, permitting thousands of middle-class whites to seize minority-owned property at bargain basement prices.

Crack

What else intensifies racism and inequality in the 1990s? Drugs. We are witnessing the complete disintegration of America's inner cities, the home of millions of Latinos and blacks. We see the daily destructive impact of gang violence inside our neighborhoods and communities, which is directly attributable to the fact that for 20 years the federal government has done little to address the crisis of drugs inside the ghetto and the inner city. It seems as if there is no drug epidemic in this country so long as young black and Latina women and men are primary victims. It seems as if there is no drug epidemic in this country so long as the drug disease is quarantined to low-income neighborhoods and voiceless ghettos. How many more of our people will we allow to be shattered by drugs? How many daughters and sons will we allow our families and friends to lose? For people of color, crack addition has become part of the new urban slavery, a method of disrupting lives and regulating masses of young people who would otherwise be demanding jobs, adequate health care, better schools, and control of their own communities. Is it accidental that this insidious cancer has been unleashed within the very poorest urban neighborhoods, and that the police concentrate on petty street dealers rather than those who actually control and profit from the drug traffic? How is it possible that thousands and thousands of pounds of illegal drugs can be transported throughout the country, in airplanes, trucks, and automobiles, to hundreds of central distribution centers and thousands of employees, given the ultra-high-tech surveillance and intelligence capacity of law enforcement officers? How, unless crack presented a systemic form of social control?

If you were living in an inner-city community in the mid-1980s, you saw the appearance of crack and felt it seep into your neighborhood and sap the will and resistance of thousands of young women and men. The struggle that we have now is not simply against the system. It's against the kind of insidious violence and oppressive behavior that people of color carry out against each other. What I'm talking about is the convergence between the utility of a certain type of commodity—addictive narcotics—and economic and social problems which are confronting the system. That is, the redundancy, the unemployment of millions of people of color, young women and men, living in our urban centers. The criminal justice system represents one type of social control. Crack and addictive narcotics represent another type. If you're doing organizing work within the black community, it becomes impossible to get people and families to come out to your community center when there are crack houses all around the building. It becomes impossible to continue political organizing when people are afraid for their own lives. This is the new manifestation of racism in which we see a form of social control existing in our communities, the destruction of social institutions, and that erosion of people's ability to fight against the forms of domination that continuously try to oppress them.

Women's Freedom

How do we locate the connections between racism and sexism? There are many direct parallels, in both theory and practice, between these two systems of domination. A good working definition of sexism is the subordination of women's social, cultural, political, and educational rights as human beings, and the unequal distribution of power and resources between women and men based on gender. Sexism is a subsocial dynamic, like racism, in that the dynamic is used to subordinate one part of the population to another.

How does sexism function in the economic system? Women experience it through the lack of pay equity—the absence of equal pay for comparable work performed by women versus men on the job. Sexism exists in the stratification of the vocation hierarchy by gender, which keeps women disproportionately at the bottom. The upper levels of the corporation are dominated by white, wealthy males, as is the ownership of productive forces and property largely that of white males. Women consequently have less income mobility, and frequently are defined as "homemakers," a vocation for which there is absolutely no financial compensation, despite 60 to 80 hours of work per week.

Sexism within cultural and social institutions means the domination of males in decision-making positions. Males control the majority of newspapers, the film industry, radio, and television. Sexist stereotypes of both males and females are thus perpetuated through the dominant cultural institutions, advertising, and broadcast media.

In political institutions, sexism translates into an unequal voice and influence within the government. The overwhelming majority of seats in the Congress, state legislatures, courts, and city councils are controlled by white men. The United States has one of the lowest percentages of women represented within its national legislature among Western democratic societies.

And finally, like racism, the wire that knots sexist mechanisms together, which perpetuates women's inequality within the fabric of the social institutions, is violence. Rape, spouse abuse, sexual harassment on the job, are all essential to the perpetuation of a sexist society. For the sexist, violence is the necessary and logical part of an unequal, exploitative relationship. To dominate and control, sexism requires violence. Rape and sexual harassment are therefore not accidental to the structure of gender relations within a sexist order. This is why progressives must first target the issue of violence against women, in the struggle for human equality and a nonsexist environment. This is why we must fight for women's rights to control their own bodies and not submit to the demagogues of the rabid right who would return us to the back alley abortionists, to those who destroy young women's lives. Those who oppose the woman's right to choose express so much love for the rights of the fetus, yet too frequently express contempt for child nutrition programs, child care, and education after the child has come into the world.

Sexism and racism combine with class exploitation to produce a three-edged mode of oppression for women of color. Economically, African-American, Latina, and Native American women are far below white women in terms of income, job security, and job mobility. The median income of a black woman who is also a single parent with children is below $10,000 annually. Thirty-six percent of all black people live below the federal government's poverty line. And more than 75 percent of that number are black women and their children.

Black and Latina women own virtually no sizable property; they head no major corporations; they only rarely are the heads of colleges and universities; they hold no massive real estate holdings; they are barely represented in Congress; and they represent tiny minorities in state legislatures or in the leadership of both major parties. Only a fractional percentage of the attorneys and those involved in the criminal justice system are African-American women. It is women of color, not white women, who are overwhelmingly those who are harassed by police, arrested without cause, and who are the chief victims of all types of crimes.

Sexism and racism are not perpetuated biologically like a disease or drug addiction; both behaviors are learned within a social framework and have absolutely no ground in hereditary biology. They are perpetuated by stereotypes, myths, and irrational fears that are rooted in a false sense of superiority. Both sexism and racism involve acts of systemic coercion—job discrimination, legal domination, and political underrepresentation. And both sexism and racism may culminate in acts of physical violence.

What correlations can be established between racism, sexism, homophobia, anti-Semitism, handicappism, and other manifestations of intolerance and violence? It is unfortunately true that people who are victimized by one form of prejudice or social intolerance sometimes fail to appreciate the oppression of other victims. There are blacks who are, unfortunately, anti-Semitic, and Jews who are racist; there are white women who are racist and oppressive to sisters of color; there are Latinos who are homophobic and oppressive to gays and lesbians; there are people of color who are insensitive to whites who are physically challenged. Yet for many of us, the experience of oppression gives us some insights into the pain and discrimination of others. I am a scholar of the civil rights movement, and I write about lynching, political franchisement, and Jim Crow. But I also lived through this experience. I personally know what it is like to go to the back of the bus. I know what it is like not to be served at a restaurant. I know what it is like not to be permitted to sit inside a heated bus terminal, but be forced to stand outside in the cold. I know what it is like not to be permitted to try on a cap or a pair of pants because you are black. When you experience this, you can never forget it.

And I believe that the experience of oppression and the struggle to overcome it, if properly understood, can be universalized. Because I have felt the pain of oppression, I can understand and feel the pain of my sisters, victimized by violence, harassment, and sexist discrimination. I can understand the anger of my Jewish sisters and brothers who must confront the hatred and bigotry of the anti-Semite. I can express my sympathy and support for lesbians and gays who experience discrimination because of their sexual preference.

Experience

What are some other characteristics of the new racism that we are now encountering? What we see in general is a duplicitous pattern that argues that African-Americans and other people of color are moving forward while their actual material conditions are being pushed back. Look at America's education system. The number of doctoral degrees being granted to blacks, for example, is falling. Between 1977 and 1987 the total number of students who received doctorates in American universities increased by about 500, to 32,278 students. In 1977, the number of African-Americans receiving doctorates was 1,116. By 1980, the year Reagan was elected, there were 1.1. million African-Americans enrolled in American colleges and various types of professional schools, and the number of black doctorates had fallen slightly to 1,032 students. The Reagan administration initiated budget cuts in education, replacing government grants for loans, and deliberately escalated unemployment for low-income people, making it difficult to afford tuition at professional schools. By 1983, the number of black doctorates dropped to 921; and by 1987 only 765 black women and men were awarded doctorates. By 1987, there were nearly 100,000 fewer black Americans enrolled in college than there were ten years ago. We're seeing the vision of equality moving away from us.

A similar story exists for the overall enrollment of African-Americans in institutions of higher education. In 1980, 1,107,000 black men and women were enrolled in a college or post-secondary institution. Six years later, that figure had declined slightly, down to 1,081,000 students. Since, however, the population base for blacks of college age (18 to 26 years) had increased significantly during these years, the decline was actually far greater than it appeared when considered as a percentage of that population group. By contrast, white college enrollment between 1976 and 1986 increased by nearly 1 million students—almost the total number of all African-Americans currently enrolled.

We can think about the problem of education under-development at the collegiate level if we backtrack the progress of young people of color from kindergarten through to their senior year in college. According to the California Post-secondary Education Commission Director's Report, the 1988 black kindergarten enrollment in California was approximately 35,290 students. Of this number, the director's report projects that only 17,645 black students from this 1988 kindergarten class, roughly 50 percent, will graduate from high schools. About 6,800 will enter community colleges, approximately 20 percent; 1,235 are projected to enter campuses of the California State University system; and another 706 will enroll in the University of California, which is only 2 percent of the original kindergarten class. How many will graduate? Only 363 black students will ultimately receive college diplomas from either California State University or the University of California, 1 percent of the initial group.

The basic pattern of elitism and racism in colleges conforms to the dynamics of Third World colonialism. At nearly all white academic institutions, the power relationship between whites as a group and people of color is unequal. Authority is invested in the hands of a core, largely white male administrators, bureaucrats, and influential senior faculty. The board of trustees or regents is dominated by white, conservative, affluent males. Despite the presence of academic courses on minorities, the vast majority of white students take few or no classes which explore the heritage or cultures of non-Western peoples or domestic minorities. Most courses in the humanities and social sciences focus narrowly on topics or issues from the Western capitalist experience and minimize the centrality and importance of non-Western perspectives. Finally, the university or college divorces itself from the pressing concerns, problems, and debates which relate to blacks, Hispanics, or even white working class people. Given this structure and guiding philosophy, it shouldn't surprise us that many talented non-white student fail to achieve in such a hostile environment.

Toward a Multicultural Democracy

How do we begin to redefine the nature of democracy? Not as a thing, but as a process. Democracy is a dynamic concept. African-Americans 25 years ago did not have the right to eat in many restaurants, we couldn't sit down in the front seats of buses or planes, we couldn't vote in the South, we weren't allowed to use public toilets or drink from water fountains marked "For Whites Only." All of that changed through struggle, commitment, and an understanding that democracy is not something that you do once every four years when you vote; it's something that you live every single day.

People of color are radically redefining the nature of democracy. We assert that democratic government is empty and meaningless without active social justice and cultural diversity. Multicultural political democracy means that this country was not built by and for only one group—Western Europeans; that our country does not have only one language—English; or only one religion—Christianity; or only one economic philosophy—corporate capitalism. Multicultural democracy means that the leadership within our society should reflect the richness, colors, and diversity expressed in the lives of all our people. Multicultural democracy enable all women and men to achieve full self-determination, which may include territorial and geographical restructuring, if that is the desire of an indigenous group, community, or oppressed nation. Native Americans can no longer be denied their legitimate claims of sovereignty as an oppressed nation, and we must fight for their right to self-determination as a central principle of democracy.

Multicultural democracy articulates a vision of society which is feminist or, in the words of Alice Walker, "womanist." The patterns of subordination and exploitation of women of color—including job discrimination rooted in gender, race, and class, rape and sexual abuse, forced sterilizations, harassment and abuse within the criminal justice system, housing discrimination against single mothers with children, the absence of pay equity for comparable work, political under-representation, and legal disfran-chisement—combine to perpetuate a subordinate status for women within society. No progressive struggles have ever been won for people of color throughout history without the courage, contributions, sacrifices, and lead-ership of women. No political agenda of emancipation is possible unless one begins with the central principle of empowerment and full liberation for all women, at every level of organization and society. Men must learn from the experiences and insights of women if we are to liberate restraints which deny us our rights as Americans and free human beings.

What else is multicultural democracy? Multicultural democracy includes a powerful economic vision which is centered on the needs of human be-ings. We each need to go out into the community and begin hammering out an economic vision of empowerment that grassroots people can grasp and understand and use. We need to break the media monologues that talk at us through the TV and begin talking with one another in the terms of our practical life experiences. What kinds of questions should we raise? Is it right for a government to spend billions and billions for bailing out fat cats who profited from the savings and loan scam while millions of jobless Americans stand in unemployment lines desperate for work? Is it fair that billions of our dollars are allocated for the Pentagon's permanent war econ-omy to obliterate the lives of millions of poor people from Panama to Iraq to Grenada to Vietnam, while 2 million Americans sleep in the streets and 37 million Americans lack any form of medical coverage? Bush and the De-mocrats recently came up with a compromise on the permanent war econ-omy. They called for a $291 billion military budget for the next fiscal year! Figure that out. It's equivalent to spending $1 trillion on military in the next three years. This is supposed to be the post–Cold War era? Who is the military-industrial complex gearing up to fight? Is the war going to be in the Soviet Union? There is already a war going on, and the war is between them and us. We're losing the war as we see millions of people slide into hunger and poverty. We're losing the war when we see children go to ele-mentary schools throughout thousands of cities and towns across America without adequate food and clothing, while no one stands up and advocates an economics of empowerment and social justice. Is it a democracy when people of color have the freedom to starve, the freedom to live in housing without adequate heating facilities, the freedom to attend substandard schools? Democracy without social justice, without human rights, without human dignity is no democracy at all.

We can unite by pooling our resources and energies around progressive projects designed to promote greater awareness and protest among na-tional communities of people of color. This could mean joint mobilizations against the 1992 Columbus Quincentennial. Any "celebration" of the so-called conquest of the Americas and the Caribbean is a sick insult to the millions of Native Americans, Latinos, Asians, and Africans who died at the sword of capitalism, the transatlantic slave trade, and colonialism. We have the opportunity to denounce 500 years of invasion, war, genocide, and racism by holding teach-ins, demonstrations, and collective protest actions while bringing greater strength and momentum to the multicultural movement. We could initiate "Freedom Schools," liberation academies which identify and nurture young women and men with an interest in community-based struggles—a curriculum which teaches young people about their protest leaders, which reinforces their identification with our collective cultures of resistance, and which deepens our solidarity by celebrating rather than stifling our cultural differences. The new majority must build progressive research institutes, bridging the distance between activists, community organizers, and progressive intellectuals who can provide the policies and theoretical tools useful in the empowerment of grassroots constituencies and national communities.

Finally, we must infuse our definition of politics with a common sense of ethics and spirituality which challenges the structures of oppression, power, and privilege within the dominant social order. Part of the historic strengths of the Black Freedom Movement were the deep connections between political objectives and ethical prerogatives. This connection gave the rhetoric of Frederick Douglass, Sojourner Truth, W.E.B. Du Bois, Paul Robeson, and Fannie Lou Hamer a clear vision of the moral ground that was simultaneously particular and universal. It spoke to the uplifting of African-Americans, but its humanistic imperative continues to reach far further.

Multicultural democracy must perceive itself in this historic tradition, as a critical project which transforms the larger society. We must place humanity at the center of our politics. It is not sufficient that we assert what we are against; we must affirm what we are for. It is not sufficient that we declare what we want to overturn, but what we are seeking to build, in the sense of restoring humanity and humanistic values to a system which is materialist, destructive to the environment, and abusive to fellow human beings. We need to enact policies which say that the people who actually produce society's wealth should control how it is used.

The moral bankruptcy of contemporary American society is found, in part, in the vast chasm which separates the conditions of material well-being, affluence, power, and privilege of a small elite from the whole spectrum of America's communities. The evil in our world is politically and socially engineered, and its products are poverty, homelessness, illiteracy, political subservience, race discrimination, and gender domination. The old saying from the sixties—we either are part of the solution or part of the problem—is simultaneously moral, cultural, economic, and political. Paul Robeson reminds us that we must "take a stand," not simply dare to dream, if our endeavors are to have lasting meaning. We cannot be disinterested observers as the physical and spiritual beings of millions of people are collectively crushed.

Can we believe in certain inalienable rights that go beyond Jefferson's terminology of "life, liberty, and the pursuit of happiness"? What about the inalienable right not to go hungry in a land of agricultural abundance? The human right to decent housing? The human right to free public medical care for all? The human right to an adequate income in one's old age? Democracy must believe in freedom, but that freedom in my terminology is something different from what "freedom" has come to mean in this country in the age of Ronald Reagan and George Bush, Clarence Thomas and David Duke. Freedom now means, unfortunately, the freedom of corporations to raise prices, the wealthy to evade taxes, or the freedom of the unemployed to dwell at the edge of starvation and desperation. Can we believe in a freedom to build a new society without racism and sexism, to work and live in our neighborhood and have access to free public medical care and decent shelter for all? If we can achieve such a democracy, if we can believe in the vision of a dynamic democracy in which all human beings, women and men, Latinos, Asian-Americans, Native Americans, come to terms with each other, we can perhaps begin to achieve Martin Luther King, Jr.'s vision when he said, "We shall overcome."

9

The Challenge of Black Leadership: African-American Empowerment for the Twenty-first Century

1994

It has been 30 years—an entire generation—since the watershed passage of the Civil Rights Act of 1964, which outlawed legal, racial segregation in public accommodations throughout America. It has been more than three decades since Dr. Martin Luther King Jr. articulated his "I Have a Dream" speech on the steps of the Lincoln Memorial, before 250,000 Americans at the 1963 March on Washington, DC. How have the challenges for black leadership changed since the end of the Civil Rights Movement?

Let us consider the state of the national black community by examining three interrelated themes. First, what are the challenges which confront African-American people today, and how are they different from those which we faced during the struggle against Jim Crow? If we examine the totality of our experience—in health care, education, economic development, criminal justice, housing and homelessness, poverty, and unemployment, we will witness an unprecedented erosion and retreat from the goal of equality, especially since 1980. We are witnessing what is, in effect, a war waged by the system against African-American children and young adults.

Second, how do we develop a strategy to move us away from the politics and tactics we held during the struggle against segregation and toward a new awareness and critical analysis of our current situation? In brief, how do we move from the effort to achieve "racial representation" within the existing system to effective "empowerment"? How do we go from "inclusion" to "transformation," the establishment of multicultural democracy?

And third, there is the question of values and vision. What values and principles will we need in order to transform the war against our young people, a war of violence, underemployment, and hopelessness, into a struggle for collective pride, social responsibility, and commitment? These values are spirit, soul, and struggle.

Throughout the twentieth century, there have been three general approaches to the struggle for black empowerment in America. Based on my research with Professor Leith Mullings of the City University of New York, we have defined these approaches as inclusion, black nationalism, and transformation. An "inclusionist" approach toward black politics has relied on coalitions with white parties or organizations to achieve reforms; it seeks access and opportunities for blacks within the existing system and utilizes the courts to pursuit legal challenges to end discrimination. Frequently, an inclusionist approach emphasizes cultural assimilation, the effort to be accepted within the American mainstream. A "black nationalist" approach to black empowerment favors the building of all-black institutions to provide goods, services, and education to African-American people; it culturally rejects the values and ideals of white America and emphasizes our unity with other people of African descent throughout the Black Diaspora. A "transformationist" or multicultural democratic approach argues that institutional racism cannot be dismantled unless the power, privileges, and property of elite whites are redistributed more democratically to oppressed Americans. A transformationist strategy calls for an internationalist perspective linking black struggles for freedom with those of other people of color and oppressed people; it favors the construction of a dynamic coalition of the oppressed in American society to extend the principles of political democracy into economic and social relations.

There are strengths and weaknesses to each of these strategies for black advancement. During the Civil Rights Movement, the basic approach taken was inclusionist or integrationist. With this strategy, we were able to outlaw legal segregation, extend voting rights to millions of people, establish reforms such as affirmative action, and expand job and educational opportunities for African-Americans and others. The number of African-American elected officials since 1964 has increased from barely 100 to 8,000; the number of black mayors during the same years rose from zero to 400. But the problem of an inclusionist approach is that it frequently confuses "symbolic representation" with genuine power. A "black face in a high place" may give African-Americans a sense of pride and symbolic accomplishment; but if that black person near the pinnacle of power fails to address the legitimate grievances and problems of our people, African-Americans as a group aren't empowered at all.

The inclusionist strategy has also failed to grasp that the basic terms of debate about the future of black people within America have changed since the 1960s. Although a minority of African-Americans are moving forward, the vast majority of our people are experiencing a deterioration in their day-to-day existence. For example, in terms of health care, an alarming gap continues to widen in the status of African-Americans versus whites. According to the National Center for Health Statistics, the life expectancy for black men has fallen to 64.7 years, before they can even qualify to collect Social Security! Millions of black women are not receiving adequate prenatal care, and infant mortality rates are, not surprisingly, twice the rate for blacks than for whites. Another recent health study found that blacks, who represent only 13 percent of the total US population, now account for 80 percent of all premature deaths (deaths of individuals between the ages of 15 and 44) because of abnormally high rates of pneumonia, asthma, bladder infections, and other diseases. Blacks, Latinos, and low-income people die sooner than upper-class whites because most have no access to regular health care services and insurance.

Yet another crisis that compounds the difficult situation of people of color is the state of public education in this country. In many cities, the dropout rate for nonwhite high school students exceeds 40 percent. Across the United States, more than 1,500 teenagers of color drop out of school each day. And many of those who stay in school don't receive any serious training to prepare them for a computer-driven, technologically advanced labor market. In short, thousands of people are applying for jobs as cashiers and bank tellers who cannot do simple arithmetic. Thousands of high school students are unable to read the simplest instructions. Meanwhile, the new jobs generated by high technology increasingly demand the ability to operate computers and analyze complex data. The gap is steadily growing between the technical qualifications and academic background necessary for such jobs and the actual level of ability of millions in the educational underclass.

It won't be long before a new form of "segregation" surfaces, threatening the prospects of millions of black youths. There won't be the Jim Crow signs of "white" and "colored" to reserve job discrimination. Instead, the new segregation of the twenty-first century will be the division between the educated "haves" and the uneducated "have-nots." Those who lack scientific, mathematical, and computer skills are already disproportionately nonwhite.

How does the legacy of racism relate to issues of economics? Walk through the heart of any American city, through the bus and train terminals, parks and side streets, and you will encounter the homeless—black, Latino, and white, ex-factory workers and the elderly, people with mental disorders and preschool children. We have a political and economic system which prides itself on being a "democracy," and yet it is unable or unwilling to address the crisis of millions of Americans sleeping each night in the streets, gutters, and alleys across this country.

Part of the problem is the growing number of people at low-income levels who must allocate a great percentage of their disposable funds just for shelter. Back in 1970, there were about 6 million households with incomes of less than $10,000 a year in 1989 dollars. There were more than 6.5 million houses and apartments throughout the country that were rented for less than $250 per month in 1989 dollars. This means that 20 years ago the vast majority of people who had low incomes were able to locate suitable housing units. And despite the image popularized by the media that public housing consists almost exclusively of African-American and Latino tenants, about 60 percent of all families living in public housing in 1990 were white.

The housing crisis for the poor reached a new level of severity under policies of deliberate cruelty during the Reagan and Bush administrations. From 1977 to 1980, during the Carter administration, the federal government added an average of 290,000 new families each year to the list of those receiving housing assistance. However, after ousting Carter from the White House in 1980, Reagan slashed federal housing allocations from $30 billion in fiscal year 1981 to barely $8 billion in 1986. The number of available housing units dropped sharply in virtually every city. In the past decade, the federal government has extended housing support to an average of 78,000 new families each year. About 9.6 million families earning low incomes are now qualified for housing assistance, but only 4.4 million households are currently receiving federal or state aid.

The federal government's blatant inaction has forced low-income people to pay more and more for housing units; not to mention that large families are increasingly being forced to live either in cramped, overcrowded conditions or in the streets. By 1989, 47 percent of all poor families were spending 70 percent of their income on shelter alone. This leaves but 30 percent for a family's food, clothing, health care, electricity, heat, school supplies for children, and transportation. Not surprisingly, the number of American homeless doubled in the 1980s. Thousands of poor children die prematurely from preventable diseases because their parents cannot afford decent health care for them. Thousands of poor children go to bed hungry every night, while their government does virtually nothing to assist them.

The social crisis of urban America threatens the prospects of an entire "lost generation" of African-American and Latino young people. The economic deterioration of our central cities, the loss of jobs, and the decline of investment are only part of the story. The loss of recreational facilities such as theaters, public parks, bowling alleys, and playgrounds reduces the environment for positive social interaction among young people. The deterioration of city services, unequal educational facilities, and higher taxes drive middle- and upper-class people out of the central cities. All of these factors coalesce to provide a context of hopelessness and social alienation.

Consider the recent proliferation of teenage pregnancies and single-parent households. In each of the past five years, more than 1 million teenage girls became pregnant. For African-Americans, the two-parent household is becoming almost extinct. Twenty-five years ago, two out of five first births by black women under the age of 35 were out of wedlock. Today, the ratio is two out of every three. A black child born today has only a one in five chance of growing up with two parents until the age of 16.

The most tragic aspect of the growth of out of wedlock births are the so-called boarder babies. About 22,000 newborn infants are abandoned in hospitals each year. Approximately 74 percent are black, another 8 percent, Latino. According to a 1991 study of the Department of Health and Human Services, more than three-fourths of all boarder babies tested positive for drugs and nearly half were born prematurely.

The most devastating impact of institutional racism and economic exploitation occurs among African-American children and young adults. In terms of education, the criminal justice system, and housing and human services, it represents nothing short of a war against young black people. For example, let us examine the statistical evidence provided by New York City and New York State. In the area of health care, six out of 10 preschool children in New York City are not immunized. There are currently only 96 nurses for 600 elementary schools in the city; nurses no longer visit middle schools and high schools. Every day in New York City, an estimated 70,500 children use drugs. Over 160,000 children—mostly black and Latino—have no health insurance. Since 1987, TB cases in New York City have doubled. And today, AIDS is the leading cause of death in New York City for children under the age of five.

In the area of housing and homelessness, there are in New York City about 90,000 homeless people today. In a typical evening, 24,000 homeless—including 9,700 children—will sleep in a city-run shelter. About 90 percent of the homeless are black and Latino. In a five-year period, about one out of every 12 black children in New York City will live in a homeless shelter.

How do we explain the persistence of racism in American life as we enter the twenty-first century? Nobel laureate Toni Morrison explains that race remains "hidden and covert," obscured from the light of a frank and honest analysis. Instead of using overtly racist epithets, Americans who believe in the inferiority of people of color rely on "code words" and subtle innuendoes to justify discrimination.

But the dilemma is deeper than prejudicial language or attitudes. The burden of discrimination is translated into radically different perceptions of the world, which separate white, upper- and middle-class America from the vast majority of black, brown, and poor people. This division even transcends the racial bifurcation outlined by the 1968 report of the Kerner Commission, which warned that America was rapidly moving toward two unequal societies—one black and one white. A more accurate description of the current racial and class impasse is to speak of two "parallel universes" in which individuals and groups coexist in the same social, political, and cultural space but perceive phenomena in sharply divergent ways.

Black urban residents, for example, have known for decades about the practice of "redlining"—in which banks and other financial institutions systematically reject loan applications from black and Latino neighborhoods. The policies of redlining are reinforced by the property insurance industry, which routinely rejects a much higher percentage of minority applications for insurance than whites. According to the research of the Association of Community Organizations for Reform Now (ACORN), this discrimination forms a nationwide pattern. For example, in Milwaukee, only 30 percent of all single-family homes owned by low-income African-Americans were insured, compared to 79 percent of all similar dwellings owned by low-income whites. In Minneapolis, only 48 percent of black single-family homes were insured versus 80 percent of homes in comparable white districts. ACORN also discovered in its research that African-Americans and Latinos invariably pay much higher rates than whites to insure homes of identical value. For example, in Kansas City, Missouri, ACORN found that insurance cost 0.88 percent of a home's value in low-income minority neighborhoods; in majority white, low-income communities, insurance cost only 0.45 percent of a home's value. Blacks pay more and receive less, but the vast majority of whites not only don't perceive this reality; they also don't even think about it.

How do we move beyond the current crisis within black America? This nation cannot continue to realize the goals of democracy unless it is willing to reorder its fiscal priorities. During the next five years, despite the collapse of Eastern Europe and the destruction of the Berlin Wall, the government is planning to spend more than $1.4 trillion for nuclear and conventional weapons. Billions of dollars will be taken from human needs and economic development. The money spent to construct 46 M-1 tanks would purchase 500 modern city buses for mass transportation. One F-16 jet fighter costs as much as 1,000 teachers' salaries for one full year. One billion dollars spent on building guided missiles creates 20,700 jobs—but $1 billion spent for public health care facilities, doctors, nurses, and staff would create 54,206 jobs. One billion dollars spent for public education, teachers' salaries, and school construction would generate 71,500 jobs.

Black America stands at a challenging moment in its history: a time of massive social disruption, class stratification, political uncertainty, and cultural ambiguity. The objectives for black politics in the age of Jim Crow segregation were simple: full equality, voting rights, and removal of "white" and "colored" signs from the doors of hotels and schools. Today's problems are fundamentally different in scope, character, and intensity: the flight of capital investment from our central cities, with thousands of lost jobs; the deterioration of the urban tax base, with the decline of city services; black-on-black violence, homicide, and crime; the proliferation of single-parent households; and the decline in the quality of our public schools. And to this familiar litany of problems, I would add one more: the crisis of the spirit. There is a growing pessimism within our ranks which asserts that there are no solutions to our overwhelming social problems, that government can't help us, that voting and participation within the political process are irrelevant, that no allies exist outside the African-American community who will help us. And the greatest doubt of all centers on the question of leadership—whether we have the capacity or the will to generate women and men who will rise to contemporary challenges. We are forced to respond to these dilemmas and to overcome our adversities. And the power to accomplish our goals, ironically enough, already exists in our own hands.

We must build a new black leadership to tackle today's problems with an originality of analysis and a new level of programmatic and policy sophistication. This new black leadership must develop policy initiatives in concert with the best scholars and researchers to construct alternatives in health care, education, housing, and the environment. Sound public policies that actually address the black community's problems must come from a collaborative process, recognizing and critiquing the weaknesses of previous policies while identifying those policies that have worked.

Black leadership should be at the forefront of defining alternatives on local, state, and national issues. In England, when a political party is defeated at the polls or is out of power, it creates a "shadow government," a group of public spokespeople who challenge the policies of those in power and present alternatives. We desperately need a black shadow government in Washington, DC, to monitor the new Democratic administration of Bill Clinton—in education, criminal justice, public transportation, economic development, housing, civil rights, and a whole range of public affairs. We need to foster a new SNCC—a Student Nonviolent Coordinating Committee—to nourish the leadership potential of today's youth and student activists. Their idealism, energy, and militancy need to be channeled for constructive political purposes.

Building a new black leadership means expanding the numbers of African-Americans who are registered to vote and conducting political education campaigns in churches and community centers. And, most important, we must realize that leaders aren't "born"; they are "made." All people ultimately get the leadership they deserve. We must construct new programs to create the leadership needed to revive movements for democracy in America, making the leap from representation to empowerment.

Power, in the final analysis, is the ability or capacity to realize one's specific, objective interests. Power is not a "thing" but a process of utilizing existing resources, personnel, and institutions for one's own objectives. If our goal is to empower the African-American community, we must have a detailed understanding of who we are and what our people want. This requires an honest and detailed analysis of where we are as a people—our genuine social problems and contradictions, our strengths and weaknesses, our internal resources and potential elements of leadership. We must actually listen to what the masses of African-American people really want and how they truly perceive the world around them. As the great African political theorist and teacher Amilcar Cabral observed, we must "hide nothing from the masses of our people. Tell no lies. ... Mask no difficulties, mistakes, failures. Claim no easy victories."

Programmatically, this means that the national black community needs a public opinion poll which regularly assesses the state of black America on a wide range of public issues. Instead of looking to the white media to learn what we think, we should utilize our own networks and resources to present our own collective views. We need to initiate leadership training seminars within black institutions which identify and educate the next generation of African-American leaders.

One achieves power by building a strategy or plan of action based on reality. We must articulate a concrete analysis of concrete conditions—not a romantic wish list of things as we would prefer them to be. We are a people of African descent, to be sure, but the vast majority of our people will live, work, and die right here in the United States. We need a plan of group development that is grounded fundamentally in the here and now, not in ancient Egypt or in the Caribbean. Our basic struggle for power is right here in America.

We must also search for common ground—the basic unity of interests which brings together people of different backgrounds, genders, sexual orientations, languages, and social classes to advance the ideals of democracy. Unity among people of color is pivotal to this process of reconstructing democracy in America. We need to realize that we represent America's future "mainstream." By the year 2000, one third of the entire American population will consist of African-Americans, Asian-Americans, Latinos, and other people of color. By 2030, a majority of most of America's cities and most southwestern states will be nonwhite. And by the year 2056, a majority of the total American population will consist of people of color. The color line will be transformed—the white majority will become a minority, and the minorities will become the numerical majority. We are the future of America, and whites must also begin to make the transition to a multicultural, pluralistic world.

We must revive a sense of political and social vision within the African-American community if we are going to move forward as a people. And the place to begin is with three simple—yet vital—elements which have underscored our entire history in America. First, black leaders must reclaim and reemphasize the meaning of "spirit" for our people. Even a casual reading of African-American history relates that our greatness as a people has been defined at those moments when we have made demands upon the larger society that are simultaneously political and morally justified. What is desired politically should also be morally and ethically correct if our policies are to transcend a level of mean-spirited self-gratification.

The bankruptcy and sickness in America's corporate and political leadership are located in its pervasive hypocrisy, a malevolent odor of hunger and homelessness, of greed and capital gains, of the accumulation of great wealth at the expense of the larger social welfare. The *New York Times* recently reported that the top 1 percent of all American households have a total net wealth which is significantly larger than the bottom 90 percent of all American households. Thus this country lurches toward the rocky shoals of racism, sexism, violence, urban decay, and class warfare.

Second, the Black Freedom Movement must reclaim the integrity and the creativity of the "soul" of our people—their sense of inner integrity and pride in their heritage; their poetry, music, and dance; their cultural traditions and worldview. One might call "soul" the creative power of cultural memory. The challenge of educators and leaders is to revive and enrich that cultural memory and consciousness.

Third, we must return to the idea that the only path toward political and economic empowerment is through "struggle." Struggle is a tradition of defiance to the dynamics of oppression, a willingness to sacrifice one's individualistic interest for the larger good. Struggle is the recognition that black people's problems are not primarily the result of individuals but of institutional forces—and so we must perceive the real sources of our oppression. We must develop long-term programs and strategies for transformation of everything that stands between ourselves and full human dignity. Black leaders must be reminded that struggle is not only a single act of protest but also a commitment to live one's life in a manner that accelerates the interests of African-Americans and other oppressed people, to motivate them to higher levels of engagement and constructive activity.

A commitment to struggle means that we must have the courage to revitalize our movement for freedom periodically. In South Africa in the 1940s, the African National Congress was essentially an "inclusionist" organization—it sought reforms and the symbolic representation of black people within the established system. Then the Nationalist Party came to power and instituted apartheid. A totally new situation existed for black people, requiring new strategies and programs. New leadership arose, personified by Nelson Mandela and Walter Sisulu; a new program of massive resistance was launched, calling for the democratic transformation of South African society.

We have a similar situation in black America today. The masses of our people recognize that most of the issues which defined the period of the Civil Rights Movement no longer exist. We face an unprecedented crisis of poverty, violence, joblessness, and social despair, and the old approaches are no longer sufficient or viable. We must struggle to transform our situation, to extend the principles of democracy to economic and social relations, to create the foundations of genuine opportunity for our people. We need a bold new leadership with a democratic vision of empowerment and equality. As Frederick Douglass reminded us more than a century ago, "Without struggle, there can be no progress."

10

Crossing Boundaries, Making Connections: The Politics of Race and Class in Urban America

Nineteen hundred ninety-four marks the thirtieth anniversary, a generation, since the Freedom Summer of 1964, when thousands of idealistic, energetic, and committed young people, black and white, went to Mississippi to register thousands of African-Americans for the first time, to make democracy a living reality. Nineteen hundred ninety-four marks the thirtieth anniversary of the challenge by the Freedom Democratic Party and Mrs. Fannie Lou Hamer, in Atlantic City, at the Democratic Party National Convention, to make the Democratic Party truly "democratic" and "inclusive." A generation has passed since the high point of the Freedom Struggle, and November 1994 marks the greatest congressional victory of the voices of conservatism, intolerance, and racism in our lifetimes. It may represent a next stage of the Reagan Revolution of 1980, which pushed back reforms for women's rights, civil rights, the rights of labor and poor people, the hungry and the homeless.

How do we reconcile our political past with the challenges of the present, and the prospects for the future? What is the meaning to our own time of the Civil Rights Movement, the struggle to deconstruct racial prejudice and to extend the principles of democracy and fairness to all members of society? What analysis and vision are required to reverse the cynicism and pessimism which feed upon the contemporary politics of inequality and intolerance and to build a new paradigm of humanism and hope? How do we cross boundaries to reach new solutions to our social problems?

Let us explore three central themes which may provide a partial blueprint for black and progressive multiracial, multicultural politics beyond the political defeat of 1994. First, let us examine the retreat from progressive politics in the 1980s and 1990s, which was created in part by the Reagan Revolution but also by the collapse of liberalism and rise of the so-called New Democrats led by Bill Clinton.

Second, let us place the political rise of the Far Right in an economic and social context—the growth of inequality throughout America. Here, we should identify the inequalities of health care, education, housing, and homelessness and the continuing burden of discrimination in the marketplace and throughout society, especially in our cities.

Third, let us explore the possible political steps necessary to reverse the trends toward intolerance and conservatism. How can we make electoral politics more relevant to issues in people's daily lives? How can we begin to change the rules of the political game to empower those who are locked out of positions of power and privilege? And finally, what issues can serve as a model for a new left-of-center paradigm, cutting across racial, ethnic, gender, language, and class boundaries and reinforcing a common program for democratic empowerment and social change? By what means, programmatic and conceptual, can we revive that idealism, that hopeful engagement and commitment of 1964, to address the new problems and issues of the twenty-first century?

Millions of Americans in the 1990s have become cynical and withdrawn from the democratic political process; they continue to ask themselves how a "democratic" country like America can have so many poor people or have 39 million people without medical insurance. Many of us are forced to try to reconcile our democratic ideals and aspirations with the actual contradictions of daily life. The values in which we believe are *constantly* undermined and compromised by a pervasive system of power, privilege, and prejudice which seeks to curtail dissent, silence critics, and limit the very *concept* of democracy.

Millions of American people believe in the ideals of political democracy—specifically, the electoral franchise, the freedom of political thought, association, and choice regarding representation—yet we live under a political plutocracy buoyed by vast financial contributions from corporate interests and maintained by a biased electoral system that rewards the privileged few and severely restricts radical, progressive, and alternative voices. Millions of American people believe in the ideal of human creativity and work, the concept of a job for everyone who wishes to work. Yet we exist under a corporate-controlled system of elitism and privilege in which the upper 1 percent of all households has a greater net worth than the bottom 90 percent. Millions of American people believe in the concept of human equality and equal treatment under the law—regardless of race, religion, gender, and sexual orientation. Yet we live in a time of growing inequalities between people, a polarization between the superaffluent "haves" and the millions of increasingly marginalized "have-nots." Black, Latino, and low-income dissent exploded on the streets of Los Angeles in 1992, yet our government refused to pass a comprehensive urban jobs program to address the root economic factors beneath this discontent.

Millions of American people believe that our nation's greatest strength is the colorful mosaic of its ethnic diversity—yet our government actively seeks to curtail immigration from most non-European countries and brutally rejects and imprisons refugees from Haiti. In short, millions of American people believe in expanding democracy to include greater rights for all Americans. Those who exercise real power in our system actively seek to curtail our voices, to limit our choices, to block and to eliminate genuine alternatives in politics. Our current political process, designed two centuries ago, must be reformed in order to reflect the new and deeply democratic aspirations of the majority of American people. Thus our challenge is to reconcile our democratic dreams with our increasingly undemocratic realities. We must democratically transform our political process to end the hypocrisy and elitism which foster alienation and frustration among voters.

In the 1980s, governments throughout Europe and North America adopted a conservative model for economic development and social relations within their societies. Employed by Ronald Reagan of the United States and Margaret Thatcher of England, this conservative model of government advanced an ideology of extreme materialism, individualism, and unveiled exploitation of labor. It declared that there was no implied or real "social contract" between citizens and their government. People had no "natural right" to benefits such as health care, education, public assistance during times of need, or shelter.

Furthermore, this conservative political perspective viewed the government as a collection agency for fleecing working people, eliminating civil rights and environmental protection laws, giving fewer and fewer social entitlements that addressed human needs. With the fall of communism and the end of the Cold War, this reactionary ideology of conservatism has come to dominate politics throughout the world. Even after the defeat of the Reagan-Bush administrations and the victory of Bill Clinton and the Democrats in 1992, most of the regressive social assumptions about the role of government have remained. Clinton's withdrawal of Lani Guinier's nomination as the Assistant Attorney General for Civil Rights, his refusal to increase the minimum wage, his failure to support working people by his position favoring the North Atlantic Free Trade Agreement (NAFTA), and his rejection of the single-payer, Canadian health care model in favor of managed competition all indicate the long-term impact of Reaganism within both major political parties.

It was in this context of retreat and rejection that the Republican Right was able to take the offensive in 1993 and this year. First came the victory of Republican Kay Bailey Hutchinson in the senatorial race in Texas. Then in Los Angeles, millionaire Republican businessman Richard Riordan overwhelmingly trounced liberal Democratic City Councilman Michael Woo in the race for mayor. In the wake of the 1992 urban rebellion in Los Angeles, Riordan appealed to frightened middle-class voters by calling for the appointment of 3,000 additional police officers.

In effect, Riordan successfully constructed an elitist, antiblack united front, which received broad, bipartisan support. He received 40 percent of the votes from registered Democrats, 50 percent of the Jewish vote, and the overwhelming majority of the white, suburban vote. In New York City that same year, conservative Republican Rudolph Giuliani, formerly the third-ranking member of the Reagan administration's Justice Department, essentially patterned his entire campaign against incumbent mayor David Dinkins after the model established by Riordan in Los Angeles.

The victories of Riordan and Giuliani, combined with the moral and political waffling and retreat by Clinton, set the stage of the second stage of the Reagan Revolution, the 1994 congressional campaign, permitting conservative Republicans to seize control of the House of Representatives for the first time since 1954. Many attributed the Republicans' victories to widespread unpopularity and disillusionment with the policies of the Clinton administration. But I would characterize the factors behind the 1994 Republican triumph as the product of what can be termed the "three D's": deception, demagoguery, and the decline of the American dream. These three D's symbolize the politics of fear which is at the heart of the Republican agenda.

For deception, we may observe the "Ten Point Program," the "Contract with America," which more than 300 Republican candidates, challengers and incumbents alike, announced on the steps of the Capitol building at the start of their campaign. The Republicans took an excursion down memory lane to the era of "Reaganism," promising massive reductions in individual and corporate taxes, a constitutional amendment requiring a balanced federal budget, term limits for members of Congress, more applications of the death penalty, increased expenditures for the military, deeper cuts in welfare, and much more. The Republicans told us that all their new programs would only cost an extra $150 billion over the next five years.

However, the Congressional Budget Office reveals that it would take another $700 billion in cuts during the next five years just to balance the current budget—even before the Republican proposals to increase military spending and to cut taxes. The Republicans didn't tell voters that reducing the capital gains tax would largely benefits high-income households. The Republicans didn't explain to voters that their programs would conservatively require slashing about 20 percent of the federal budget across the board—from farm subsidies to Social Security. They didn't tell us that their proposed tax credit for children would provide absolutely nothing to families too poor to owe taxes. No wonder the *New York Times* editorialized that the Republicans' "Contract with America" was little more than "duplicitous propaganda."

For demagoguery, we might turn to the dangerous alliance brewing among Republicans, the Radical Right, and extremist elements in the religious fundamentalist movement. The 1992 Republican Convention in Houston featured the voices of intolerance and bigotry, led by reactionaries such as Patrick Buchanan. Now, state by state, the Radical Right has seized control of the GOP state apparatus in Virginia, Minnesota, Iowa, Oregon, and Washington, among others. In Texas this summer, the Radical Right purged the state's GOP Chairman Fred Meyer, ousted the state executive committee, and drafted the most reactionary state party platform in the country. Among the Texas Republican Party's dogmatic tenets are demands to repeal the minimum wage, to outlaw a woman's constitutional right to choice for reproductive freedom, to withdraw the United States from the United Nations and return its monetary system to the gold standard, and to eliminate bilingual education programs. Droves of moderate Republicans and even some hard-core Reaganites shuddered at this level of demagoguery.

The worst example of demagoguery was the senatorial race in Virginia, featuring Oliver North against incumbent Senator Chuck Robb. Conservative Republican Senator Charles Grassley of Iowa has accurately described North as "a nut." North was a convicted liar before Congress because of false testimony during the Iran-Contra hearings. Although unsuccessful despite spending more than $17 million, North will probably return as a Far Right candidate for the Senate again in 1996. One observer who witnessed the recent North campaign describes him as potentially "the most preposterous US Senator since the notorious racist Theodore Bilbo" of Mississippi. Or as Colin McEnroe, a columnist for the *Hartford Courant*, commented on North: "There's a Norman Bates sort of thing going on in his eyes."

What explains the popularity of Ollie North as well as other extremist candidates who promise much but can deliver little? The backlash against the Democrats is fueled not as much by logic as by fear and frustration. Since the mid-1970s, the real standard of living for most middle-income Americans, adjusted for the rate of inflation, has declined. Families today are working at two, three, or more jobs and aren't getting ahead. Their sacrifices to send their children to college and to set aside something for their own retirement seem unrewarded and even futile. The decline of the American dream creates fertile ground for the politics of fear, deception, and demagoguery.

But let us be frank: a central factor in the success of the Far Right is the reality of racism and the manipulation of racial stereotypes within our political culture and society. The decisive cutting edge of Reaganism and political reaction is racism. Race and gender were primary factors which fueled the victories of Republican congressional candidates in 1994. According to Voter News Service exit polls, in 1992 the overall vote was divided by 54 to 46 percent in favor of the Democratic candidates. White males that year tended to favor Republicans, but only slightly, 51 percent versus 49 percent. This year, the general electorate favored Republicans slightly, 51 percent to 49 percent. However, white males as a group overwhelmingly endorsed Republicans, by a margin of 63 percent to 37 percent. Since white males make up 42 percent of all voters, their nearly two to one endorsement of Republicans was chiefly responsible for the Democratic defeat.

A breakdown of the white male vote by income and education is even more revealing. A majority of white males, who have less than a high school education and less than $15,000 annual income, were more likely to vote Democratic than Republican. Conversely, 70 percent of the white men who earn $75,000 and above voted for Republican congressional candidates. Sixty-nine percent of all white males with some college education and 67 percent of white men who are college graduates supported Republicans.

In many individual races, the votes by white males provided the margin of victory. In California, 60 percent of all males and over 67 percent of all white men voted for Republican Governor Pete Wilson, who ran successfully on a platform embracing Proposition 187, which outlawed governmental services and health programs to undocumented immigrants. By contrast, 75 percent of all black voters, 69 percent of all Latinos, and 51 percent of all people regardless of race earning less than $15,000 per year voted for Wilson's Democratic opponent, Kathleen Brown. In Michigan, 61 percent of all males and more than 67 percent of all white men supported successful Republican senatorial candidate Spencer Abraham, a former aide to Vice President Dan Quayle. Conversely, 91 percent of all African-Americans voted for Abraham's Democratic opponent, Congressman Bob Carr.

And in New York State, Democratic gubernatorial candidate Mario Cuomo received the strong support of African-Americans (86 percent), Latinos (78 percent), Jews (61 percent), people without a high school diploma (58 percent), and members of union households (51 percent)—in short, racial and ethnic minorities, low-income and poor people, and blue collar workers. Republican challenger George Pataki, by contrast, won the votes of people earning $100,000 and more annually (55 percent); white Protestants (62 percent); whites regardless of gender and income (58 percent); and white men (67 percent).

Let us have a historical perspective on the burden of race, the legacy of discrimination and hatred in American politics. The 1994 congressional campaign victories of the Republicans represent the culmination of a historical process which actually began a generation ago. After the political reforms of 1964 and the defeat of Jim Crow segregation, racial politics and a white backlash helped elect Richard Nixon in 1968. He subsequently pursued a "Southern Strategy" of appealing to the supporters of segregationist George Wallace and opposing school desegregation. Nixon tried to slam the door on the movement for racial equality; but Watergate undermined his conservative efforts. In 1980, racial politics crystallized behind white ethnic voters and the middle class, which endorsed the conservative candidacy of Ronald Reagan. As president, Reagan aggressively tried to roll back affirmative action, equal opportunity legislation, women's rights, and the rights of labor—remember the administration's repression of the air traffic controllers' strike in 1981. However, the Iran-Contra scandal shattered the conservative offensive momentarily. Now, 30 years after Fannie Lou Hamer's moving and eloquent challenge to the Democratic Party, 31 years after the memorable address of Martin Luther King Jr. on the steps of the Lincoln Memorial at the historic March on Washington, DC, a third racial backlash across white America has emerged.

We cannot hope to defeat the third wave of racial intolerance and reactionary politics by offering a pale imitation of the Far Right's conservative program to voters under the highly ambiguous banner of New Democrats. If given a choice between an imitation and the "real thing," voters will choose the real thing every time. We can reverse the politics of fear only with a vision of democratic empowerment, greater equality, and multicultural opportunity, bringing millions of disillusioned and alienated Americans into the political process. This requires an affirmative vision of job creation, quality health care, transportation, improved education, and the satisfaction of other human needs. Instead of retreating into the past, riding backward with Reaganism in our rearview mirror, we need to move forward toward a multicultural politics of hope and human development. And at the very center of such politics must be an ethical and social vision of antiracism and human equality.

We must honestly recognize just how deeply rooted racial stereotypes are within American political culture. The best evidence of this was provided in a 1993 national survey of over 2,200 American adults funded by the National Science Foundation, which was designed to measure contemporary racial attitudes. The study's directors, including Stanford University political scientist Paul Sniderman and University of California at Berkeley Professors Philip Tetlock and Anthony Tyler, stated that "the most striking result" of the survey "is the sheer frequency with which negative characterizations of blacks are quite openly expressed throughout the white general population." Not surprisingly, white conservatives had little reluctance in expressing their prejudices about African-Americans. But what surprised researchers was the deep racial hostility expressed by white liberals.

According to Sniderman, 51 percent of the white conservatives but also 45 percent of the white liberals agreed with the statement that "blacks are aggressive or violent." Thirty-four percent of the conservatives and 19 percent of the liberals "agreed that black are lazy." Twenty-one percent of the conservatives and 17 percent of the liberals concurred that African-Americans are "irresponsible." This explains why it is so difficult to pass meaningful legislation through Congress which addresses the inequality and discrimination which black people face everyday: white liberals basically dislike blacks as much as white conservatives do.

Racial stereotypes mask the central dynamics of what racism is and why it exists. Racism is nothing more or less than white privilege, white power, and white violence. And unless white Americans seriously are forced to confront their stereotypes about people of color, there will be no racial dialogue or peace in this country.

Racial politics is grounded in the reality of economic and social inequality for millions of Americans. There are many striking ways in which the harsh realities of inequality can be measured. For example, the criminal justice system has become the principal means for regulating the masses of unemployed, undereducated young black and Latino people. As of January 1, 1994, the American prison population, including those confined in penitentiaries, jails, and prisons of all kinds, exceeded 1.4 million people. There are roughly 650,000 African-Americans in prison today. The average black prisoner is 29 years old or less; the majority of black prisoners were unemployed at the time of their arrests. Nationwide, our prison population is projected to double within the next seven years and double again after another seven years. At that rate statistically, before the year 2073 we will have more Americans of all races and classes inside of prison than outside of prison.

The bitter recession of 1991–1992 forced several million middle-income Americans into unemployment lines for the first time, increased personal bankruptcies, and destroyed many lives. The media projected hundreds of stories on the "economic squeeze" of middle-income people unable to pay their home mortgages and college tuition bills for their children. But virtually ignored by the media and politicians were the millions of Americans in the lowest fifth of all income earners. This group includes millions of female-headed households with children who barely survive on Aid to Families with Dependent Children (AFDC); 10 million adults who are unemployed or who have stopped looking for work; millions of elderly who rely on Supplement Security Income payments and small pensions to survive; and several million Americans who are either homeless or dependent on others for temporary shelter. This is the "other America" described vividly by Michael Harrington more than 30 years ago.

A recent study of the Washington-based Center on Budget and Policies Priorities found that of the 30 states providing general assistance—a short-term program for indigent adults who are not elderly or physically challenged—14 cut funding and 13 froze the level of benefits in 1992–1993. About 1.5 million American adults depend on general assistance just to survive. But in Michigan, 82,000 recipients of this program lost all cash and medical assistance. Illinois cut its general assistance program by curtailing coverage to six months beginning in 1993. Ohio slashed its general assistance program in half, cutting benefits to single adults to only $100 a month.

During this recession, state after state turned against the problems of the poor. Massachusetts threw 10,000 poor people off its general assistance program and cut benefits by $56 million. California reduced AFDC payments by 4.5 percent and froze funding levels for the next five years. Maine reduced funding for low-income housing by 90 percent. And the District of Columbia slashed emergency housing assistance to the homeless by 43 percent.

The politics of turning against the poor is not only inhumane and antidemocratic; it is also extremely subversive. Pushing down the incomes and standard of living at the bottom of society inevitably reduces the wages and job prospects of people in the middle. By doubling the number of homeless people and denying cash payments to indigent adults, we only make our streets less safe and our environment more hostile for everyone. When millions lack food for their children or have no medical insurance, the fabric of our entire society is destroyed. All of our problems are interconnected. When we turn against the poor, we ultimately turn against ourselves.

Most white middle- and upper-class Americans refuse to recognize the oppressive dynamics of inequality, especially as they relate to what's happening in our nation's urban areas. Again, consider the striking racial profile of those voting for conservative candidates in the 1994 congressional election in the context of urban policy. White affluent Americans as a group have grown tired of the demands for economic development, social justice, and equality which continue to emerge from the representatives of African-American and Latino communities. They have grown weary of the thousands of homeless and mentally ill people who live on the streets, sidewalks, and alleys in our major cities. They have grown accustomed to television investigative programs on the deterioration of our inner-city schools, the proliferation of youth gangs and violence, or the dilemmas of urban unemployment and plant closings. This majority of white mainstream America desperately wants to close its eyes to the urban crisis. It has constructed electronic walls of security and physical isolation around itself, promising protection from the growing storms of human unrest and social destructiveness that periodically sweep across the avenues and neighborhoods of urban America. Most Democrats and Republicans alike want to run away from the crisis of social reality. But in the final analysis, there will be no security guards, no sophisticated alarm systems, no concrete barriers to keep the turmoil of our central cities from the well-manicured lawns, country clubs, and comfortable enclaves of white suburbia.

We need to have the courage to make the connections, to project a progressive politics of the "living space" to conceive of reconstructed and revitalized urban neighborhoods which bring together people of diverse class backgrounds, ethnic groups, languages, cultural and social traditions. The theory which states that elections are decided by white conservative males ignores the multicultural reality of contemporary American society. In the past 10 years, there has been a 40 percent increase in the number of Americans who speak a language other than English in their homes. In New York City, more than 40 percent of all residents speak a language other than English at home. By the year 2000, 33 percent of all Americans will be people of color: Latinos, Asian-Americans, Pacific Island Americans, American Indians, and African-Americans. The Asian-American population is projected to grow from 7.2 million in 1990 to over 20 million by the year 2020. Demographically, the Latino population now outnumbers African-Americans in four of the 10 largest cities in America—Los Angeles, Houston, Phoenix, and San Antonio. Between 1980 and 1990, according to the Census Bureau, the Latino population surpassed African-Americans in dozens of cities, including Arlington, Virginia; San Francisco and Pasadena, California; Las Vegas, Nevada, Providence, Rhode Island; Patterson, New Jersey; and Danbury and Waterbury, Connecticut. In New York City, African-Americans made up 25.6 percent of New York City's population, with Hispanics totaling 23.8 percent.

Now is the time for African-American leaders to take steps to reach out to Latinos, especially the powerful Mexican-American community. Blacks and Latinos usually share identical interests and goals on a host of issues: health care, job training and employment opportunities, education, affirmative action, housing, and social services. Both groups benefit from a civil rights agenda; both are overwhelmingly working-class and urban people. Black Americans must recognize the ethnic diversity within the Latino population, the major political and social class divisions which separate the largely Republican Cuban-American community of south Florida from the mostly liberal Democratic Dominican and Puerto Rican neighborhoods of Harlem. We must learn to articulate an agenda for black empowerment which simultaneously respects and listens to Latino interests.

We always need to remember that the unequal conditions of health care, education, housing, and employment are not fundamentally or solely problems of race. Most Americans who live in poverty—in destitution—are not people of color. There are about 9 million Latinos and 12 million blacks living below the federal government's poverty level—but there are also more than 22 million poor whites. In 1990, the majority of the recipients of food stamps was not black or Latino but white. About 4 percent of all American families live in federally subsidized or public housing units. Their median family income is below $9,000 annually. More than 50 percent of these families are white. And of the more than 25 million individuals on Medicaid, over 70 percent of them are white. We need to keep in mind that hunger knows no color, that poverty and unemployment touch millions of lives in the white community. When we accept the stereotype that the civil rights agenda on economic issues is for blacks only—or for minorities only—we ignore the grim realities affecting millions of white households every day.

How do we make common connections across race and class boundaries? Let's examine the issue of environmentalism, but within a multicultural, radical democratic context. Several years ago, the United Church of Christ's Commission on Racial Justice issued a major report, *Toxic Wastes and Race in the US*. The study revealed that three out of five blacks lived in communities with abandoned toxic waste sites and that blacks made up higher percentages of the populations of urban areas with the highest number of toxic waste sites. Although African-Americans are less than 12.5 percent of the total US population, for example, they account for 43 percent of Memphis, which has 173 uncontrolled toxic waste sites; 28 percent of St. Louis, with 160 sites; 24 percent of Houston, with 152 sites; and 37 percent of Chicago, with 103 sites. Heavily black Sumter County, Alabama, alone accounts for nearly 25 percent of the nation's total capacity for commercial hazardous waste disposal.

The environmentalist movement within white middle-class American must confront the reality that the state of the environment is inextricably connected with the existence of social justice, the possibility for all members of society to have a share in the decisionmaking, the resources, and the power within the social order. Environmental racism is a symptom of the inequality of power relations between people of color, working people, and the poor and those who have power, resources, and privilege. Unless we are prepared to examine the connections between political relations, the more substantive socioeconomic power relations, we will never address the roots of the problem of urban inequality.

Upper-class whites who lament the endangered status of the spotted owls of the Pacific Northwest, for instance, or who are deeply concerned about the plight of the whales, but who show little awareness or interest in the harsh realities of poverty, death, and disease in our own ghettos, barrios, and Indian reservations, are prisoners of a limited vision of democracy. We must redefine environmentalism to include the questions of land tenure, zoning, and utilization of natural resources in urban areas. Black Americans are victims of environmental racism because we do not control the decisions about land utilization, zoning of factories and businesses, and transportation of hazardous wastes and chemical throughout our communities. We have to demand that our elected officials become more knowledgeable and more directly responsible regarding environmental issues and their relationship to the health and safety of black people. We need to educate young people to realize that we need a new civil rights protest movement to attack and condemn the processing of hazardous chemicals and wastes in our neighborhoods.

We will succeed in challenging the power of the corporations to destroy the environment only when we mobilize in concert with those among us whose children and families are the greatest victims of these policies. Our approach must be to listen to the actual voices of the people, to make the connections linking questions of the environment to the pressing daily concerns of poverty, unemployment, homelessness, disease, and the destructive power of the criminal justice system.

We need to create a powerful, democratic political realignment, based on a new progressive social contract that empowers the masses of American working people. But such unity must go beyond simply stating what is "wrong" about our political and economic systems. It isn't enough for us to declare what we are "against." We must also affirm what we are "for." We must advocate an affirmative, dynamic social vision of the kind of democracy we need to construct for America's next century.

The place to begin is to identify and bring together all groups which experience alienation, discrimination, and oppression within our society: members of trade unions; women; gays and lesbians; the unemployed, the homeless, and people on fixed incomes; people of color—African-Americans, Latinos, Asian-Americans, and others; and all Americans who do not have a basic quality of life, such as health insurance, adequate shelter, and education. We must go beyond interest-group politics, which looks at social change like a game of poker in which someone wins, while others must lose. In our new democratic society, everyone must win.

We must get to know one another, sharing our common experiences, learning a common language of political action and social commitment. As Malcolm X observed a generation ago, we must move from a "civil rights" struggle to a "human rights" perspective, which has the power to mobilize millions. It is only through day-to-day struggles and joint dialogue that we will learn to transcend the barriers of misunderstanding between groups and political tendencies. Progressive unity among the broadest social forces in America can be constructed only at the grassroots level—in thousands of union halls, women's centers, churches, and schools.

It isn't enough to complain about politicians and the "system." The power to achieve change is already in our hands. The next movement for a deeper and more meaningful democracy requires us to go beyond the limits of our current political imagination. We are, today, part of a long tradition of Americans who have endeavored over several centuries to achieve a more democratic and socially just society—from the abolitionists, women's suffragists, Populists, and early labor union activists of the nineteenth century, to the activists of nearly a generation ago who opposed Jim Crow segregation and the Vietnam War in the 1960s. Among us are the people who believe in a democracy expressed in the modern feminist movement; we share solidarity with those gay rights' activists who fought at Stonewall; we the people should share our commitments to the dignity of labor by our expressions of support for those countless women and men who still walk picket lines at hundreds of factories, plants, and shops across this country; we the people must support the rights of undocumented workers and oppose the racist, exclusionary policies aimed against Latino working people; and we the people must embrace the struggles to democratize our political system, making it easier for third parties to gain ballot access and restricting the flow of millions of corporate dollars into the electoral process. "We the people" means democracy for the many rather than for the few. And such a democracy can be constructed only through the collective contributions, sacrifices, and ideas of all its people. The great African-American poet Langston Hughes spoke for all of us three generations ago with the poem entitled "America":

> I, too, sing America
> I am the darker brother
> They send me to eat in the kitchen
> when the company comes.
> But I laugh, and eat well, and grow strong.
> Tomorrow
> I'll be at the table when the company comes.
> Nobody will dare say to me
> 'Eat in the kitchen,' then.
> Besides, they'll see how beautiful I am
> and be ashamed.
> I, too, am America.

We, too, are America: African-Americans and Latinos, women and working people, gays and lesbians, the unemployed and the physically disabled, the homeless and the poor, those without health care, housing, or hope. We, too, are America, and we shall not retreat until genuine equality and social justice are shared by all. And toward that end, we dedicate ourselves to the empowerment of all humanity and to the continued enrichment of the human spirit.

11

Violence, Resistance, and the Struggle for Black Empowerment

A spectre is haunting black America—the seductive illusion that equality between the races has been achieved, and that the activism characteristic of the previous generation's freedom struggles is no longer relevant to contemporary realities. In collective chorus, the media, the leadership of both capitalist political parties, the corporate establishment, conservative social critics and public policy experts, and even marginal elements of the black middle class tell the majority of African-Americans that the factors which generated the social protest for equality in the 1950s and 1960s no longer exist.

The role of race has supposedly "declined in significance" within the economy and political order. And as we survey the current social climate, this argument seems to gain a degree of creditability. The number of black elected officials exceeds 6,600; many black entrepreneurs have achieved substantial gains within the capitalist economic system in the late 1980s; thousands of black managers and administrators appear to be moving forward within the hierarchies of the private and public sector. And the crowning "accomplishment," the November 1989 election of Douglas Wilder as Virginia's first black governor, has been promoted across the nation as the beginning of the transcendence of "racial politics."

The strategy of Jesse Jackson in both 1984 and 1988, which challenged the Democratic Party by mobilizing people of color and many whites around an advanced, progressive agenda for social justice, is dismissed as anachronistic and even "reverse racism." As in the Wilder model, racial advancement is projected as obtainable only if the Negro learns a new political and cultural discourse of the white mainstream. Protest is therefore passé. All the legislative remedies which were required to guarantee racial equality, the spectre dictates, have already been passed.

It is never an easy matter to combat an illusion. There have been sufficient gains for African-Americans, particularly within the electoral system and for sectors of the black petty bourgeoisie in the 1980s, that elements of the spectre seem true. But the true test of any social thesis is the amount of reality it explains, or obscures. And from the vantage point of the inner cities and homeless shelters, from the unemployment lines and closed factories, a different reality behind the spectre emerges. We find that racism has not declined in significance, if racism is defined correctly as the systemic exploitation of blacks' labor power and the domination and subordination of our cultural, political, educational, and social rights as human beings. Racial inequality continues, albeit within the false discourse of equality. Those who benefit materially from institutional racism now use the term "racist" to denounce black critics who call for the enforcement of affirmative action and equal opportunity legislation.

Behind the rhetoric of equality exists two crises, which present fundamental challenges to African-Americans throughout the decade of the 1990s. There is an "internal crisis"—that is, a crisis within the African-American family, neighborhood, community, cultural and social institutions, and within interpersonal relations, especially between black males. Part of this crisis was generated, ironically, by the "paradox of desegregation." With the end of Jim Crow segregation, the black middle class was able to escape the confines of the ghetto. Black attorneys who previously had only black clients could now move into more lucrative white law firms. Black educators and administrators were hired at predominantly white colleges; black physicians were hired at white hospitals; black architects, engineers, and other professionals went into white firms. This usually meant the geographical and cultural schism of elements in the black middle class from the working class and low income African-American population, which was still largely confined to the ghetto.

As black middle class professionals retreated to the suburbs, they often withdrew their skills, financial resources, and professional contacts from the bulk of the African-American community. There were of course many exceptions, black women and men who understood the cultural obligations they owed to their community. But as a rule, by the late 1980s, such examples became more infrequent, especially among younger blacks who had no personal memories or experiences in the freedom struggles of two decades past.

The internal crisis is directly related to an external, institutional crisis, a one-sided race/class warfare which is being waged against the African-American community. The external crisis is represented as the conjuncture of a variety of factors, including the deterioration of skilled and higher paying jobs within the ghetto, and the decline in the economic infrastructure; the decline in the public sector's support for public housing, health care, education, and related social services for low to moderate income people; the demise of the enforcement of affirmative action, equal opportunity laws, and related civil rights legislation; the increased racial conservatism of both major political parties and the ideological and programmatic collapse of traditional liberalism; and most importantly, the conscious decision by the corporate and public sector managerial elite to "regulate" the black population through increasingly coercive means.

The major characteristic of the internal crisis is the steady acceleration and proliferation of *violence,* in a variety of manifestations. The most disruptive and devastating type of violence is violent crime, which includes homicide, forcible rape, robbery, and aggravated assault. According to the *Sourcebook of Criminal Justice Statistics* for 1981, the total number of Americans arrested was nearly 9.5 million. Blacks comprise only 12.5 percent of the total US population, but represented 2.3 million arrests, or about *one fourth of all arrests.* Black arrests for homicide and nonnegligent manslaughter were 8,693, or about 48 percent of all murders committed in the US. For robbery, which is defined by law as the use of force or violence to obtain personal property, the number of black arrests was 74,275, representing 57 percent of all robbery arrests. For aggravated assault, the number of African-Americans arrested was 94,624, about 29 percent of all arrests in this category. For motor vehicle theft, the number of blacks arrested and charged was 38,905, about 27 percent of all auto theft crimes. Overall, for all violent and property crimes charged, blacks totaled almost 700,000 arrests in the year 1979, representing nearly one third of all such crimes.

One of the most controversial of all violent crimes is the charge of forcible rape. Rape is controversial because of the history of the criminal charge being used against black men by the white racist legal structure. Thousands of black men have been executed, lynched, and castrated for the imaginary offense of rape. Yet rape or forcible sexual violence is not imaginary when African-American women and young girls are victimized. In 1979, there were 29,068 arrests for forcible rape. Black men comprised 13,870 arrests, or 48 percent of the total. Within cities, where three fourths of all rapes are committed, blacks total 54 percent of all persons arrested for rape.

The chief victims of rape are not white women, but black women. The US Department of Justice's 1979 study of the crime of forcible rape established that overall most black women are nearly *twice* as likely to be rape victims than are white women. The research illustrated that in one year, about 67 out of 100,000 white women would be rape victims; but the rate for black and other nonwhite women was 115 per 100,000. In the age group 20 to 34 years, the dangers for black women increase dramatically. For white women of age 20 to 34, 139 out of 100,000 are rape victims annually. For black women the same age, the rate is 292 per 100,000. For attempted rape, white women are assaulted at a rate of 196 per 100,000; black women are attacked sexually 355 per 100,000 annually.

There is also a direct correlation between rape victimization and income. In general, poor women are generally the objects of sexual assault; middle class women are rarely raped or assaulted, and wealthy women almost never experience sexual assault. The statistics are clear on this point. White women who live in families earning under $7,500 annually have a 500 percent greater likelihood of being raped than white women who come from households with more than $15,000 income. The gap is even more extreme for African-American women. For black middle-class families, the rate of rape is 22 per 100,000. For welfare and low-income families earning below $7,500 annually, the rate for rape is 127 per 100,000. For attempted rape, low-income black women are victimized at a rate of 237 per 100,000 annually.

Rape is almost always intra-racial, not interracial. Nine out of 10 times, a white rapist's victim is a white female. Ninety percent of all black women who are raped have been assaulted by a black male. Sexual violence within the African-American community, therefore, is not something "exported" by whites. It is essentially the brutality committed by black men against our mothers, wives, sisters, and daughters. It is the worst type of violence, using the gift of sexuality in a bestial and animalistic way to create terror and fear among black women.

The type of violence which most directly affects black men is homicide. Nearly half of all murders committed in any given year are black men who murder other black men. But that's only part of the problem. We must recognize, first, that the homicide rate among African-Americans is growing. Back in 1960, the homicide rate for black men in the US was 37 per 100,000. By 1979, the black homicide rate was 65 per 100,000. In other words, a typical black male has a *six to seven times* greater likelihood of being a murder victim than a white male.

The chief victims of homicide in our community are young African-American males. Murder is the fourth leading cause of death for all black men, and the leading cause of death for black males age 20 to 29 years. Today in the US, a typical white female's statistical chances of becoming a murder victim are one in 606. For white men, the odds narrow to one chance in 186. For black women, the odds are one in 124. But for black men, the chances are one in 29. For young black men living in cities who are between age 20 to 29, the odds of becoming a murder victim are *less than one in 20.* Black young men in American cities today are the primary targets for destruction—not only from drugs and police brutality, but from each other.

The epidemic of violence in the black community raises several related questions. What is the social impact of violence within our neighborhoods? What is the effect of violence upon our children? And most importantly, how do we develop a strategy to reverse the proliferation of black-against-black crime and violence?

Violence occurs so frequently in the cities that for many people, it has become almost a "normal" factor. We have become accustomed to burglar alarms and security locks to safeguard our personal property and homes. More than one in three families keep a gun in their homes. However, we also need to keep in mind that in most of the violent crime cases, the assailant and the victim live in the same neighborhood, or are members of the same household. Half of all violent deaths are between husbands and wives. Many others include parents killing their children, or children killing parents, or neighbors killing each other. There are hundreds of murders among blacks for the most trivial reasons—everything from fighting over parking spaces to arguing over $5.

Black men are murdering each other in part because of the deterioration of jobs and economic opportunity in our communities. For black young men, the real unemployment rate exceeds 50 percent in most cities. Overall jobless rates for black men with less than a high school diploma exceed 15 percent. High unemployment, crowded housing, and poor health care all contribute to an environment of social chaos and disruption, which create destructive values and behaviors.

The most tragic victims of violence are black children. Black children between the ages of one and four have death rates from homicide which are four times higher than for white children the same age. According to the Children's Defense Fund, black children are arrested at almost seven times the rates for white children for the most serious violent crimes and are arrested at more than twice the white rates for serious property crimes. More than half of the arrests for African-American teenagers are for serious property crimes or violent crimes. For instance, the arrest rate for black youth aged 11 to 17 for forcible rape is six times higher than for whites. In terms of rates of victimization, nonwhite females are almost 40 percent more likely than white females to be raped, robbed, or victims of other violent crimes.

How do we understand the acts of violence committed by and against our children? We must begin by focusing on the cultural concept of identity. What is identity? It's an awareness of self in the context of one's environment. Identity is based on the connections between the individual and his or her immediate family and community. We don't exist in isolation of each other. We develop a sense of who we are, of who we wish to become, by interacting with parents, friends, teachers, ministers, coworkers, and others.

Our identity is collective, in that it is formed through the inputs of thousands of different people over many years. If the people relate to an individual in a negative manner, an antisocial or deviant personality will be the result. If children are told repeatedly by teachers or parents that they are stupid, the children will usually do poorly in school, regardless of their natural abilities. If children are told that they are chronic liars and untrustworthy, they will eventually begin to lie and steal. If they are physically beaten by their parents frequently or unjustly, they will learn to resort to physical violence against others. People are not born hateful or violent. There's no genetic or biological explanation for black-against-black crime. Violence is *learned* behavior.

Violence between people of color is also directly linked to the educational system. If the curriculum of our public schools does not present the heritage, culture, and history of African-Americans, if it ignores or downgrades our vital contributions to a more democratic society, our children are robbed of their heritage. They acquire a distorted perspective about themselves and their communities. If they believe that African-American people have never achieved greatness in the sciences, art, music, economics, and the law, how can they excel or achieve for themselves? Despite the many reforms accomplished to create a more culturally pluralistic environment for learning, many of our public schools are in the business of "miseducation" for people of color. Our children are frequently "cultural casualties" in the ideological warfare against black people.

The dynamics of violence within the African-American community create such chaos and destructiveness that they provide a justification for the public and private sectors' retreat from civil rights initiatives. The argument of the dominant white elites proceeds thus: "Blacks must bear the responsibility for their own poverty, crime, illiteracy, and oppression. Affirmative action is consequently harmful to blacks' interests, since it rewards incompetence and advances individuals not on the basis of merit but race alone. Blacks should stop looking to the government to resolve their problems, and take greater initiatives within the private enterprise system to assist themselves. Through private initiatives, moral guidance, and sexual abstinence, the status of the Negro will improve gradually without social dissent and disruption."

We need to recognize that, fundamentally, there would be no internal crisis among African-Americans if the political economy and social institutions were designed to create the conditions for genuine democracy and human equality. The external crisis of the capitalist political economy is responsible for the internal crisis. All of the private initiatives, and all of the meager self-help efforts mounted at the neighborhood level, and the doubling of the number of black entrepreneurs and enterprises, would not in any significant manner reverse the destructive trends which have been unleashed against our people. Institutional racism and class exploitation since 1619 have always been, and remain, the root causes of black oppression.

The epidemic of violence, in combination with the presence of drugs, has directly contributed to another type of violence—the growth of African-American suicide rates, especially among the young. From 1950 to 1974, the suicide rate of African-American males soared from 6.8 per 100,000 to 11.4 per 100,000. In the same years, the black female suicide rate rose from 1.6 per 100,000 to 3.5 per 100,000. A 1982 study by Robert Davis noted that nearly one half of all suicides among blacks now occur among people between age 20 to 34 years. Within this group, black males who kill themselves account for 36 percent of the total number of suicides. Davis also observes that within the narrow age range of 25 to 29, the suicide rate among black males is higher than that for white males in the same age group. For black men and women who live in urban areas, the suicide rate is twice that for whites of the same age group who live in cities.

These facts must be understood against the background of the social history of African-Americans. Traditionally, suicide was almost unknown within the black community during slavery and the Jim Crow period. Blacks found ways to cope with stress and the constant disappointments of life, from singing the blues to mobilizing their sisters and brothers to fight against forms of oppression. Frantz Fanon's psychiatric insight, that struggle and resistance for the oppressed are therapeutic, is confirmed by the heritage of the Black Liberation Movement. But when people lose the will to resist oppression, when they no longer can determine their friends or enemies, they lack the ability to develop the mental and spiritual determination to overcome obstacles. Suicide, once an irrational or irrelevant act, becomes both rational and logical within the context of cultural and social alienation.

The American legal system in the 1980s and 1990s also contributed to the violence within our communities in several ways. The patterns of institutional racism became far more sophisticated, as former President Reagan pursued a policy of appointing conservative, racist, elitist males to the federal district courts and the US Circuit Courts of Appeals. By 1989 Reagan had appointed over 425 federal judges, more than half of the 744 total judgeships. Increasingly, the criminal justice system was employed as a system of social control for the millions of unemployed and underemployed African-Americans. The essential element of coercion within the justice system, within a racial context, is of course the utilization of the death penalty.

According to one statistical study by David C. Baldus based on over 2,000 murder cases in Georgia during the 1970s, people accused of killing whites were about 11 times more likely to be given the death penalty than those who murdered blacks. Over half of the defendants in white-victim crimes would not have been ordered to be executed if their victims had been African-Americans. Research on the death penalty in Florida during the 1970s illustrates that Florida blacks who are accused and convicted of murdering whites are five times more likely to be given the death penalty than whites who murder other whites.

Under the conditions of race/class domination, prisons are the principal means for group social control, in order to regulate the labor position of millions of black workers. Our free market system cannot create full employment for all; and the public sector is unwilling to devote sufficient resources to launch an economic reconstruction of the central cities, which in turn would greatly reduce the drug trade. Consequently, prisons become absolutely necessary for keeping hundred of thousands of potentially rebellious, dissatisfied, and alienated African-American youth off the streets.

Between 1973 and 1986, the average real earnings for young African-American males under 25 years fell by 50 percent. In the same period, the percentage of black males aged 18 to 29 in the labor force who were able to secure full-time, year-round employment fell from only 44 percent to a meager 35 percent.

Is it accidental that these young black men, who are crassly denied meaningful employment opportunities, are also pushed into the prison system, and subsequently into permanent positions of economic marginality and social irrelevancy? Within capitalism, a job has never been defined as a human right; but for millions of young, poor black men and women, they appear to have a "right" to a prison cell or a place at the front on the unemployment line.

The struggle against violence requires a break from the strategic analysis of the desegregation period of the 1960s. Our challenge is not to become part of the system, but to transform it, not only for ourselves, but for everyone. We must struggle against an acceptance of the discourse and perceptions of the dominant white political criminal justice and economic elites in regards to black-on-black violence. If we focus solely on the need to construct more prisons and mandatory sentences for certain crimes, the crisis will continue to exist in our cities and elsewhere. People who have a sense of mastery and control in their lives do not violate their neighbors or steal their property.

An effective strategy for empowerment in the 1990s must begin with the recognition that the American electoral political system was never designed to uproot the fundamental causes of black oppression. Most of the greatest advances in black political activism did not occur at the ballot box, but in the streets, in the factories, and through collective group awareness and mobilization. Our greatest leaders in this century—W.E.B. Du Bois, Marcus Garvey, Paul Robeson, Malcolm X, Fannie Lou Hamer, Ella Baker, Martin Luther King, Jr., and many more—were not elected officials or government bureaucrats. Yet because of the electoral focus of most of the current crop of middle class black elites, we now tend to think of power as an electoral process. But there is also power when oppressed people acquire a sense of cultural integrity and an appreciation of their political heritage of resistance. There is power when we mobilize our collective resources in the media, educational institutions, housing, health care, and economic development to address issues. There is power when African-American people and other oppressed constituencies mobilize a march or street demonstration, when we use a boycott or picket line to realize our immediate objectives.

A strategy for African-American empowerment means that black politicians must be held more closely accountable to the interests of black people. Power implies the ability to reward and to punish friends and enemies alike. Can blacks continue to afford to conduct voter registration and education campaigns, and then do nothing to check the voting behavior of our elected officials? Accountability must be measured objectively according to a list of policy priorities, and not determined by political rhetoric at election time. One method to consider could be the creation of "people power" assemblies, popular, local conventions open to the general black public. Politicians of both major parties would be evaluated and ranked according to their legislative or executive records, and their responses on specific policy questions. Neither the Democratic nor the Republican Party can be expected to provide this level of direct accountability.

We are losing the battle for the hearts and minds of millions of young African-Americans who have no personal memory of the struggles waged to dismantle the system of Jim Crow segregation. They have no personal experience on the picket lines, in street demonstrations, and in the development of community-based organizations which reinforce and strengthen black families, black religious, civic, and social institutions. The path forward is to create a new generation of black leaders who recognize that the effort to achieve social justice and human equality is unfinished, and that the status of black people in America could easily deteriorate to a new type of repressive environment comparable to legal segregation in the pre–Civil

Rights South. We must identify and cultivate the leadership abilities of young people who display a potential and an interest in progressive social change.

We need to recognize that power in American society is exercised by hierarchies and classes, not by individuals. Part of the price for the individualism and blatant materialism within certain elements of the black upper middle class since the 1970s has been their alienation from the dilemmas confronting the black working class, the poor, and unemployed. Class elitism of any type, for a segment of the oppressed community, contributes to a disintegration of solidarity and a sense of common values, goals, and objectives. To end the dynamic of violence, we need to recognize that freedom is not rooted within individualism, in isolation from the majority. No single black woman or man in America will ever transcend the impact of racism and class exploitation unless all of us, and especially the most oppressed among us, also gain a fundamental level of cultural awareness, collective respect, material security, and educational advancement. This requires a new vision of the struggle for power, a collective commitment to the difficult, yet challenging project of remaking humanity and our social environment, rooted in a vision beyond self-hatred, chemical dependency, and fratricidal violence. This must be at the heart of our strategy for cultural resistance and empowerment for the 1990s and beyond.

12

Malcolm, Martin, and the Mandates of Justice

We live in a time in which the black community seems to be nearly devoid of effective leadership. The representatives of the growing black middle class seem self-centered and divorced from the daily struggles of low income and unemployed African-Americans. In some quarters we have a "de-racialized leadership," black professional and managerial elites who credit their successes to personal accomplishment and individual excellence, rather than link their own upward mobility with the fate of 32 million black folk. Our venerable organizations like the NAACP seem hopelessly in disarray, with bickering and acrimony encircling the national board and leaders. The Congressional Black Caucus, recently defunded by the new Republican majority in Congress, has failed to present a powerful alternative which could capture the imaginations of African-American people. Most of the black mayors of our major cities seem befuddled and confused, uncertain whether to compromise with the Republicans and corporate conservative interests or to stake out political ground to the left, mobilizing their desperate constituents to the fight for meager resources. As the material conditions of our cities deteriorate, as the bitter winds of unemployment, alienation, and black-on-black violence cut sharply through our neighborhoods, there rises a deep and desperate yearning for the voice of justice and human dignity. With clenched fists and bitter tears, one hopes for an Elijah or a Joshua who will advocate one's cause, who will fight the good fight, righting wrongs and healing wounds.

In our collective memory as black people, we recall what courage in leadership can mean. From the Second Reconstruction, the modern Civil Rights Movement, there are two outstanding profiles of visionary leadership: Malcolm X and Martin Luther King, Jr. Even today, there is the regrettable tendency to juxtapose these figures against each other, suggesting that they represented two antagonistic poles of hostile political opinion. Usually, the mainstream media, political and academic establishment, as well as the black middle class, lavish praise on Martin Luther King, Jr. and draw unfavorable comparisons between the civil rights leader and Malcolm X. Malcolm is usually projected as the uncompromising advocate of black nationalism, while Martin is praised as the supporter of racial integrationism, the peaceful inclusion of black people into the institutions of white authority and power. Malcolm, always brooding and alienated, is depicted as the architect of armed revolution and confrontation, while Martin's well-known advocacy of nonviolence and interracial dialogue is applauded. Malcolm is presented as the hostile critic of white liberalism, while Martin is depicted as the friend of both the Kennedy and Johnson administrations. Yet historical memory is always fragmented and selective, partial and incomplete. Our images of Malcolm and Martin are drawn less by what they actually accomplished as individual political actors, and much less by the outlines of our own reconstructed recollections, than by the weight of what we collectively are told about them within contemporary culture. Martin moves from the role of a creative and insightful political leader to the semi-frozen state of becoming a cultural icon, with coldly chiseled features. Since Spike Lee's cinematic version of *X*, younger people often have difficulty disaggregating the images of actor Denzel Washington from the actual historical figure of Malcolm. For many black nationalists, Malcolm also experiences a metamorphosis, moving from history into the stage of the cultural icon, with his image duplicated on T-shirts, caps, and various articles of clothing.

The great danger with this form of lionization is that, regardless of well-meaning motivations, it is destructive and dangerous, particularly for the oppressed. The real value of historical greatness is not the simple-minded praising of figures like King and Malcolm X: it is found by learning the lessons which their public lives and thought provide. Both of these men were profoundly human. They made errors, mistakes, misjudgments of all kinds. But both had a tremendous capacity to learn from their experiences and to listen to their critics. Most importantly, both refused to be imprisoned by the boundaries of long-standing public statements concerning their ideological orientations. They pursued in their own ways the struggle for justice for their people, and were both prepared to move in new and often uncharted directions in that effort.

For more than a decade, Malcolm X had made his public reputation as the articulate representative of Elijah Muhammad and the Nation of Islam. But the eclectic mix of conservative black nationalism and rigid religiosity could not adequately speak to the sense of militancy and political urgency rising up from American ghettoes in the early 1960s. Reluctantly at first, Malcolm was pressured to speak less on strictly religious topics and increasingly on political matters which addressed the concerns of many blacks who were not members of the Nation of Islam. As Malcolm grew in popularity within the more radical wing of the desegregation movement, his critics inside the Nation of Islam grew. By late 1962, *Muhammad Speaks,* the Nation of Islam's newspaper, had largely ceased to cover Malcolm's public activities and speeches. As Malcolm broke from the Nation in March 1964, he sought to articulate a program of action which would mobilize a whole spectrum within the black community.

Establishing the Organization of Afro-American Unity, Malcolm broke from his conservative black nationalism to advocate a political strategy which was progressive and internationalist. He no longer defined all whites uncritically as the categorical enemies of black people. Malcolm X now understood that the struggle to uproot racial discrimination was structurally linked to worldwide patterns of poverty and colonialism. He denounced the early stages of America's involvement in Southeast Asia, and prepared to submit to the United Nations a list of human rights violations which the United States government had committed against black people. Malcolm X denounced the tendency of reform-minded integrationists to invest their energies and efforts solely within the electoral political system, and deplored the 1964 presidential campaign of Lyndon Johnson versus Barry Goldwater as a contest between the "fox" versus the "wolf." But the essential point made by Malcolm, in his writings and speeches, was that black Americans would never gain equality or empowerment by integrating themselves within an unfair, unjust system. This "transformationist" perspective was also consistent with many of Malcolm's views when he was within the Nation of Islam. "It is not a case of [dark mankind] wanting integration or separation," Malcolm declared, "it is a case of wanting freedom, justice, and equality. It is not integration that Negroes in America want, it is human dignity."

Similarly, Martin Luther King, Jr. had moved along a parallel political path. From the early days of the Montgomery Bus Boycott in 1955 through the Selma March a decade later, Martin had been at the heart of the struggle to desegregate American society. He had successfully led the battle for the landmark passage of the Civil Rights Act of 1964 and the Voting Rights Act of 1965. Equally importantly, he had become the political conscience for millions of Americans who were committed to the realization of social reforms which would eliminate the second class status of Negroes. But the political climate changed with the stunning Republican congressional victories in November 1966, and the steep military escalation of the Johnson administration in Vietnam. Urban radical uprisings from Watts to Detroit marked a new degree of impatience and dissatisfaction with the modest pace of liberal programs. Martin was forced to rethink his whole approach to politics, and was challenged to reexamine his basic assumptions about strategies for social change.

Like Malcolm X, in Martin's turbulent final year, he moved dramatically toward an approach toward black empowerment which was "transformationist." He no longer called for incremental, indecisive changes within the racial status quo. Martin never repudiated from his commitment to nonviolence, or the philosophy of humanistic change. But the social urgency of the times which was sweeping the world, from the experiments in Tanzania by Julius Nyerere of "Ujamaa socialism," to the political mobilization of millions of young people by Mao Tse-tung in China during the "Cultural Revolution," found its expression within the fabric of black America. As millions of Americans questioned the logic of Vietnam, how could the Civil Rights Movement stand outside this debate? Was the essential struggle for civil rights within the framework of American democracy, King asked himself, or was it a broader, international crusade for human rights and social liberation for the oppressed of all colors and cultures?

During the staff meetings of the Southern Christian Leadership Conference in late August 1967, Martin systematically linked the crisis of Vietnam with the necessity to reorder national priorities. According to historian Vincent Harding, Martin had come to the conclusion that "Negroes must therefore not only formulate a program; they must fashion new tactics which do not count on government goodwill but serve, instead, to compel unwilling authorities to yield to the mandates of justice." Martin now understood the structural limits of liberal reform, even in the context of political democracy. What was necessary was to connect the struggle for civil rights with the democratic restructuring of America's economic system. "The dispossessed of this nation—the poor, both white and Negro—live in a cruelly unjust society," Martin insisted. "They must organize a revolution against that injustice, not against the lives of the persons who are their fellow citizens, but against the structures through which the society is refusing to . . . lift the load of poverty."

Martin used his political and moral authority more dynamically than ever before: leading demonstrations to oppose the Vietnam War, calling for a protest campaign for nonviolent direction action in Washington, DC, challenging his old associates to move beyond tradition liberalism. Just before his assassination, Martin had come to Memphis on the side of striking black sanitation workers who were struggling for decent wages and better working conditions. The battle which had once been defined as the effort to obtain a seat at the front of a public bus had become the movement to dismantle all forms of social injustice, colonialism, and exploitation.

For both Malcolm and Martin, the language and political logic of both black nationalism and integration became too restrictive and too confining. If black Americans' struggles were to assume an international significance, we had to acquire an international perspective. The goal of our movement could not be defined narrowly in separatist or inclusionist contexts: to "fight the power" meant to transform the system for the benefit of all. If there are the foundations of a social theory which can liberate African-Americans, they begin by taking theoretically and conceptually what is common to both Malcolm X and Martin Luther King, Jr. By learning from their examples, we may begin to challenge ourselves and to realize that the full meaning of our own movement embraces "the mandates of justice."

13

Louis Farrakhan and the Million Man March

"There is a great divide, but the real evil in America is not white flesh or black flesh. The real evil in America is the idea that undergirds the setup of the western world, and that idea is called white supremacy." So declared Louis Farrakhan on 16 October in his two-hour keynote speech before hundreds of thousands of black men from across America who had gathered in front of the Capitol for the "Million Man March."

The demonstration was the culmination of a year-long mobilization, led by Farrakhan, leader of the Nation of Islam, and former National Association for the Advancement of Colored People (NAACP) secretary Benjamin Chavis, and endorsed by more than 200 national black organizations. Although the march's official position was at first to exclude women—Farrakhan's advice to women was to stay at home, pray, and watch the children—several women's organizations also endorsed the event, including the National Council of Negro Women and the National Black Women's Political Congress.

Farrakhan's call included a demand for "atonement"—that African-Americans should recognize "wrongs done and make amends," and apologize for all offenses "against the Creator." The march agenda spoke relatively little about contemporary public policy issues, such as affirmative action, immigration, and welfare reform. Instead, it emphasized the need for blacks to assume "personal responsibility" for their own circumstances, and challenged African-American males to provide leadership for their families and communities.

Farrakhan's controversial history, including public statements describing Jews as "bloodsuckers" and Judaism as "a gutter religion," at first led most

US politicians and the media to dismiss or condemn plans for the mobilization. Many prominent black feminists, including Angela Davis, publicly condemned the march's position that women could not participate. Many black gay men were turned off by Farrakhan's homophobia, such as in his 1993 statement "We must change homosexual behavior and get rid of the circumstances that bring it about." Many black progressives criticized the march for not attacking the Republicans' "Contract with America."

Yet it is to Farrakhan's credit that he recognized the deep emotional and cultural crisis at the heart of the African-American community. Those who participated in the gathering all described a deep sense of fellowship. Men wept openly, embracing each other, committing themselves to new levels of personal and civic engagement. Many explained that they had not come to Washington in support of Farrakhan's political agenda. Rather, they were there to express a deep desire for the black community to come together, in a process of healing.

In one opinion poll, 85 percent of all African-Americans expressed support. Thousands of people returned to their homes with a new dedication to participate in black organizations. For example, although the National Urban League and its affiliates refused to endorse the march, many blacks returning from it contacted this moderate civil rights body to volunteer their services.

Even so, one must keep in mind that the majority can be wrong. In 1991, the majority of African-Americans favored the appointment of Clarence Thomas to the US Supreme Court. Thomas's subsequent conservative tenure has represented a disaster for black people. Mass popularity is no guarantee that the masses are pointed in the right direction.

So what explains the cathartic outpouring of emotion and enthusiasm that characterized the day in Washington? One fundamental factor is the destruction or elimination of an entire generation of progressive African-American leaders since the civil rights movement. Beginning with the assassinations of Malcolm X and Martin Luther King, the American government has aggressively attempted to isolate or imprison black leaders on the left. The Black Panther Party was specifically targeted and wrecked by the FBI and local police. Since then, hundreds of progressive black elected officials have been indicted and imprisoned.

Jesse Jackson's Rainbow Coalition seemed to represent a breakthrough by blacks to mainstream electoral politics. In 1988, Jackson received more than 7 million votes for the presidency. But the defeat of his left social democratic program and the decline of the Coalition left a deep vacuum in US politics.

Another lost opportunity was represented by Benjamin Chavis's short and controversial leadership of the NAACP, the nation's largest civil rights organization, in 1993–94. Chavis's program represented a fundamental challenge to the reformist, inclusionist strategy of traditional civil rights leaders and most black elected officials. He expanded the NAACP membership to reach out to alienated urban youth and the most oppressed sectors of the black community. He initiated a constructive dialogue among a broad spectrum of leaders and constituencies, seeking the grounds for practical cooperation, and advocating what was in effect a left social democratic agenda: expansion of government investment in the inner cities, full employment, a universal health care system, construction of low- to middle-income housing, and vigorous enforcement of affirmative action and civil rights legislation.

When Chavis was attacked for engaging in a dialogue with Farrakhan, he carefully distinguished his own politics from those of Farrakhan's Nation of Islam. In the *New York Times* in July 1994, he reiterated his support of the "long and honorable alliance" between African-Americans and Jews, emphasizing that "neither I nor the NAACP have ever embraced anti-Semitic beliefs, nor would we countenance them." But, he explained, it was wrong to claim that a dialogue with Farrakhan implied an acceptance of his philosophy.

Within days, however, charges that Chavis had misappropriated NAACP funds to cover up allegations of sexual harassment eroded the moral and political base of his leadership. Funds dried up, as funders demanded his expulsion. A compliant board, some of whom had benefited from the internal corruption and patronage within the NAACP hierarchy, summarily fired him.

Despite his sacking, Chavis still commanded substantial influence among key sectors of the black middle class, churches, and many NAACP branches. By recruiting him as "national chairperson" for the Million Man March, Farrakhan and the Nation of Islam were able to reach new constituencies where previously they held only marginal influence. Chavis, in turn, was prepared to jettison much of his previous left-of-center politics for a black nationalist program centered on patriarchy, "atonement," and self-help conservative economics.

At an ideological level, the march represented a kind of pragmatic united front, anchored in cultural nationalism and the racial politics of the aspiring black middle class. Neither Farrakhan nor Chavis has significant influence within black labor unions or the Coalition of Black Trade Unionists. Their core program was designed to appeal in the broadest possible terms to racial solidarity, while saying next to nothing about the growing class stratification within the black communities.

Perhaps the primary reason the march acquired such widespread support was the general recognition that blacks are faced with an unprecedented crisis within the US political and economic system. Politically, both major parties have largely repudiated the legacy of civil rights reforms and the social welfare expenditures of the "Great Society." While politicians have campaigned aggressively against affirmative action, minority economic programs, and majority-black legislative districts, blacks have been caught in a cycle of unemployment, growing social inequality, and imprisonment. Indeed, the single most important material reality of American society in the 1990s is the vast polarization of classes, the unprecedented rise in personal incomes and profits among a small minority of American households, and the expansion of social misery, falling incomes, and inequality for the majority of the population of the country.

As of 1993, the top 1 percent of all income earners in the US had a greater combined net wealth than the bottom 95 percent. According to a survey of the 85 largest metropolitan areas in the US, between 1973 and 1989, average incomes fell by 16 percent. In the New York borough of Manhattan, the poorest one-fifth of the population in 1990 earned an annual average income of $5,237. The richest one-fifth earned $110,199.

The same profile of inequality exists in every American city. In Los Angeles, the median annual incomes of the poorest and the wealthiest fifth in 1990 were $6,821 and $123,098, respectively. In Chicago, the figures were $4,743 and $86,632; in Detroit, $3,109 and $63,625. Millions have been pushed into unemployment and poverty, while for America's privileged and powerful elite, things have never been better.

The conservative political agenda, from Reaganism to Newt Gingrich's "Contract with America," rests fundamentally on this core reality of escalating inequality. The ruling elites have to hide these statistics, or at least blame the hardships of white working-class people on the behavior of blacks, Latinos, and other people of color. "Race" is deliberately manipulated to obscure class inequality.

The primary response by elected officials and the corporate elite has been the massive expansion of public and private security forces, and the incarceration of literally millions of black, Hispanic, and poor people. Between 1980 and 1990, the number of police in the US doubled. And in addition to the 554,000 officers employed by local and state police forces, there are now 1.5 million private security officers. Much of the new suburban housing being built today in "planned communities" is surrounded by walls, wired for electronic surveillance, and guarded by private security personnel.

It was in this context in 1994 that the US Congress passed President Clinton's $30-billion Omnibus Crime Bill. As author Phil Gasper has observed, the Crime Bill's provisions included "$10.8 billion in federal matching funds to local governments to hire 100,000 new police officers over the next five years, $10 billion for the construction of new federal prisons, an expansion of the number of federal crimes to which the death penalty ap-

plies from two to 58 (the bill also eliminated an existing statute that prohibited the execution of mentally incapacitated defendants), a so-called
'three strikes' proposal which mandates life sentences for anyone convicted
of three 'violent felonies,' and so on."

Even more striking has been the massive expansion of the US prison system. In 15 years, the prison population tripled, from 500,000 in 1980 to
1,500,000 in 1995. In California alone, between 1977 and 1992, the prison
population soared from less than 20,000 to over 110,000.

The racial oppression that defines US society is most dramatically apparent in the criminal justice system and the prisons. Today, about half the in-
mates in prison and jails, more than 750,000 people, are African-Americans. About 30 percent of all African-American males in their twenties are
today either in prison, on probation or parole, or awaiting trial. A recent
study in the District of Columbia estimated that 70 percent of black men
would be arrested before the age of 35, and that 85 percent would be arrested at some point in their lives.

These statistical profiles of racial oppression should not obscure the class
dimensions of who is arrested and imprisoned in the US. In 1989, more
than 14 million Americans were arrested; about 2 percent of the total male
labor force in the US today is in prison. According to a 1991 survey, about
one-third of all prisoners were unemployed at the time of their arrests,
while two-thirds of all prisoners have less than a high school level education and few marketable skills. The prisons of the US are vast warehouses
for the poor and unemployed, for low wage workers and the poorly educated, and most especially, for Latino and African-American males. White-
collar criminals, who embezzle hundreds of millions of dollars, are rarely
given prison sentences. The wealthy and powerful almost never go to
prison for the crimes they commit. But for the most oppressed, prison is
frequently an improvement in life circumstances: free health care, three
meals a day, shelter, and some modest training programs. Today, there are
hundreds of thousands more black men in prison than are enrolled in colleges or universities. Statistically, a young black man has a greater likelihood of being arrested than obtaining a job that adequately supports him
and his family. It is this tough reality that gives Farrakhan such legitimacy
among millions of African-Americans.

Yet this is why the march's emphasis solely on the plight of black males is
so short-sighted. No one doubts the physical and psychological agony of
African-American men. But the burden of unemployment, inferior education, and nonexistent health care weighs equally upon black women. And
in many other respects, African-American women must bear an overwhelming burden alone: raising their children, working at two or more jobs
to survive, and struggling in human terms often without the personal inti-

macy or sharing of a partner. To construct a politics grounded in patriarchy, however "benevolent," is to denigrate the real struggles, responsibilities, and interests of our sisters.

The racial essentialism of the "Million Man March" obscures the growing reality of class polarization among blacks. One example of the political and class divisions just beneath the surface within the African-American community is provided by the phenomenon of General Colin Powell, the former chairman of the Joint Chiefs of Staff. In a *USA Today*/CNN/Gallup poll this month, far more whites than blacks supported Powell for the presidency. In head-to-head competition against Clinton, Powell as the Republican candidate would win a majority of whites' votes, by 54 to 37 percent. But African-Americans overwhelmingly endorsed Clinton over the black challenger, by 68 to 25 percent.

Among African-Americans, Powell's support is weakest among the most oppressed, those with low incomes, lacking a college education, who live in the south. Powell's greatest support among blacks comes from those with college degrees, whose incomes are $30,000 and above, and who believe the O.J. Simpson verdict was wrong. The black middle class, the chief beneficiaries of affirmative action and minority economic set-asides, is searching for an acceptable political alternative to advance its own class interests. In this sense, Colin Powell and Louis Farrakhan represent two sides of the same political coin. Middle-class Republicanism and conservative black nationalism have similar social and economic philosophies: self-help, less reliance on government, entrepreneurial capitalism, hostility to trade unionism and the left.

The great unknown in the aftermath of the "Million Man March" is the political future of Jesse Jackson. For months, Jackson refused to endorse the march, on the grounds that it lacked a strong public policy agenda, and, to some extent, because it focused too narrowly on black policy issues. Jackson changed his mind, and his speech at Washington resounded with much greater clarity and vision than anything Farrakhan represented.

Jackson declared: "We come here today because there is a structural malfunction in America. Why do we march? Because the media stereotypes us. We are projected as less intelligent than we are, less hard-working than we work. . . . Why do we march? Because we are trapped with second-class schools and first-class jails. What is the crisis? Wealth going upward; jobs going outward. Middle class coming downward; the poor expanding rapidly."

Following the march, Farrakhan committed the Nation of Islam to conduct a massive voter registration campaign, bringing millions of new black voters to the polls in 1996. This represents a challenge to the remnants of the Rainbow Coalition and the traditional civil rights establishment. Does Jackson embrace Farrakhan's leadership, or does he attempt to regain the political initiative? Can Jackson revitalize multi-cultural, multi-racial, left-of-center politics, speaking beyond black and white? If he fails, black America may increasingly turn within itself, moving away from the possibility of multi-racial democratic reform.

Before Benjamin Chavis's expulsion as NAACP leader, he urged the black freedom movement to eschew the politics of racial chauvinism and social isolation from progressive constituencies. Chavis wrote: "Let us not be distracted from our central task: building a nation where we are not separate and unequal, where no group is relegated to poverty, and where race or creed does not determine one's destiny." Although Chavis has become Farrakhan's lieutenant, his previous observation remains the central challenge for both black and progressive US politics. A strategy that addresses poverty and imprisonment should understand the burden of race, but must also speak a language of class. A social vision that transcends the narrow confines of black nationalist separatism remains vital to the reconstruction of American democracy.

PART 2

The Third World
and the Politics
of Peace

14

Zimbabwe and the Problematic of African Socialism

1983

In recent months, the American media have delivered a grim eulogy for the "democratic experiment" of Zimbabwe. The government of Prime Minister Robert Mugabe has received intense criticism from the Right and, not surprisingly, from some elements of the Left sympathetic to Mugabe's rival Joshua Nkomo, leader of the opposition ZAPU party (Zimbabwe African People's Union). Over 1,000 people have been killed in conflicts between the majority Shona and the minority Ndebele. Western aid and investment in Zimbabwe have been halted; reporters and opponents of Mugabe's dominant ZANU party (Zimbabwe African National Union) talk of the creation of a "black police state." Most of the US Left has basically reserved judgment on Zimbabwe. There are, however, numerous points of debate which should be taken up concretely by the American Left that illustrate the thorny problems of socialist transformation inherent in the Third World. Specifically, I would like to address three issues in a very limited and preliminary manner: (1) the overall problem of economic development and agricultural production within the entire African continent; (2) the recent hostilities in Matabeleland, or southern Zimbabwe, and the role of South Africa within this political crisis; and (3) a criticism of the US Left's approaches toward the problematic of African socialism.

The African Context of Underdevelopment

No analysis of Zimbabwe's present crisis is possible outside of a brief review of the fundamental historical burden facing all African nations today: the legacy of colonialism and systematic underdevelopment by the capitalist West. The brutal realities can be summed up in a brief set of statistics: 22 of the 30 poorest nations in the world are black Africa; from 1970 to 1980, the economics of eight black nations shrank, and the combined debt of all 30 countries in these years soared by 1,000 percent; only three countries currently grow enough food to feed their indigenous populations. Even the *Wall Street Journal* noted recently, "Africa is a continent of poor soils and unfriendly climates. Markets are too small and scattered to support local manufacturing. Distances are too vast for effective transportation and communication. . . . Africa's economies are based on external demand, on prices set by the West for raw materials that, with few exceptions, can be bought from any number of sellers." None of the countries "make the manufactured goods the others need. None of them want the weak, overvalued currencies of their neighbors. And it's cheaper anyway to buy maize and sugar, bicycles and hoes, from the West than from each other."

The International Monetary Fund (IMF) has meted out its most severe "medicine" to the new African regimes. Under IMF pressure, notes the *Journal*, "Zimbabwe devalued its dollar by 20 percent in recent months. It has frozen wages and raised the price of maize, its staple food, by 40 percent. Sudan devalued the pound, introduced incentives on its state farms and raised the price of sugar. The list goes on: Kenya, Botswana, Zambia, Malawi, the Ivory Coast, all them are acceding to the IMF." Zimbabwe's acquiescence to IMF demands followed a series of economic problems. Many African workers' salaries were increased by one third to two thirds after independence, while white professionals earning above $20,000 had their wages frozen. The economic recession of 1982, a severe drought which reduced agricultural output, and the decline of gold prices produced a burgeoning balance of payments deficit. The growth rate of the GNP declined from 15 percent in 1980 to only 2 percent in 1982.

Socialist construction is not possible unless there is an accumulation of a surplus drawn from the great mineral and natural wealth of the continent. Thus, Western investment and technical services are to some degree a necessary and inevitable aspect of development, even under Marxist governments. Thus in recent months, for instance, Mozambique has invited technicians from US and Dutch companies to bid for oil concessions under agreements which guarantee 50 percent of the profits to the state. Specialists from France, Brazil, East Germany, Sweden, and the Soviet Union are prospecting for new coal reserves, which are currently estimated at 300 million tons. Star-Kist Foods of California recently met with Maputo officials to initiate fishing activities along the Indian Ocean coastline. Zimbabwe is thus following the path charted in part by both Angola and Mozambique. To date, there has been only one major firm from the US, the Heinz Corporation, which has established an important factory since Zimbabwe's independence. Zimbabwe's pressing need for foreign exchange and for the development of a local industrial and commercial infrastructure must of necessity involve relations with the capitalist West.

Agriculture reconstruction in Zimbabwe has been agonizingly slow, but steady. Three years ago, 6,000 Rhodesian white settlers controlled over one half of Zimbabwe's farmland. Under the Mugabe government, 5 million acres of land have been sold or seized, and then given to 20,000 black families. By 1985, the whites will control roughly one quarter of the land, and another 162,000 African families will receive farmland. As African journalist Jean-Francois Lisee has noted, "Primary education is compulsory and free, and there are twice as many children in classrooms now than in white Rhodesia. Free medical care for the poor has been introduced, and, while doctors are in short supply, rural women are being trained in first aid and preventive care." Like other African Marxists, Mugabe is desperately attempting to improve the necessary environment for Western investment on a cooperative basis. Given the destabilizing role of South Africa, the IMF, and the presence of many white settlers from the *ancien regime*, it is a difficult task.

The ZAPU-ZANU Conflict

Much of the Western media coverage, ethnocentric as always, has focused on the so-called "plight" of the remaining white settlers. At the high point of white hegemony, about 250,000 whites lived in Rhodesia. Since 1980, about 75,000 whites have departed—and although the rate of white flight has declined sharply, over 17,000 whites left in 1982 alone. Mugabe has attempted to induce whites with administrative, agricultural, and technical skills to remain in the country. Even today, most whites families maintain a host of servants, and profit from a standard of living which in African terms can only be described as decadent. To ensure that their wealth remains inside Zimbabwe, the government insists that an emigrating white take only $1,000 in money and no furniture. A handful of white settlers have been killed and threatened in the recent period of unrest, to be sure— but there is absolutely no reason to sympathize with their current situation. Indeed, their deaths should not evoke one single tear or merit a drop of ink. What must concern us is the fratricidal struggle between the Shona and the Ndebele, and whether this may lead to a kind of Biafran civil disorder, from which only South Africa will benefit. It is imperative to keep in mind, too, that hostilities between these two very different peoples predate the colonial era, and that the "Patriotic Front" and the détente between ZAPU and ZANU were only due to political necessity. The collapse of the Ian Smith regime and the end of formal hostilities with the racist settler militia did not permit a long transitional period through which a programmatic unity between the two liberation forces could be forged.

The recent military actions of the Mugabe government are remarkably restrained, given the level of internal attacks which that nation has endured in the previous two years. These acts of terrorism and sabotage include the destruction of roughly $32 million worth of government arms and ammunition; the destruction of Zimbabwe air force jets; the bombing of ZANU's headquarters in downtown Harare; the murder of nearly 100 civilians, tourists, and police by Nkomo's forces in Matabeleland. In December 1982, after the deserters committed a number of fresh executions and kidnappings, Mugabe finally decided to act. The North Korean–trained Fifth Brigade, comprised largely of Shona and numbering 2,000, systematically went through Matabele territory to uproot the terrorists. Sadly, about 1,000 civilians, deserters, and others suspected of terrorism were executed; 450 ZAPU members were placed under arrest; and the two top military leaders loyal to Nkomo, General Lookout Mask and Dumiso Dabengwa, were charged with treason. Nkomo promptly fled the country. Media charges of atrocities committed by the Fifth Brigade were used to freeze Western support to the government, including a $17 million grant from Sweden. A pending grant of $60 million from the US, scheduled to begin in October 1983, is also in jeopardy. But as Zimbabwe press secretary Dan D. Manyika explained to the *Washington Post,* Mugabe "had no other options" left to restore order. Only after an "armed assault on the prime minister's home," attacks on "military and police outposts," and the abduction of tourists, "thereby affecting the tourism industry," and the destruction of water development equipment worth millions of dollars" did "the government send troops into Matabeleland to clear the mess. It is clear that ZAPU dissidents and followers alike won't recognize any government not headed by Mr. Nkomo," Manyika concluded.

A second but somewhat overlooked element in the current ZAPU-ZANU struggle is the omnipresence of the *apartheid* regime in Pretoria. As Prime Minister P.W. Botha informed a *New York Times* correspondent in mid-February, his regime would consider "request for aid" from counterrevolutionary groups across black Africa. "If fellow Africans are threatened by the evils of Communism, we shall assist them," Botha promised. "I'm an African and I believe Communism is bad for Africa." The Botha regime's covert support for Jonas Savimni's UNITA inside Angola is of course well known. Since February, there have been substantial reports indicating that BOSS (apartheid's secret police) and military agents have been involved in the extensive sabotage within Zimbabwe since its independence. South Africa now maintains at least four training camps for anti-Marxists dissidents, and perhaps as many as 1,000 former "loyalists" from the puppet government of Bishop Abel Muzorewa are currently training there. Late in 1982, pro-Nkomo deserters were running low on supplies and ammunitions. The great cache of AK-47s and other Soviet-built weapons captured by South African troops in their war against SWAPO inside Namibia are now appearing inside Zimbabwe and are being used by some Nkomo forces Two points are now clear: the Ndebele (17 percent of the country's population) are an insufficient force to gain effective political hegemony; and therefore, any acts of dissidents terrorism serve not only to disrupt Zimbabwe, but also to reinforce apartheid's powerful economic grip over the entire region.

With Nkomo's recent flight into exile, there exists some hope that the ZAPU leadership will come to terms with the government. ZAPU Vice-President Josiah Chinamano has quickly distanced himself from Nkomo, and has vowed to support Mugabe's "policy of unity, peace, and reconciliation." Privately, a few ZAPU lieutenants have admitted to government ministers that Nkomo was "the biggest stumbling block to cooperation between the parties." The Soviets, the chief supporters of Nkomo during the guerrilla war, have refused to support their old friend. Zambian officials also close to Nkomo declare that "it would be grossly wrong" for the country "to embroil itself in the already sad and tangled mess," according to the *Times of Zambia*. "It would also be very wrong for Mr. Nkomo to even seemingly seek refuge in Zambia." Perhaps the Soviets and Zambian leader Kenneth Kaunda are waiting to see whether a covert relationship exists between the apartheid regime and the rebels in Matabeleland. Meanwhile, the campaign of terror has eroded critical international support for Mugabe's government, and has jeopardized his economic programs.

Criticism of Mugabe's Government

Western leftists usually commit two types of errors when confronting socialist construction in the underdeveloped world. Either the new national state should rapidly eradicate the authoritarian structures of the old regime, and create the social and cultural conditions which approximate Western bourgeois civil society, or the state must relentlessly pursue a permanent revolution among the masses, holding no measure of accommodation with the indigenous private sector and the local petty bourgeoisie. Social democrats take the first position, upholding irrational and indeed ahistorical standards of civil and political behavior for transitional states which can barely feed themselves, much less have the luxury of a social surplus from which the material conditions for socialist construction may take place. How can Mugabe tolerate a "bourgeois freedom of the press" when the masses do not control sufficient capital to publish a constructively oppositional paper, and where the white colonizers and investors could destabilize the young government via the media—as they have done elsewhere in the Third World? But can Mugabe exempt white farmers from their holdings overnight without creating massive urban food riots, widespread hunger, and the political conditions suitable for apartheid and US-backed intervention? Here the metaphysical Left, the petty bourgeois elites who criticize Nicaragua, Mozambique, Grenada, and Zimbabwe from the "Left," err by advocating so-called permanent warfare against the middle strata and other transitional regimes. In this context, the theory of permanent revolution underestimates the importance of the peasantry and the middle strata in the process of socialist transition. Left sectarians seemingly support only those revolutions which have never occurred, and condemn revolutions which are actually taking place.

Just the internal problems confronting the Zimbabwe African National Union are enormous by any political standard. First, despite ZANU's description as a Marxist party in the Western press, in actuality it is more of an anticolonialist front. Mugabe comes from the Zezuru subgroup of the Shona, who are not the dominate clan among the Shona language group. He has a more militant Leninist wing in the party, lodged within the former guerrilla circles, which has pushed for even firmer measures against Joshua Nkomo's followers. There are also a goodly number of ZANU administrators, farmers, and party officials who, despite their rhetorical claims to socialism, are quite satisfied with plans to expand the corporate sector in the country, and who would like to pursue an economic policy not unlike that of Jamaica's former leader Michael Manley. Internal party fractures have always made things difficult for the Prime Minister and the party. Indeed, no party congress has ever been held since 1964! What holds ZANU together is not a common Marxist ideology, but the practical necessity of uprooting counterrevolutionaries inspired by Nkomo, and the gradual transferal of economic power from the settler white elites to the African masses without an exodus of much-needed intellectuals, administrators, technicians, and capital investment.

On what terms can constructive criticism of Zimbabwe be placed? One specific area of concern is that of organized labor. In early 1983, the government passed new restraints on African workers. Under certain conditions strikes can be illegal; the government has the prerogative of ignoring and invalidating union elections if the winner is not to its liking; the state can even dictate the movement of workers in a manner that parallels the South African system of "influx control." These legal controls over labor are reminiscent of the constrictions demanded by Kwame Nkrumah in the aftermath of labor unrest in Ghana in 1961. The labor problem in this instance was finally resolved with the purging of labor militants and the absorption of trade unions as an ineffectual arm of the state apparatus. For Nkrumah, the fact that trade unions lacked any real independence meant the loss of an effective proletarian force on the Left, and ultimately led to his own 1966 overthrow by the military. For Mugabe, the choices to be made between the interests of African labor versus the growing African bureaucracy must be predicated by Nkrumah's failure.

The Mugabe government must immediately come to terms with the elements of ZAPU and the Ndebele leadership who disavow the dissidents. In the long run, Nkomo's departure may become a turning point in the Shona-Ndebele conflict, if there is some kind of limited regional autonomy that can evolve for Matabeleland within the overall framework of the central government. Mugabe must guarantee the Ndebele national minority a share of effective state power. The decision to accept IMF intervention in the troubled economy must be seen from the vantage point of other Third World nations—especially Jamaica—as a step backwards from socialist construction. No workers' state worthy of the name can be built unless the African working class has structural independence from the state apparatus, and has decisive input into all economic policy-making. Despite these and other contradictions, however, Mugabe merits the critical support of the Left here, and elsewhere, as he and the people of Zimbabwe attempt to build a new society.

Sin Libertad:
United Nations Appeal for
Puerto Rican Independence

Mr. Chairman and distinguished members of this United Nations Special Committee on Decolonization, I address this international body on behalf of the United States People's Delegation and the Puerto Rico Solidarity Committee.

As a political sociologist and historian, I will attempt briefly to outline the historical evolution of racism, slavery, colonialism, and economic exploitation in Puerto Rico. I will make special references to the pivotal role of American capital and the US government in the economic underdevelopment of the Puerto Rican nation, in the suppression of civil liberties and human rights, and in the exploitation of the Puerto Rican national minority within the United States. I shall also, as the great-grandson of a slave, endeavor to address the special sense of solidarity I feel toward the Puerto Rican demand for independence, justice, and self-determination.

A History of Slavery and Colonialism

It would assume encyclopedic proportions to document fully the heritage of slavery, peonage, and social exploitation which is at the foundations of Puerto Rican political and socioeconomic history. The Spanish Caribbean (which included Santo Domingo, Cuba, Jamaica prior to 1665, and Puerto Rico) was the basis for the expansion of African slavery and colonial exploitation into all the Americas. Historians estimate conservatively that

77,000 Africans were imported into Puerto Rico for agricultural production. Hundreds of thousands more were brought to Puerto Rico directly from Africa, and were subsequently sold or transported to other Spanish plantations in the region. In the nineteenth century, Cuba and Puerto Rico surpassed Haiti as the world's chief supplier of sugarcane. This economic growth was due in no small measure to the fierce exploitation of black labor.

A body of laws emerged in Puerto Rico and in other Spanish possessions mandating strict provisions for acts of rebelliousness. No more than three Africans were allowed to meet without the presence of a white colonial; slaves absent from the masters for more than one week were given 100 lashes and were forced to wear "iron fetters tied to their feet" for another two months. Slave rebels were often decapitated, raped, or burned at the stake. Profits generated at the expense of Puerto Rican laborers were so great that the Spanish only reluctantly ended slavery in the island in 1873— 70 years after it was abolished in Haiti, 60 years after its demise in Argentina and Colombia, and 25 years after emancipation in all French and Danish West Indian colonies. Historians Luis M. Diaz Soler, author of *Historia de la Esclavitud Negra en Puerto Rico,* and Jose L. Franco, author of *Afroamerica* and *La Presencia Negro en el Nuevo Mundo,* document the rich African legacy which is an integral aspect of Puerto Rican culture, and the brutal means by which the Spanish colonial regime used to accumulate capital at the expense of this servile labor force.[1]

A historical perspective on the Spanish political economy of slavery is important because it clarifies the roots of American colonialism and the current economic exploitation of Puerto Rico. The Spanish American War of 1896 was the United States' decisive step toward becoming a worldwide imperialist power. As historian Ramon Eduardo Ruiz notes, "In return for an empire that embraced the Philippines, mid-Pacific islands, Puerto Rico, and Cuba, fewer than one hundred lives were lost. To Theodore Roosevelt, who undoubtedly voiced the sentiment of his countrymen, 'It wasn't much of war, but it was the best war we had.'"[2]

One disturbing dilemma for the American imperialists was the issue of race. Over 300,000 Puerto Ricans in 1900 clearly held Negro ancestry. An even larger number of Puerto Ricans would have been classified as "black" by American racists. Thus, as African-American historian John Hope Franklin observed, the new American colonial regime had to export and promote the virulent brand of white supremacy into the island, while establishing the economic conditions necessary to expropriate surplus value from the labor force. Franklin writes:

In 1900, when the first organic act of Puerto Rico was passed by [Congress], the Southern members of that body—and some Northern members, too—were concerned not only with the fact that the Puerto Ricans should be carefully supervised in the operation of their government but also that the Negroes of the island would not enjoy such political liberties as to inspire the Negroes of the United States to fight for greater political opportunities. The governor and all of the important officials were to be appointed by the President of the United States; and Americans were to outnumber Puerto Ricans on the important Executive Council. The second organic act of 1917 remodeled the local government to resemble one of the states of the United States. . . . The power of appointing all of the major officials of the island, however, was reserved for the President of the United States.[3]

The inevitable result of this racist and elitist state apparatus, according to Franklin, was "the concentration of the wealth in the hands of a few," "considerable profits" reaped by American investors, a "high mortality rate [and] abject poverty of the masses of the people."[4]

United States domination after 1898 created a more diversified economy, but perpetuated and in every respect deepened class exploitation. Tobacco manufacturing rose and suddenly declined in the first quarter of the twentieth century, to be replaced by needle trades which fed "on the pathetically cheap labor of thousands of women and children in rural squalor." By the 1930s and 1940s, as social scientists Ricardo Campos and Frank Bonilla note, "economic and social conditions approached intolerable levels. The goading anomalies of the sugar economy—the short work season, the wretched wage scale, the steady withdrawal of lands from subsistence cultivation, the pitiless encroachment on small landowners, the flagrant withdrawal of desperately needed wealth from a nation living from hand-to-mouth—brought tensions to a new peak."[5]

As official unemployment rates reached 37 percent by the outbreak of World War II, the US government attempted to redefine the terms of Puerto Rico's colonial status. What eventually evolved was "Operation Bootstrap."[6] Capital was invited to the island on its own terms: low taxes, low wage rates, no environmental protection laws, little unionized labor, and a puppet state apparatus which would guarantee high profit margins. In subsequent decades, US corporate expansion increased. Capital investment jumped from $1.4 billion in 1960 to $24 billion in 1979. Corporations now included petrochemicals, pharmaceuticals, banks, the tourism sector (hotels, etc.), and high technology. "At the close of the 1970s," Campos and Bonilla note, "90 percent of the net industrial income (variable capital and profits) in Puerto Rico was generated by United States firms. . . . In 1979 these profits constituted 42 percent of those reaped in Latin America by United States investors. Not only industry and commerce but banking, air and sea transport, tourism and numberless 'services' are virtual monopolies controlled by United States capitals."[7]

The "social costs" of American corporate expansion into Puerto Rico were, and continue to remain, devastating. Puerto Rican agriculture once sustained a food supply for a growing population: now 80 percent of local food consumption is imported, mostly from the US. Real unemployment on the island is currently between 30 to 45 percent. Sixty percent of the population exists below the US-established poverty level. Fifty-three percent of all Puerto Ricans survive on Food Stamps and other Federal government programs. As attorney and Puerto Rican activist Judith Berkan notes, the island's ecology has been harmed "by the export of industrial and military activities which destroy and pollute."[8]

Corporations subjected to few controls by the state repeatedly dispose of industrial and chemical wastes with little regard for the health and safety of the local population. Puerto Rican women have traditionally been subjected to all forms of sexual oppression, from rape to sexual harassment in the workplace. Since the 1940s, government-backed sterilization campaigns have attempted to resolve the "problem" of overpopulation by the most inhumane and brutal means. Poverty and unemployment have often divided families, and continue to undermine the social and cultural integrity of the working masses.

Puerto Rican Exploitation Within the United States

Working people of Puerto Rico have been forced to seek employment within the United States for generations. In New York City alone, the Puerto Rican population increased from 60,000 in 1940 to approximately 250,000 in 1950.[9] Along with other immigrants and people of color—Mexicans, Filipinos, Chinese, Haitians, Jamaicans, and African-Americans—they were generally confined within the lowest sectors of the labor force. The dual labor market which existed to squeeze super profits from this Third World workforce perpetuated the social conditions for poverty.

As the Puerto Rican population exceeded 800,000 in New York City, Chicago, Boston, and other US cities by 1960, the features of permanent domestic underdevelopment became even more clear. In 1970, to cite only one set of official statistics, the median family income of Puerto Ricans in the US was only $4,969. This contrasts with the 1970 median family income of African-Americans at $5,074; Irish-Americans, $8,127; and Italian-Americans, $8,808.[10]

Since the mid-1970s, the American state has faced a massive fiscal crisis, and it has looked to Puerto Rican, Chicano, black, and other low income workers to bear the political and economic burden for restoring profit margins. Thus Puerto Rican youth in New York City suffer from 50 percent unemployment rates. Necessary social services in public medical care, housing, and welfare have been drastically reduced or eliminated outright. About 40 percent of all Puerto Rican families live below the poverty level, and public programs for bilingual education have been cut. Under the administration of Ronald Reagan, the Puerto Rican community has been one of the hardest hit in terms of "mass unemployment, financial instability," and "social pain and misery."[11]

The Illusion of Puerto Rican Democracy

It is still claimed by American politicians and colonial bureaucrats that Puerto Rico is an example of true participatory democracy for the Caribbean and Latin America. There are active political parties, primarily the Popular Democratic Party (PPD) and the New Progressive Party (PNP), which engage in regular elections. The masses of Puerto Rican people supposedly are represented in an elected Senate and House. Any preliminary investigation of the realities behind these formal structures of US-style democracy reveals the absolute negation of self-determination.

Both the pro-Commonwealth PPD and the pro-statehood PNP represent the Puerto Rican comprador elites and those elements of the petty bourgeoisie committed to the continuation of colonial rule and US corporate hegemony on the island. Through their control of the electoral process, including their domination of the public bureaucracy and the Electoral Board, these colonial parties are able to regulate and manage political culture. Voting is defined as the only acceptable means through which the population can express its political will.

But even at the ballot box, the forces of colonial repression leave nothing to chance. In 1972, voting fraud was so prevalent that the major parties had to negotiate the allocation of votes. In the election of 1980 there were many reported instances of gross election violations. As one observer commented, "Boxes [of uncounted ballots were] even found in garbage cans at the Electoral Commission."[12] Under circus-like conditions, with the omnipresence of outright corruption in even the highest circles of government, the people of Puerto Rico have no viable free choice at the polls. This has led to a growing percentage of abstentions in general elections—28 percent in 1980—and a sense of alienation and political apathy. Thus "politics" has been transformed into a conduit for the interests of elites and corporations to suppress the will of the majority.

Puerto Ricans both within the colony and the US who actively denounce these electoral political frauds, and who advocate independence and self-determination, are subjected to state repression. Pedro Albizu Campos, a graduate of Harvard undergraduate college in 1916 and Harvard Law School in 1921, was a leader of the first generation to suffer from US imperialism. As a proponent of Puerto Rican independence, he was tried and convicted for the crime of advocating freedom for his people. Imprisoned from 1937 to 1943, and again during the 1950s, he died in April 1965.

Hundreds of other martyrs have suffered Albizu Campos' fate. For decades, the CIA, FBI, and various law enforcement agencies have hounded, suppressed, imprisoned, tortured, and persecuted advocates of independence. In October 1977, progressive trade union leader Juan Rafael Caballero was kidnapped, tortured, and executed. The next year, two independence leaders were butchered in a police ambush in Puerto Rico. In November 1979, Angel Rodrigues Cristobal was beaten to death while in custody in Tallahassee, Florida.[13] Grand jury repression continues to mount; since last year's testimony was heard, criminal contempt charges—with demands for lengthy prison terms—have been brought against independentistas who have refused to cooperate in the suppression of their movement.

Regional Geopolitical Context

The continued occupation and political-economic exploitation of Puerto Rico must also be understood in the context of recent US foreign policies in the Caribbean, Central America, and Latin America. Since the mid-1970s, a progressive political trend has culminated in the victories of liberation and anti-colonialist forces. The triumphs of the Sandinistas in Nicaragua, the New Military Council of Suriname, and the New Jewel Movement of Grenada were sufficient to place the political question of US hegemony in the region into problematic status.

The Carter Administration has responded to the crisis by making bellicose statements and military maneuvers against the people of revolutionary Cuba. In 1979 it announced plans to create an "inter-American peacekeeping force" to respond to local "emergencies."[14] Puerto Rico assumed a central position in US plans to "stabilize" the geopolitical situation. Also in 1979, units of the Puerto Rican National Guard were "federalized" and stationed in the Dominican Republic. By 1980, members of the Barbados Defense Force were sent to Puerto Rico to train at Camp Salinas.

With the advent of the Reagan Administration, the full implications of a more aggressive American policy in Latin America become apparent. In 1981 and 1982 the Puerto Rican National Guard took part in war maneuvers along with the American and NATO troops. US sources states openly that these war maneuvers were designed to "[develop] the capacity of military intervention against Cuba and Grenada." In February 1983, the National Guard was sent to Honduras, near the northern boundary of Nicaragua. Simultaneously, the Reagan Administration openly violated US laws by conducting a vicious campaign against Nicaragua, which involved the CIA, Somocista, and counter-revolutionary terrorists. As noted by the Caribbean Project for Justice and Peace, the crucial function of the Puerto

Rican Guardsmen is to play the role of a Spanish-speaking Foreign Legion, buttressing local dictatorial regimes. US policy "could eventually involved the utilization of soldiers of the National Guard of Puerto Rico in repressive activities within Honduras and in military operations against the progressive forces in El Salvador and the Sandinista regime in Nicaragua."[15]

The fact that Central America and the Caribbean countries are engaged in social unrest shows what the general results of US economic and political policies in the region have been during the twentieth century. The Reagan Administration's efforts to turn back the historical clock to the "Big Stick" policies of Theodore Roosevelt only worsen the damage that has already been done. Typical of the crude arrogance of the Reagan Administration is the following statement, made on Puerto Rico's "Commonwealth Day," by Jeane Kirkpatrick: "Puerto Rico is neither a domestic nor international matter. It is a geopolitical bastion of the United States." This statement by the US Ambassador to the United Nations completely and contemptuously disregards the previous resolutions of this committee.

Clearly, the Reagan Administration wants to impose a "Reaganite" and conservative style of governance around the world. Using the sterile rhetoric of anti-Communism, the Reagan Administration is attacking all movements for political reform and social justice, especially in the Third World nations. History and common sense tell us that no viable democracy can exist for Puerto Rico unless it achieves self-determination and independence.

African-American Solidarity with the People of Puerto Rico

Of all Americans who sympathize with the goals of the Puerto Rican independence movement, perhaps the African-American community shares the deepest sense of solidarity. We are also the historical product of slavery and racism; we intimately understand the weight of political repression which has been placed against our own demands for human rights and social justice. We have experienced high rates of unemployment, the lack of adequate human services, inferior schools, and the never-ending attacks against our own political activists and leaders, from Paul Robeson and W.E.B. Du Bois, to Malcolm X and Martin Luther King, Jr. Our solidarity with the Puerto Rican nation is deeply rooted in a common cultural heritage, and a common legacy of economic exploitation. We understand and agree that our common liberation will not be achieved until American monopoly capitalism is erased from human existence. Domination abroad and institutional racism at home are the twin pillars of American capitalist oppression.

Our greatest African-American scholar, W.E.B. Du Bois, a founder of the National Association for the Advancement of Colored People (NAACP), took a special interest in the plight of Puerto Rico. Du Bois supported the political work of Albizu Campos, and rallied to his defense.[16] In June 1922, Du Bois informed readers of his NAACP journal, *The Crisis*, that the "liberation of Puerto Rico was inevitable."[17] In February 1929, he attacked the US policies in the island for perpetuating economic exploitation.[18]

A half century later, Congressman Ronald V. Dellums, an African-American socialist, introduced a bill in the House of Representatives which called for the "Transfer of Powers to Puerto Rico" in compliance with United Nations requirements. In the bill, Congressman Dellums openly states that "the move toward the elimination of colonialism and all vestiges of colonialism in all parts of the world is now irreversible. . . . The practices followed by the United States with respect to Puerto Rico have been developed in open contradiction to the principles upon which this Nation was founded. . . . Therefore the people of Puerto Rico [must] freely decide their political status without any intervention whatsoever of any government. . . . Puerto Rico constitutes a full-fledged Latin American nation."[19]

In the anticolonialist and anti-imperialist spirit of Pedro Albizu Campos and W.E.B. Du Bois, and with the active support and solidarity of all freedom-loving peoples across the world, we rededicate ourselves to the end of this sordid chapter of colonial history in Puerto Rico. The worldwide struggle against racism, imperialism, and corporate domination demands the independence of the nation of Puerto Rico. *Venceremos!*

NOTES

1. Robert W. Fogel and Stanley Engerman, *Time on the Cross: The Economics of American Negro Slavery* (Boston: Little, Brown, 1974), pp. 18, 19, 33, 34; Jose L. Franco, "Maroons and Slave Rebellions in the Spanish Territories," in Richard Price, ed., *Maroon Societies: Rebel Slave Communities in the Americas* (Baltimore: Johns Hopkins, 1979), pp. 35–48; and Jose L. Franco, *La presencia negra en el nuevo mundo* (Havana: Casa de las Americas, 1968).

2. Ramon Eduardo Ruiz, *Cuba: The Making of a Revolution* (New York: W.W. Norton, 1970), p. 21.

3. John Hope Franklin, *From Slavery to Freedom: A History of Negro Americans*, Third Edition (New York: Vintage, 1969), p. 426–427.

4. Ibid.

5. Ricardo Campos and Frank Bonilla, "Bootstraps and Enterprise Zones: The Underside of Late Capitalism," paper presented by Frank Bonilla at "US Today" Symposium, Instituto de Investigaciones Sociales, Universidad Nacional Autonoma de Mexico, Coyoacan, Mexico, July 1981, pp. 1–2.

6. A very misleading but typical account of Puerto Rican economic "development" along capitalist lines is Earl Parker Hansen's *Transformation: The Story of Modern Puerto Rico* (New York: Simon and Schuster, 1955).

7. Campos and Bonilla, "Bootstraps and Enterprise Zones," pp. 5–6.

8. Judith Berkan, "PRSC at the UN," *Puerto Rico Libre,* Vol. 6 (Winter 1981), p. 13.

9. For Puerto Rican migrations to the United States, see History Task Force, Centro de Estudios Puertoriquenos, *Labor Migration Under Capitalism: The Puerto Rican Experience* (New York: Monthly Review Press, 1979).

10. See US Bureau of the Census, "Persons of Spanish Origin in the United States: November 1969," *Current Population Reports,* Series P–20, No. 2131 (Washington, DC.: US Government Printing Office, 1970), p. 34; and US Bureau of the Census, "Characteristics of the Population by Ethnic Origin: November 1969," *Current Population Reports,* Series P–20, No. 221 (Washington, DC.: US Government Printing Office, 1970).

11. Victor Quintana, "'Nuestra Comunidad': The State of the Puerto Rican Community," *Puerto Rico Libre,* Vol. 6 (Spring 1983), pp. 5, 8.

12. Judith Berkan, "1980 Elections—Puerto Rico," *Puerto Rico Libre,* Vol. 6 (Winter 1981), p. 3.

13. Berkan, "PRSC at the UN," p. 13.

14. James Petras, "US Foreign Policy in the Post Somoza Period," *Puerto Rico Libre,* Vol. 6 (Winter 1981), p. 10.

15. Quoted in Luis Prado, "Puerto Rican Proxy Troops: New Stage of the Inter-American Conflict," *Puerto Rico Libre,* Vol. 6 (Spring 1983), p. 3.

16. See W.E.B. Du Bois to warden, Atlanta Penitentiary, July 7, 1941, in Herbert Aptheker, ed., *The Correspondence of W.E.B. Du Bois,* Vol. II (Amherst, Massachusetts: University of Massachusetts Press, 1976), pp. 291, 294.

17. W.E.B. Du Bois, "Opinion," *The Crisis,* Vol. 24 (June 1922), p. 55.

18. W.E.B. Du Bois, "As the Crow Flies," *The Crisis,* Vol. 36 (February 1922), p. 41.

19. "Congressman Dellums Introduces Transfer of Powers Bill," *Puerto Rico Libre,* Vol. 6 (Winter 1981), pp. 15–16.

16

Nuclear War and
Black America

After the bombing of Hiroshima and Nagasaki, Albert Einstein noted that "the unleashed power of the atom has changed everything except our way of thinking." The struggle for black Americans' civil rights since the end of World War II has occurred beneath the specter of nuclear war. Major civil rights leaders and black intellectuals—most prominently Paul Robeson, W.E.B. Du Bois, and Martin Luther King, Jr.—have spoken out against the nuclear arms race. But for many black Americans, our essential way of thinking about issues of war and peace has not been integrated into our long-standing desire for civil rights, economic opportunity, and racial equality. More than ever before, the necessity to link the issues of "jobs, peace, and freedom" demands a new level of analysis of the impact of the arms race upon black American society.

The root causes for nuclear arms proliferation and its political and economic consequences for American society can be briefly stated. The United States was the first nation to develop the atomic bomb and has been the only country, to date, which has used this devastating weapon against any civilian population. Within three years after Hiroshima, the Americans had developed the first intercontinental bomber capable of delivering atomic bombs at most Soviet cities and military installations. The Soviet Union endeavored to catch up, first successfully testing an atomic weapon in 1949, and developing their own intercontinental bombers by 1955. Each new US advance in technology and weapons systems was eventually matched by the Russians: the hydrogen bomb (US in 1952, USSR in 1955); intercontinental ballistic missiles (US in 1958, USSR in 1957); submarine-launched ballistic missiles (US in 1960, USSR in 1968); multiple warhead missiles (US in 1964, USSR in 1973). With a clear head start in nuclear weapons development, by 1964 the United States held the capacity to completely destroy Soviet society. The Americans had 7,000 strategic missiles, and more than 1,000 bombers; the Russians had on balance only one-fifth as many.

During the late 1960s and 1970s, the Soviets strained their domestic economy in order to close the arms gap with the US. By 1983, rough parity existed between the two superpowers: the US with over 11,000 strategic warheads versus 7,800 Soviet warheads. Both sides had the capacity to suffer a "first strike" from their opponent, and still deliver sufficient firepower to level the other many times over. This equivalence of nuclear weaponry has led many millions of Americans and Europeans to call for a "freeze" in order to reduce the growing risk of nuclear war. The Reagan Administration, however, has just stepped up the arms race by authorizing the deployment of Cruise and Pershing II missiles in Western Europe. Both are "first strike" weapons, designed to start a nuclear war. The Cruise missile is only 20 feet long, and would be difficult, if not impossible, to verify under any arms agreement. Given that a series of American presidents have publicly or privately threatened the use of tactical nuclear weapons for decades—from Eisenhower's threat to use the nuclear bomb in the Mideast and China in 1958 to Nixon's warnings of the possible use of the bomb over North Vietnam in the early 1970s—the Soviets will predictably respond to the Reagan Administration's escalation with one of their own. We are thus closer to a worldwide nuclear holocaust today than at any time since the 1962 Cuban missile crisis.

What would a nuclear war mean for black America? Demographically, the black population is the most "urban" of all other ethnic and social groups within the US. About one out of every eight African-Americans lives in metropolitan New York City and Chicago alone; almost 9 million blacks live in the nation's 15 largest cities, and half of all blacks live in the 60 largest urban areas. US military planners assume that in the first half hour of a general war, the 200 largest US cities and almost every military base or missile site would be struck by at least one Soviet warhead, delivering the explosive power of at least 657 Hiroshima bombs (one megaton). Under a best-case scenario, if the US managed to destroy over two-thirds of the Soviets' missiles, the Russians could still destroy American society. According to Senators Edward M. Kennedy and Mark Hatfield, with only 2,000 warheads "the Soviets could target 10 to 20 warheads on each city with a population over 1 million. . . . They could allocate 5 to 10 warheads to each of the next hundred largest cities and still have enough left over to target a warhead on each of the next thousand cities. That would be enough to saturate every metropolitan area in the United States and reach towns with populations no larger than a few thousand." In this initial exchange, at least 80 percent of the total black US population would be instantly obliterated, or would soon die from injuries.

Some foster the faint hope that many inner-city residents could be saved by taking cover in the basement of churches, office buildings, and subways. In March 1982, Reagan Administration officials requested $4.2 billion in civil defense funds to prepare Americans for a nuclear attack. One Reagan official, Deputy Under Secretary of Defense T.K. Jones, even insisted that most Americans could survive a nuclear war. "Everyone's going to make it if there are enough shovels to go around," Jones stated. "Dig a hole, cover it up with a few doors and then throw three feet of dirt on top. It's the dirt that does it." The 1979 report of the Congressional Office of Technology Assessment stands in sharp contradiction to the Reagan Administration's rosy predictions. If a one megaton bomb struck downtown Detroit at night, for instance, 70,000 people would be vaporized, and every building within a 1.7 mile radius would be leveled. Three miles out, all homes are destroyed, half the people are either killed instantly, and the rest are injured seriously. Five miles from downtown, most of the buildings catch fire, and about half the people are either killed or injured. People who looked at the Detroit nuclear blast or fireball from Ann Arbor, Michigan, would be blinded. It is likely, however, that the Soviets could employ a 20 megaton bomb on metropolitan Detroit, in which case 3,212,000 people would be killed, and another 536,00 would be injured, leaving roughly 110,000 survivors to cope with the radioactive fallout, malnutrition, genetic damage, heat prostration, and the lack of medical care. In short, "deep fallout shelters," according to former National Security Agency director Noel Gayler, "would become deep tombs."

Blacks Support Freeze

The sheer insanity of the nuclear and conventional arms race with the Soviet Union has culminated into a massive disarmament movement with widespread public support. In November 1982, over 11.6 million Americans voted in favor of a nuclear freeze between the US and USSR. In cities with sizable black populations, the margin of victory was between 3 to 1 to 4 to 1. Washington, DC, for example, cast 77,521 votes in favor of a nuclear freeze, with only 23,369 votes against. In Philadelphia, the vote was 231,787 to 75,149; in Chicago, 404,173 to 135,325. Two hundred seventy-six City Councils across the nation passed freeze resolutions, and both chambers of eleven state legislatures. In Congress, the Congressional Black Caucus (CBC) has been the leading voice favoring meaningful reductions in defense expenditures. In May 1982, the CBC proposed an alternative budget which called for increased spending for human needs and reductions in war programs. The proposal was, quite predictably, trounced, receiving only 86 favorable votes, with 322 opposed. Congressman Ronald V. Dellums (D-California) introduced HR-6696, an alternative appropriations bill which would have sliced about $50 billion from the currently bloated war budget of $240 billion. Billions of dollars for the Cruise and MX missiles, the Pershing II, and the Trident II would be transferred to job programs, health care, and other essential social services. Yet the Dellums bill received only 55 votes. Despite the fact that a clear majority of Americans—black, Hispanic, and white—favor a weapons freeze and a reallocation of funds toward human needs, neither Congress nor the White House is listening to the public.

Yet even within the black community, there are many who would define the national debate over the nuclear arms race as a "white issue." For example, one of the chief objections of Bayard Rustin to the August 27, 1983, March on Washington, DC, was the decision of march coordinators to include the "peace" slogan with other traditional civil rights demands. In an open letter to other black leaders, Rustin and Norman Hill of the A. Philip Randolph Institute stated, "The achievement of programmatic unity among ourselves becomes more difficult to the inclusion of peace, thereby making the success of the event even more problematic." Wisely, Coretta Scott King, Congressman Walter Fauntroy, and others refused to capitulate to this argument. But problems still remain at a grassroots level in many communities in making the linkages between civil rights reforms and the peace movement. Some of my own black students haven't even heard of the nuclear freeze; others voice the opinion that military spending may even be good for the economy. Given the overall depression-level economic conditions within the black community—19 percent unemployment, and over 50 percent unemployment among youth—any type of federal spending which creates jobs, even in defense plants, becomes somewhat attractive.

Moreover, for substantial segments of the black population, there is a popular belief, rooted in historical experience, which says that "a war is good for the economy." This attitude is especially evident black Americans in their thirties and early forties, and among black senior citizens. The former entered the job market during the Vietnam War. Many black high school and college graduates had a relatively easy time getting jobs. In 1969, for example, black youth unemployment was much less than half of today's figure. That same year, black males with families had official jobless rates of only 2.5 percent. The ratio of black families' median income levels to those of whites narrowed from 51 percent in 1958 to 63 percent in 1969. After the reduction of US troop involvement in Southeast Asia, economic conditions rapidly deteriorated for blacks.

The latter group's favorable attitude toward defense spending was created by World War II. In November 1941, black unemployment stood at 28 percent. The New Deal had helped to reduce black joblessness, but the nation as a whole was still trapped in an unprecedented depression. In the next three years, 11 million young men and women went into the armed services. Billions were spent in defense-related industries, and millions went to work. In these same instances, war-related spending did increase job opportunities for black people. But the simple fact usually overlooked is that any type of federal spending—whether for guns or hospitals, cruise missiles or day care centers—will generate jobs. The real question for black Americans is, How many jobs are created by spending the identical amount of money?

Jobs Versus Missiles

In 1983, an investment of $1 billion in the production of guided missiles would create 20,700 direct and indirect jobs. The identical amount of capital, if spent in the production of steel and iron, would generate 34,700 total jobs—an increase of 67.6 percent in employment. One billion dollars spent to upgrade and to expand inner-city bus, subway, and train systems would create 39,500 jobs on average. If we allocated $1 billion for hospitals and public health facilities, we'd produce 54,260 direct and indirect jobs. And $1 billion spent for public education and schools for our children would generate 71,500 jobs—345 percent more jobs than in guided missiles production. Yet even these statistics are misleadingly low. The Bureau of Labor Statistics recently determined that only 28 percent of the employees involved in guided missiles production are "production workers." Typically, in older industries such as automobile, steel, and rubber plants, production workers are 70 percent or more of all employees. Many of those hired in defense industries are highly trained white collar workers—scientists, engineers, computer analysts.

Any profile of the modern black labor force should quickly dispel the notion that African-Americans will be the chief beneficiaries of Reagan's arms buildup. One out of four black adult workers is found in manufacturing, 14 percent are in public administration, and 13 percent work in wholesale or retail trade. One in five black families today does not have a single income earner. The majority of blacks in white collar categories work as clerical employees or in lower paid administrative posts. Federal spending for hospitals, to subsidize basic industries, or for education and welfare would dramatically increase the number of potential jobs for blacks, specifically because they are already in these areas of the labor market. Conversely, only 29 of the 3,348 doctorates in the physical sciences in 1981–82 were

African-Americans. For doctorates in advanced mathematics for the same year, six out of 720 were black; in computer science, one out of 220; and in engineering, 20 out of 2,644. Spending for the Cruise and Pershing II missiles not only escalates the arms race, but it literally destroys hundreds of thousands of jobs yearly for black Americans.

Marion Anderson of Employment Research Associates of Lansing, Michigan, estimates that military spending in 1977 and 1978 caused a net loss each year of more than 1 million jobs. She calculates that each $1 billion of Pentagon spending causes the net loss of 9,000 job opportunities in the private sector and 35,000 jobs in the state and local government sectors. How does this relate to black unemployment? Anderson's research concludes that "there were over 480,000 fewer jobs for blacks in civilian industry because of the military budget. These are the civilian jobs lost or never created when people are heavily taxed to pay for the military and are unable to spend the money upon their own needs." A sector by sector analysis for the years 1970–1978 indicates that 28,100 blacks' jobs were lost annually in nondurable goods as a result of military expenditures. In residential construction, the net annual job loss was 21,350 jobs; for service related enterprises, 191,300 jobs were lost yearly; and another 150,450 were lost in state and local governments. Anderson concludes, "Every time the Pentagon's budget goes up to $1 billion, 1,300 jobs disappear from black Americans." Even blacks who are currently working on military contracts suffer lessened job opportunities, pay, and mobility for workers. Moreover, in the 21 states where 90 percent of the black population live, 17 show a loss of black employment when the military budget goes up. New Yorkers suffers a net loss of 58,000 jobs for blacks; Ohio, 12,000; Florida, 14,000; Michigan, 19,000; and Illinois, 24,000 jobs.

Flight of Economic Infrastructure

But even these devastating statistics on the loss of blacks' jobs must be understood within a broader socioeconomic context. The Reagan Administration projects a budget of $1.6 trillion for both conventional and nuclear weapons over the next five years. Take out your hand calculator, and compute this set of disturbing facts: If you spent $1 million per day, from the birth of Christ to the year 2000, you would spend less than one half of what Ronald Reagan wants to spend on defense in the next five years.

By any standard, this is an unprecedented shift of national resources and manpower from human needs–oriented production to the mechanisms of death. As a direct result, such spending will destroy the basic economic infrastructure of America. Business expansion can only take place where there is an economic and social infrastructure that exists which encourages growth. No business can grow or even remain in a community without adequate water, mass transportation systems, sewage, decent schools, and necessary social services.

Today, more than 8,000 miles of the US interstate highway system and 13 percent of its bridges must be rebuilt. Over the next 10 years, just to maintain highways outside our urban areas that are not part of the interstate system will require $700 billion. It will cost $31 billion in federal and state expenditures just to maintain the present sewage systems. It will cost $41 billion to repair and/or replace the 200,000 deficient bridges in the US. Major cities will have to spend $110 million to just maintain water systems. And the metropolitan transit systems are at the state of collapse. About one out of four public transportation systems may halt operation by 1988 because of the Reagan Administration's elimination of federal funds. These factors alone, even without the threat of nuclear conflict, would threaten to destroy America economically. Bad roads and bridges alone keep 25 percent of US towns out of growth business. For example, the typical street has about a 25-year life. Cleveland is only replacing or resurfacing all its streets at a rate of once every 49 years. New York City's rate is once every 700 years. The breakdown in public transportation means workers cannot get to work on time, or at all; the breakdown in the sewer systems limits business expansion; the collapse of public education means poorly trained individuals who are unfit for employment within the new technological age. State and city governments cannot afford to pay for these necessary economic expenses. And the arms race continues to keep blacks' unemployment rates at high levels.

What are the human consequences of the arms race and Reagan's war budget? Professor Harvey Brenner of Johns Hopkins University has found that a rise of 1 percent in the unemployment rate translates in one year to 37,000 additional deaths. This figures includes 920 additional suicides; 650 additional homicides; 500 additional deaths from cirrhosis of the liver. This also doesn't count the 4,000 additional admissions to state mental hospitals. Every time US unemployment goes up by 1 percent, $68 billion are lost in national production, and $20 billion are lost in tax revenues.

We do not have to wait for a nuclear war with the Soviets for American society to be destroyed—Reagan's war spending is killing thousands of us literally every year.

More than any other segment of American society, black Americans are the chief victims of the nuclear arms race. As urban residents, we will be among the first to die in a nuclear war; as blue collar, service, and low income white collar workers, we suffer higher rates of unemployment due to military expenditures. Martin Luther King, Jr. understood clearly that the battle for civil rights could not end with the achievement of desegregation. The basic goal of the black freedom movement must be the creation of social justice and a more democratic and peaceful society for all Americans.

"Somehow we must transform the dynamics of the world power struggle," Martin declared, "from a negative nuclear arms race which no one can win, to a positive contest to harness [humanity's] creative genius for the purpose of making peace and prosperity a reality for all of the nations of the world."

17

Race and Democracy in Cuba

For several decades, the Cuban Revolution has influenced the political thought of an entire generation of intellectuals across the Black Diaspora. For Frantz Fanon, Cuba represented the first decisive defeat of Western imperialism in his native Caribbean region. For LeRoi Jones, then a "beat" poet traveling to the island in July 1960, Cuba represented the militant vanguard of the world youth in revolt against the old order. Harold Cruse was also inspired by the Cuban revolutionary experience. In 1962 he noted that "the effects of the colonial revolutions are reaching the American Negro and arousing his nationalist impulses."

Black activists in the mid- and late 1960s saw in Cuba both a bastion of political support for their own domestic struggles as well as a theoretical paradigm for advancing their movements. Robert Williams, a former NAACP leader in North Carolina and an advocate of blacks' armed self-defense, was given asylum in Cuba. One year after the Black Power explosion in the US, SNCC activist Stokely Carmichael was invited by the Bertrand Russell Peace Foundation to attend the Organization of Latin-American Solidarity conference in Havana.

In his speech before the conference he declared, "We share with you a common struggle ... [and] a common enemy, white Western imperialist society. Our destiny cannot be separated from the destiny of the Spanish-speaking people in the United States and of the Americas." Within several years, delegations of the Black Panther Party were also touring the island.

Cuba continues to serve as a model of international solidarity to the Black Diaspora for several reasons. Of all socialist nations, it has provided the greatest level of assistance, given its limited domestic resources, to the struggles of nonwhite peoples. After the overthrow of the Haile Selassie regime in 1974, for instance, Ethiopia had barely 90 doctors; Cuba promptly supplied that nation with 200 additional physicians, as well as other technicians. By the early 1980s, Cuba had sent several hundred military advisers to Mozambique, as well as hundreds of agricultural, chemical, and planning technicians. As of 1982, over 1,200 Mozambican students were studying in Cuba.

Certainly the most significant example of solidarity was the case of Grenada. Cuba's contribution in medical personnel, teachers, and agricultural technicians totaled $3 million annually. Even for non-Marxist black leaders, Cuba's radical domestic reforms were worthy of emulation. In *Uhuru Na Ujamaa,* to cite only one instance, Julius K. Nyerere praised Cuba's "experiments in adult education" as providing techniques which "could usefully be adapted to meet our needs."

What is interesting, given the impact of Revolutionary Cuba upon the political thought of the black world, is the relative obscurity of political analysis concerning the evolving status of Cuba's black population, within an overall context of theoretical and political solidarity with the government and people of Cuba. Over the past 25 years, there have been a few isolated and discredited voices charging socialist Cuba with maintaining racism domestically. After running a radio station called "Radio Free Dixie" on the island, Williams moved to China and in 1967 attacked his former hosts: "Afro-Cubans are beginning to feel the pinch of subtle but fast-returning racism." Afro-Cuban Charles Moore charged in an essay in *Presence Africaine* in 1965 that "prejudice continued," and that "Cuban Negroes played no greater part in Cuban politics than they had before 1958—if anything, less." Other critics noted that the Central Committee of the Cuban Communist Party in the mid-1960s was composed of less than 10 percent Cubans of African descent, and observed that Walterio Carbonell, a black Communist who in 1953 had supported Fidel, had served time in a rehabilitation camp "on the ground that his folkloric investigations had racist overtones." Much of this body of criticism can be dismissed as reactionary propaganda, because sufficient evidence exists illustrating that most Afro-Cubans have long endorsed the Revolution. As early as 1962, North American sociologist Maurice Zeitlin found in his independent surveys that over 80 percent of the black and mulatto population was "wholly in favor of the Revolution," compared to 67 percent of white Cubans. It is equally certain, as Robert Chrisman asserted in 1977, that the Revolution "altered the material base of the Cuban society and changed the economy in such a way that there was no longer any need for the exploitation of blacks and women."

Cuba's commitment to destroy racism, and to eradicate the material foundations for its perpetuation, is unequaled in the socialist world. But the weight of the racist superstructure of the past, conscious and subconscious ideological assumptions, and cultural patterns and social relations transcends the particular social formation which gave it life. With rare exceptions—notably the works of Chrisman and anthropologist Johnnetta Cole—most black North American radicals have been reluctant to pursue the difficult question of race relations in a postcapitalist society, within a political context of solidarity. Standing "at the foot of the Sierra Maestra mountains" on the morning of July 26, 1960, Cruse raised a central question concerning the Revolution: "What did it all mean and how did it relate to the Negro in America?" Cruse also recognized the need to discuss "the obvious and unclarified position of the Cuban Negro. . . . Yet we were all treated with such overwhelming deference, consideration and privilege, it was difficult to be critical." Yet the failure to extend constructive and sympathetic criticism, within the context of the revolutionary process, compromises the very essence of solidarity.

Revolutionary Cuba is instructive for yet another reason. Cuba was the first nation with a significant black population to experience a socialist revolution in the Western Hemisphere. More precisely, before 1959, Cuba was ruled by the military regime of Fulgencio Batista in conjunction with US imperialism and the majority of the Cuban bourgeoisie. Institutional racism, women's oppression, the suppression of trade unions, and the lack of adequate educational, housing, and health facilities were "normal" Cuban symptoms. Even when certain "bourgeois democratic" forms were tolerated, the economic, cultural, and racial exploitation of the Cuban masses continued. The Cuban Revolution as a social process sought not only to oust Batista from power, but to create genuine democracy for the workers, peasantry, and oppressed Afro-Cubans.

As economist Paul A. Baran observed, "At the outset, the horizon of the Castro movement coincided on the whole with the horizon of the broad liberal wing of the Cuban bourgeoisie, with the view that a *political* turnover could no longer be postponed, with the insight that *some* economic reforms were indispensable if the people of Cuba were to emerge from their misery." But within months, the popular movement was forced to "transcend the political objectives of a bourgeois *coup d'état*, and to carry the revolution to its ultimate goal—a *social* transformation of the country."

After a quarter century of social transformation, Cuba has become a "revolutionary democracy." This process has been made more difficult, certainly, by the implacable opposition of the United States and the subversive, terrorist activities of right-wing Cuban exiles financed by the Central Intelligence Agency. The first task of any state in the transition from capitalism to socialism is survival: contesting the residual power and ideology of the bourgeoisie and petty bourgeoisie, defending itself against direct assaults—such as the 1961 Bay of Pigs invasion—and arming loyal sectors of the civilian population.

But "hegemony," as Antonio Gramsci reminds us, consists of force and ideological consent. A revolutionary state must meet the material needs of the working class and farming population: universal education, expanded public housing, rural development, accessible health care, and other essential services. Moreover, in the context of a racialized society, the state must make every effort to combat and to uproot racist ideology, and to urge the participation of blacks within every level of public decision-making.

Robert Chrisman, the publisher/editor of the *Black Scholar,* invited me to participate in a week-long tour of Cuba on April 22–29, 1984. Chrisman had visited Cuba previously on eight separate occasions, and was able to obtain a special invitation to a select group of African-American intellectuals. The members of our delegation included Mary Kenyatta, dean at Williams College; Paulette Pierce, sociologist at Queens College; political theorist and professor at Seton Hall University, William Sales; author Louise Meriwether; *Black Scholar* general manager Larry Loebig; Chrisman; and myself. My concerns were two-fold: to analyze the reality of race in Cuba, and to assess the social achievements and political structures of revolutionary democracy.

Cuba's Racial Heritage

The contemporary status of Afro-Cubans was largely predetermined historically by four overlapping factors: the legacy of slavery, development of a counter-hegemonic black Cuban culture, the reality of race within Cuba's Wars for Independence against Spain during the nineteenth century, and the more immediate condition of racial segregation and class exploitation during the regimes of Machado and Batista after World War I. Estimates of the total number of African slaves imported into the island between 1500 and 1850 begin at 700,000 and proceed upward.

The slave trace was not officially abandoned in the country until 1862, and slavery itself ended in 1886, roughly a half century after its demise in neighboring Jamaica. Haiti's successful slave revolution of 1790–1804 inspired Cuban sugar producers to take over the world sugar market and ironically enlarged and extended the life of slavery in this process. As Eric Williams noted, "Cuban sugar production increased more than forty times between 1775 and 1865." British imports from the island increased "sixfold between 1817 and 1832."

Yet inside the harsh crucible of enslavement, Africans developed a culture of resistance. As Phyl Garland has observed, the Yoruba of Nigeria adopted Shango, the "god of war and lightning, an erotic sensual god," to their new cultural context. From the Catholic Spanish oppressors, they acquired a new language–but the Afro-Cuban religion of Santeria, the dances and songs, and the cultural world-view were distinctly Afrocentric. In Cuba, Africans in "an alien culture had developed a duality of behavior that enabled them to survive."

By the late nineteenth century, Cuban race relations reflected therefore an uneven mixture of classical Hispanic standards of culture with the organic culture of the African slaves. Historian Franklin Knight observes that "in the context of Cuban plantation society, the term 'white' covered a wide spectrum of peninsular Spaniards, Cuban and Latin American-born creoles, East Indians, Chinese, and Mexican Indians." Free mulattos or coloreds comprised from 15 to 20 percent of the island's total population throughout the 1800s. Dark-skinned blacks were consigned to jobs as "maids, gardeners, and coachmen." But, unlike in the United States, color was only one index of social and economic status.

This racial/cultural diversity is manifested most strikingly in the Wars of Independence in 1868–78 and in 1895. The two outstanding Cuban revolutionaries of 1868 represented the two antipodes of national culture: Carlos Manuel De Cespedes, lawyer and Oriente slave owner, and the courageous political descendant of Toussaint L'Ouverture, Antonio Maceo. De Cespedes freed his slaves, and in his challenge to Spanish domination, the "grito de Yara," concluded that national independence could not be realized unless "all men [were] equally free, as the Creator intended all mankind to be." Maceo, called "the Bronze Titan," led the military forces of former slaveholders and former slaves and held the more powerful Spanish to a stalemate for a decade.

The process of genuine national liberation was cut short with the US intervention in 1898 and its subsequent six decades of economic and political domination. Yet the fact remains that the democratic revolutionary process, unlike that of North America, was profoundly committed to the realization of racial equality, and indeed in its actual military thrust was personified by a black general, Antonio Maceo.

Importing Jim Crow

The core of Cuba's twentieth-century racial dilemma was created by US imperialism. As Johnnetta Cole comments, nineteenth-century Cuban racism "never reached the intensity and blatantness of the US variety. However, the coming of the 'Yankees' meant not only economic exploitation . . . but also the transporting of US-style Jim Crow to Cuba." Within the civil society or superstructure, a rapid deterioration of relations occurred.

Surveying the island after World War II, Howard University Professor Rayford Logan noted that few blacks or mulattos were hired "in the better white collar positions." Few blacks found employment as streetcar or bus conductors because, it was alleged, "the white passengers resented the closer personal contact." Despite the fact that the 1940 Cuban Constitution prohibited racism, "the existence of the justly famous Negro Club Atenas in Havana is evidence that Negroes feel that they are not welcome in certain quarters, for the writer believes that Negroes do not as a rule voluntarily segregate themselves."

Logan, who was "white" in appearance, "went every day for a month to the Florida restaurant in Havana. The only colored persons who came there were three strolling musicians. The visitor to Cuba . . . cannot fail to observe that the clientele of the best establishments are largely white and the color becomes darker as one goes down in the scale. Moreover, there are a few establishments in Cuba where Negroes definitely are not welcome."

With Batista's fall, the young revolutionaries sought to fulfill the democratic racial legacy of De Cespedes, Maceo, and José Martí. Implicitly they understood the dialectical relationship between national liberation and the destruction of racial inequality. In early 1959, Castro gave a major address, "Proclamation Against Discrimination," which "exposed the discrimination that existed in Cuba in both work centers and places of recreation, and proclaimed the right of every Cuban to employment, schools, and recreational areas." The general material approach of the Revolution—to create free health care, education, low-cost public housing, and full employment—has obviously meant, as Cole asserts, that "black Cubans have experienced the greatest gains from the revolutionary process . . . since, in any society, moves toward equality will provide the most gains for those who have suffered the greatest deprivation."

The political decisiveness with which the Cuban state has uprooted racism in the production sectors, however, gives way to a cultural ambiguity within the civil society. This ambiguity can be expressed in two rather different cultural lines of argument. In the context of African-American history, these divergences are what separates Frederick Douglass from W.E.B. Du Bois. Both leaders fought every manifestation of racism and opposed all forms of Jim Crow.

But anti-racism for Douglass also dictated his opposition to the existence of separate black churches, and his well-known hostility to the militant nationalism of a Martin Delany and Henry Highland Garnet. Du Bois was, however, a cultural pluralist as well as a "radical democrat." At critical times he advocated separate, all-black economic and social institutions; in the early 1960s he warned that desegregation should not be achieved at the cost of the destruction of the unique African-American historical and cultural heritage.

Since 1959 one can observe, in a radically different historical context, positions which echo simultaneously both Douglass and Du Bois. The first tendency would be expressed in the following manner: the Revolution is committed to the abolition of racism, which is directly defined as the recognition of color and caste differences within the population. To be absolutely color-blind in human relations was therefore to be a "revolutionary"; to recognize the divergent patterns of cultural and social life embodied within pre-1959 racial categories was to perpetuate them and therefore to be a "racist."

During my recent visit to the island, most of the Cubans I talked with expressed, directly or indirectly, this "color-blind" version of anti-racism. At the Simon Bolivar High School, located about 35 miles southwest of Havana in the countryside, both teachers and administrators insisted that students were completely oblivious to color distinctions. "We have no racism here, no vices," the principal Raul Quintana Esta stated. "We are determined to construct a completely new society freed of racial oppression." Texts highlight the contributions of Afro-Cubans to the nation's revolutionary heritage.

In Santiago, Felix Arronyo, the Vice President of the city's Municipal Assembly of the People's Power, related that all statistics on the Afro-Cuban population are deliberately repressed. "According to our criteria, color has nothing to do with a person becoming a delegate and in having the highest level of responsibility. We never keep the data, because we never wish to discriminate." Arronyo, an Afro-Cuban, noted that the President of the Municipal Assembly also happened to be black. However, "we are not worried about the ethnic composition of our Assembly." In politics, as well as in economic and social life, a person is judged according to "merit" rather than the fact of one's racial heritage.

Cultural Pluralism

The "Du Boisite" position of cultural pluralism is also present—and indeed, was partially expressed within the Cuban Communist Party when the advisability of the programmatic demand for "an autonomous Negro state in Oriente" was discussed during the 1930s. Cuba's political and social links with the African continent were stressed in the post-revolutionary period by Che Guevara. In his speech before the United Nations General Assembly in December 1964, Che asserted, referring to both the brutal assassination of Prime Minister Patrice Lumumba and to the UN's continued role in reinforcing imperialism, "The scales have fallen from our eyes and they now open upon new horizons, and we can see what yesterday, in our conditions of colonial servitude, we could not observe—that 'Western civilization' disguises under its showy front a scene of hyenas and jackals." White mercenaries in the Congo were "bloodthirsty butchers who feed on helpless people! That is what imperialism does to men; that is what marks the 'white' imperialists." Subsequently, Che spent nearly one year inside the Congo training Africans to fight a guerrilla war.

Yet Cuba's connection with the "African diaspora" in a domestic cultural context was not made fully clear until the Angolan civil war a decade later.

When the Popular Movement for the Liberation of Angola (MPLA) requested Cuban support to defeat counter-revolutionaries supported by both the US and South Africa, the Cuban government correctly identified the struggle as simultaneously anti-racist and anti-imperialist.

Dr. Melba Hernandez, Cuba's ambassador to Vietnam, explained that Cubans "are obviously, by origin, Latin-African. We cannot be indifferent to the sacrifices made by the African peoples, the same Africans who came to our shores exploited as slaves." The Cuban "revolutionary process" had educated millions of Cubans to comprehend the essential unity of Angola's struggle for self-determination with their own. Two decades before, Hernandez noted, "a large pat of our population" would have been indifferent to the Angolan people, rejecting them as "*blacks* . . . in a pejorative way."

Castro's 1976 speech "We Stand with the People of Africa," delivered before a Havana rally of over 1 million, reiterated Hernandez's position: "African blood flows freely through our veins. Many of our ancestors came as slaves from Africa to this land. As slaves they struggled quite a great deal. They fought as members of the liberating army of Cuba. We're brothers and sisters of the people of Africa and we're ready to fight on their behalf." One former Black Panther Party member exiled in Cuba during these years has informed me that Castro's major speech had a "profoundly emotional" and "liberating" impact upon Cuban whites. "Suddenly white matrons proudly claimed African heritage," bragging to friends about their forgotten Afro-Cuban grandmother or great-grandfather. "To be African in appearance" was suddenly highly valued and esteemed.

But the essential contradiction of race remains. During a 1977 visit to Cuba, noted cultural worker Bernice Reagon visited a museum which displayed a history of Cuban paintings. Most of the pre-1959 art did not draw upon the multiracial Cuban experience. One notable exception was the painting "The Rape of the Mulattos," by Carlos Enriquez. "Although the painting was done as protest against the pre-revolutionary police," Reagon noted, "there was a gross misrepresentation in the portrayal of the rape victims." One woman was depicted as "sensuous, buxom, in low-cut Latin dress style. She appeared to be almost a willing sexual object."

Official Anti-Racism

Nevertheless, virtually everyone I talked with in Cuba agreed on one point: racism is officially not tolerated, and the entire population feels a direct and personal link with the struggle for African and Caribbean liberation. Most white Cubans, especially those who have become adults during the Revolution, seem oblivious to racial distinctions. However, cultural diversity is an integral element in black Caribbean political life, and recognition of cultural pluralism within a nation is not succumbing to racism. But it is clear that most Afro-Cubans do not share the black American political perspective on racial matters.

Health, Education, and Housing

The struggle for socialist democracy is not metaphysical. State power is meaningless unless the social structure is radically transformed to promote the general social welfare of the masses. As African theorist Amilcar Cabral observed: "Keep always in mind that the people are not fighting for ideas, for things in anyone's head. They are fighting for material benefits, to live better and in peace, to see their lives go forward, to guarantee the future of their children. National liberation [must] bring a real improvement in conditions of life. It is pointless to liberate a region if its populations then remain without essential goods."

Perhaps the most serious social problem before the Cuban Revolution was the dire state of public health. Under Batista, there was only one physician per 1,000 people, and only one dentist per 3,000 people. The wealthy classes could afford private medical treatment; the poor usually went without it. The majority of farmers and laborers never saw a doctor, and consequently fell victim to malaria, tuberculosis, and typhoid. Infant mortality rates in Cuba only 25 years ago were 62 per 1,000. The average life expectancy of a Cuban between 1945–1960 was 57 years. Conservatively, one-third of the total population suffered from malnutrition: one family out of 25 ate meat regularly, and only one family in 50 had eggs. With the triumph of the Revolution, about half of the nation's doctors, nurses, and health administrators fled the country, creating a major crisis in the medical field.

Today Cuba has one of the best public health care systems in the world. In the 1960s, the government channeled scarce resources into building a vast medical system, which would be absolutely free of charge for all citizens. With the assistance of friendly Latin-American and socialist states, hundreds of paramedics were quickly trained. Nurses were given greater responsibilities to assist the expansion and administration of the national medical system. By 1965, about 500 new doctors were being produced annually. Today over 2,000 doctors are trained each year, and within two years, 3,000 will be produced annually. Before the years 2000, Cuba will have 65,000 doctors nationwide, or one physician per 200 people. In contrast, black America today has roughly one black doctor per 2,000 blacks.

Any doubts I could have had about Cuba's health system were quickly allayed after a tour of the Hermanos Ameijeiras Hospital, a massive 25-story building located in central Havana. Completely air-conditioned, the hospital has 300 rooms which can accommodate up to four beds each, 25 operating rooms, two intensive care centers, a polyclinic which can handle

1,500 outpatient cases per day, and laboratories equipped with modern scientific equipment for research in nuclear medicine, biochemistry, microbiology, and pathology. The emergency ward has two operating rooms and a staff that can treat up to 800 patients daily. The hospital also has an auditorium that can seat 342 persons, a conference hall for another 100 persons, and 17 classrooms for 16 students each. The total range of health care facilities provided include specialized services in cardiovascular surgery, gastroenterology, nuclear medicine, radiology, neurology, and other fields.

Dr. Cenobio Gonzales led the tour of the hospital, and provided additional background on Cuba's medical system. Dr. Gonzales explained that 26 years before he had lived in New York City, working as a presser in a lower Manhattan dry cleaners. With a sense of humor, he added, "We are glad for you to visit this hospital as a journalist and not as a patient." Dr. Gonzales explained that Hermanos Ameijeiras was only one example of the massive hospital building program.

Since the early 1960s, 19 new metropolitan hospitals have been constructed. By 1990, a total of 35 hospitals each with 300 to 800 beds will be in service. These major hospitals are complemented by a network of 200 smaller municipal hospitals with 300 to 400 beds each, and with 18 to 22 medical specialists; and a series of provincial hospitals with 700 to 800 beds and more than 30 medical specialists each. "At this time, we're perfecting the system," Dr. Gonzales stated. "Our goals are to increase services in the primary levels in dermatology, orthopedics, ophthalmology, etc. The larger hospitals should focus solely on research, surgery, emergency care, and so forth."

Family Doctor Plan

The latest innovation is "the Doctor of the Family" plan, which began in some parts of Cuba in October 1983. As Dr. Gonzales explained, "One doctor is assigned to one hundred and twenty families" in a particular neighborhood or village. "He lives in the area, and emphasizes preventive medicine. He regularly visits the families when they are sick and well. Thus the physician serves a broader social function." All medical treatment, including dental work to the most expensive medical care, is absolutely free of charge. "This is not a hospital for the bourgeoisie," Dr. Gonzales declared. "What is important in the institution is not its structure, nor in the technical level of instruments. You can find the same materials in other countries. The difference is who receives our services, and how they are discharged."

Patients are encouraged not to eat in their rooms, but in dining room areas throughout the hospital. Patients are escorted to cultural activities and sports events, Dr. Gonzales notes, "so they can feel better from a psychological point of view." Cuba's Ministry of Culture "is developing a whole range of programs to place original paintings, sculpture, and other art of Cuban artists" into all hospitals. "A hospital can be a pleasant and cozy place."

The results of Cuba's medical achievement are found in United Nations' statistics. Not a single case of polio has been reported in Cuba since 1961. Malaria claimed its last victim in Cuba in 1967. The infant mortality rate declined by 1983 to 16.8 per 1,000—compared to 14.2 per 1,000 for white Americans and 24.2 per 1,000 for blacks in the US. The Cuban man has an average life expectancy of 73 years—about ten yeas longer than African-American males. As Dr. Gonzales noted, "This is an achievement of a socialist society. It is a better nourished society; therefore people are healthier, and lead longer lives."

US researchers confirm this analysis, noting that one fourth of the total island's population are served free meals in schools, factories, and in agricultural collectives daily. Cuba's successes at the Olympic games and in international athletic competition are the direct result of a better national diet, regular exercise, and a massive emphasis placed on preventive health care.

Housing

Similar advancements have been achieved by the Cuban people in the area of housing. Before the Revolution, housing conditions for many Cubans were little better than sharecroppers' shacks in the Mississippi Delta. In rural areas, indoor toilets were considered a luxury item. Even as late as the mid-1960s, less than half of all Cuban homes had electricity.

The Cuban government developed a unique plan to provide new shelter for millions of citizens in the subsequent years, based on the simple idea that workers themselves could build their own homes with materials provided by the state. Alamar, a series of apartment complexes located about eight miles east of downtown Havana, was initiated in 1971 to provide new housing for Cuban families. Today, Alamar has 70,000 residents, with a projected capacity of 150,000 inhabitants. When touring the new city, I was most impressed with the quality of construction, and the egalitarian method of labor used to build the apartments.

Workers are organized into "micro-brigades" averaging 33 people each. They are assisted by skilled construction workers, and are given on-the-spot training in building techniques. With prefabricated materials, the micro-brigades build their own apartment units. The smallest apartment buildings have 20 family dwellings; the largest buildings are 18 stories high. The city's layout was designed by urban planners and architects, and is a testament to human creativity.

Alamar complex is a complete "city" in every respect, with 14 day care centers, eight primary schools, three junior high schools, one high school, one college, five supermarkets, three department or commercial stores, and two medical clinics. Buses regularly transport residents to and from central Havana. However, most adults who live in Alamar also work there. The industrial and business district of the complex has several textile factories, two candy factories, one large firm which cooks and processes meals for schools and factories, and one large commercial laundry. My guide at Alamar, Elena Perez, was a former architecture student who worked in the complex. She noted that Alamar provided theaters and an outdoor amphitheater for residents, and that swimming pools, soccer fields, baseball diamonds, and basketball courts were within walking distance of every apartment building.

Rents are only 6 percent of a worker's monthly income. In some projects, such as the José Martí development in Santiago, no rent is charged at all. The basic assumption is that housing, like health care, is a fundamental human right. Each apartment has a full bath, kitchen, dining room, two to three bedrooms, and at least one outdoor terrace. Unmarried couples are permitted to live together in single apartments, and even if the residents do not pay the rent, there are no forced evictions.

Education

Prior to the Revolution, Cuban education scarcely existed. Over one quarter of the population was illiterate. Nationally, about 44 percent of the children aged 6–14 did not attend school; in the predominantly black Oriente Province, 60 percent of all children had no schools. Only 7 percent of the rural teenagers in the 1950s attended high schools. As political scientist Hugh Thomas observed, most schools "consisted of a single room, where the same teacher had to teach all classes."

Many schools had no books and supplies; teachers were often inept or semiliterate themselves. Teaching "inspectors were also both incompetent and corrupt," and "promotion depended on political patronage or seniority. A social survey conducted in 1956 among peasant families suggested that in the whole country about 45 percent had never been to school and, of those who had been, nearly 90 percent had not got beyond the third grade." Thomas concludes that the educational situation "was bad enough to cause the parents of such children, themselves unschooled, to back any revolutionary cause which promised change."

The Castro government immediately emphasized an expansion of educational facilities upon assuming power. Under José Martí's slogan "To be literate is to be free," the government was determined to eradicate illiteracy.

Within 18 months, nearly all in the country acquired the ability to read and write. By 1961 over 80 percent of all children were attending schools; university enrollments soared, and thousands were trained in professional schools.

Social scientists Donald W. Bray and Timothy F. Harding note that the minimum educational goal for everyone was raised to the thirteenth grade in 1967, "one year of technical training beyond completion of secondary school." New schools in metallurgy, industrial engineering, fishing, and agriculture were initiated. "Special tests and programs were developed on a massive scale to place children or adults who had dropped out of school, and students who were encouraged to accelerate so as to join their age-groups as soon as possible. Scholarships at the secondary and university level including full support and an allowance were made available so that parents actually experienced financial relief by having their children study." By the early 1970s, "27.6 percent of the people in Cuba were studying in some form of organized instruction, compared with an average of 16.8 percent for Latin America as a whole."

Political Power and Social Contradictions

A revolutionary democracy is a "dictatorship of the proletariat," whose ultimate objective is the realization of equality and empowerment across all sectors of society. Equality, defined as the abolition of classes, can only be achieved when the workers have (1) direct and uninhibited access to all decision-making institutions; (2) popular, mass-participation apparatuses which safeguard their state power; and (3) control over the means of production. In the years after the Revolution, confronting the omnipresent specter of North American invasion and internal subversion by agents of the former bourgeoisie, the Cubans developed mass-based, popular political organizations which reach literally into every city block.

The National Association of Small Farmers organizes in rural districts; the Union of Communist Youth and the Young Pioneers mobilize students. But the principal mass organization is the CDR—the Committees for the Defense of the Revolution—which has 6 million members. The CDRs are organized on the national, provincial, municipal, neighborhood, and block levels. Each city block has a CDR, whose members are involved in general public health measures, sanitation, neighborhood patrol, and other volunteer activities. CDR leaders encourage local children to attend schools, resolve family or neighborhood quarrels, and lead political discussions and study groups.

One CDR I visited in Havana was typical of thousands of such organizations. On this block there were 14 local leaders, seven men and seven women. The youngest was a man about 20 years old, and the oldest was about 70. The principal leader was a young woman of 22. For one middle-aged man, the CDR represented a break from the economic dependency and political backwardness of the past. "Under Batista," he related, "we were educated in the consumer mentality. When we needed a spare part, we went to Woolworth." The economic blockade of the US "forced us to develop new industries, for women to go into labor, and for us to create a strong sense of solidarity at the local level."

One highly articulate middle-aged woman noted that the CDR tried to nurture an attitude of responsibility among the youth. "A man thinks according to the way he lives. In our society," she stated, "our children live in an environment of constant ideological struggle. When a whole people are involved in socially important tasks, as in our country, the children will learn through example."

The most influential political organization of Cuban society, obviously, is the Communist Party. But even in this regard, compared to most Third World or Marxist countries, the presence of the Communist Party, or its key leader, Fidel Castro, is not apparent on every street corner. Most of the political posters I saw during my tour were not of Fidel or the Communist leadership, but depicted historical figures from Cuba's long revolutionary past, such as José Martí, Antonio Maceo, and Che Guevara.

The basic governmental structure in Cuba, called "People's Power," departs from most Communist states as well. All elections begin at the municipal and neighborhood levels. In every electoral district, there are between 150 and 3,000 voters. Each district of "People's Power" is subdivided into "areas" of several hundred persons, where public meetings are held to nominate municipal delegates from the neighborhoods. Persons nominated to run from various "areas" run against each other for the district's seat. After 30 days, there is a direct and secret ballot; voters must be 16 years or older. The candidate winning a majority is elected, but if no one wins 50 percent, the top two candidates face each other in a run-off election in one week.

Once the municipal delegates are elected, the municipal assemblies in turn elect representatives to the provincial assembly. Provincial assemblies elect national delegates who set national legislation in Havana. What is interesting about the Cuban electoral system is that voters are given a selection of from two to eight candidates, and membership in the Communist Party is not required to run for office.

Throughout the country, about 30 percent of the municipal delegates who won local office were not Communists. In the April elections this year, 98.6 percent of all eligible voters cast ballots—all the more impressive in a country where there is no legal requirement to vote. Three of this year's delegates in Havana were only 16 years old, and the youngest was a teenage girl who was not a member of the Communist Party.

Socialist Economy

The basic economic system of Cuba is, of course, socialism, although elements of capitalism are permitted to exist and even to thrive. In rural areas 25 years ago, almost all of the best farmland was owned by a small elite of Cuban families and American businesses. The Revolution seized these estates, and over the years created agricultural collectives for the landless peasantry. Only about 15 percent of all Cuban agricultural output today is in private hands.

At a meeting with a top administrator of Cuba's Central Planning Board, the economic central nervous system which employs 900 people and coordinates national production, we learned that Cuba's key focus for 1986–1990 will be in industry. Two new nickel plants are being developed, both with a capacity to produce 30,000 tons of nickel annually. Other growth areas include the fishing industry, citrus products, electricity, and, in the future, nuclear power.

Cuba has experienced many of the problems which plague state-managed economies, but certain priorities have been achieved. The gross wage differentials between the peasants and the powerful have long been eliminated. The minimum monthly salary for everyone in Cuba is 85 pesos; the maximum salary, 450 pesos; and the average salary, 170 pesos. Most medical doctors, for instance, would earn about 370 pesos per month, and skilled laborers could receive probably half that amount. But state control ensures that certain consumer items, when available, are accessible to all. A quart of milk in Cuba costs only 20 cents; a pair of leather shoes, 15 to 20 pesos; and average lunch at a restaurant, 70 cents.

All workers, from janitors to Castro himself, receive 30 days' paid vacation per year. Cuba is still heavily dependent upon sugarcane as its principal export crop, and despite 25 years of planning, citizens candidly complain about shortages in consumer goods. But when compared to the previous political and economic order, it is clear that the great majority of Cuban laborers, farmers, and the poor have materially benefited from the Revolution, despite its problems.

The political, social, and economic realities of revolutionary Cuba continue to change. The Revolution has made its share of mistakes, particularly in the area of social and cultural relations. In the 1960s, educators frequently condemned "tight trousers and miniskirts" among the youth. Fidel added his own authority to the debate in a lecture commemorating the eighth anniversary of the founding of the CDR, on September 28,

1968. Long hair, fancy clothes, and "extravagant" behavior, Castro warned, lead to moral decay and political chaos.

For several years, overly eager police officers carrying pairs of scissors or clippers would stop long-haired Havana youth at random, and promptly administer haircuts. When I toured the city, however, these rigid cultural standards had been reversed. Walking through the central city at night, I saw literally hundreds of young adults in designer jeans, tank tops, and transparent blouses. Throughout the streets of Santiago and Havana music is continuos: sometimes a mixture of African rhythms and a Latin beat, which is the heart of Cuban music, but frequently the sounds of Aretha Franklin, Marvin Gaye, and Stevie Wonder.

Occasionally our delegation came across a sight I expected to find only in black America: young Afro-Cuban males, donning knit caps, bopping along with huge portable radios. The status of homosexuals, however, remains unclear. The 1971 Educational Congress of Cuba passed a resolution denouncing homosexuality and declared that gays and lesbians were not suitable to become teachers. Government officials declared at the time that "homosexuals per se cannot be revolutionary." Gay professors were ordered out of the classroom and sent to work in the sugarcane fields. At Alamar complex, I was told that homosexual couples would not be permitted to live together in public housing.

Social contradictions of this type—a reluctance to accept cultural and human diversity, or an underestimation of the progressive tendencies of certain sectors of the population—can compromise the revolutionary process. One prime example, which had direct economic consequences, was in the development of rural cooperatives. Fidel admitted before the Sixth Congress of the National Association of Small Farmers, in May 1982, that the cooperative movement was retarded because he "overestimated [the farmers'] individualism, and underestimated their level of [political] awareness." But Castro also noted, "The most sacred duty of every revolutionary is to admit his mistakes. I always try to think back on events and analyze every one of the acts with which I've been involved."

This commitment to rigorous self-criticism, the ability to confront and to resolve contradictions among the people without authoritarian measures, is the essence of democracy within the process of public decision-making. On racial, social, and economic matters, despite continuing difficulties and errors, Cuban revolutionary democracy is continuing to develop toward the goal of equality and a classless society. As such, Cuba serves as a model and an inspiration for all who are engaged in a struggle to uproot racism and capitalism.

18

Free South Africa Movement: Black America's Protest Connections with South Africa

1985

In late 1984, two separate events occurred on opposite sides of the globe which culminated in the most dramatic and unexpected social movement in recent US history. Last September, approximately 50,000 mine workers went on strike inside South Africa. Mobilizing millions of nonwhites, the United Democratic Front, a multiracial coalition of more than 600 groups, initiated a series of protest actions. The targets of the demonstrations were both the lack economic rights for the black majority and the newly ratified constitution, which prohibits democratic rights to Africans. Tensions peaked on 5–6 November, when 1 million workers staged a general strike. The apartheid regime responded in the only language it comprehends. Almost 200 people were murdered, several thousand were detained without charges, and roughly 6,000 laborers were dismissed from their jobs.

On 6 November in the US, Ronald Reagan was reelected to a second term in office by a historic "mandate." As in the struggles inside South Africa, the dimension of race was crucial in the national political culture. Approximately 66 percent of all white voters endorsed Reagan, compared to barely 10 percent of the black electorate. Reagan received key support from white Southerners (72 percent), "born-again" white Christians (80 percent), and whites with annual incomes above $50,000 (68 percent). One important factor contributing to blacks' hostility towards the Reagan Administration was its record of close cooperation with apartheid. During his

1984 presidential campaign, civil rights leader Jesse Jackson repeatedly attacked the President's policy of "constructive engagement" with Pretoria—the decisions to back IMF loans to South Africa, the US training of the South African Coast Guard, the sending of 2,500 electric shock batons to apartheid's police force, and the establishment of offices in Johannesburg designed to stimulated US investment in the country. Jackson's emphasis on South Africa forced the Democratic Party's 1984 platform to include a call for the immediate release of African National Congress leader Nelson Mandela, and the freeing of "all other political prisoners in South Africa." This was the first time that any major US party has denounced apartheid unconditionally. In early August 1984, black Congressman George Crockett obtained a nonbinding congressional resolution urging the President "to use his good offices" to secure Mandela's release. Given Reagan's fresh electoral victory, it seemed probable that the administration would do absolutely nothing to pressure Pretoria over the next four years. Similarly on domestic issues, the administration was likely to escalate its attacks on civil rights legislation, public housing, and social services essential to the black community. Activists felt that some form of aggressive protest was necessary to restore the momentum from the Jackson campaign, as well to provide active solidarity to the militants inside South Africa.

The prime architect of the Free South Africa Movement (FSAM) was Randall Robinson, executive director of Transafrica, a Washington, DC–based lobbying agency. Robinson and two other supporters of last year's Jackson campaign, US Civil Rights Commissioner Mary Frances Berry and black Congressman Walter Fauntroy, decided to hold a nonviolent protest at the South African Embassy on 21 November. The choice of "nonviolent" tactics was inevitable: Fauntroy had been a close associate of Dr. Martin Luther King, Jr. and was the coordinator of the 1983 March on Washington. The three leaders obtained an interview with the South African ambassador, and upon their arrival, announced their intention not to leave the building. Embassy officials panicked and called police, and the black leaders were "pleasantly surprised" when they were arrested for trespassing.

Within several days, other members of the Congressional Black Caucus held nonviolent demonstrations in front of the South African Embassy and were arrested. Rosa Parks, the initiator of the famous 1955 Montgomery, Alabama, bus boycott movement, and the Reverend Joseph Lowery, leader of the Southern Christian Leadership Conference, soon followed. In weeks, the FSAM began to acquire national dimensions. Virtually all of the leaders of Jackson's "Rainbow Coalition," plus many other liberals who had supported either Walter Mondale or Gary Hart for the Democratic nomination, volunteered to be among those arrested. In New York City, among the first leaders arrested for blocking the door of the South African consulate were judge William Booth; the Reverend Herbert Daughtery, chairman of the National Black United Front; Roman Catholic Bishop Emerson J. Moore; and New York City Clerk David Dinkins. Feminists Gloria Steinem, Bella Abzug, and leaders of the National Organization of Women were arrested. Even groups which had vigorously opposed Jackson's candidacy found it difficult to disagree with the new movement. Initially a few Orthodox and Conservative Jewish groups refused to join the protests, primarily because of Israel's extensive economic and political links with the apartheid regime. But within two weeks, virtually all of the major Jewish organizations, including leaders of the American Jewish Congress and the Union of American Hebrew Congregations, had taken part in the demonstrations. Even "celebrities" got involved: among those arrested included two children of the late Senator Robert F. Kennedy, tennis star Arthur Ashe, actor Harry Belafonte, and recording artist Stevie Wonder.

Most of the media coverage focused on the Washington, DC, and New York City demonstrations, but thousands of blacks and progressive whites initiated actions in other cities as well. On 6 December, Fauntroy and Lowery led several hundred demonstrators in a "pray-in" protest at the home of the honorary South African consul in Mobile, Alabama. The next day, in Berkeley, California, 1,000 students staged an anti-apartheid rally, blockading the central administration building for three hours, resulting in 38 arrests. Simultaneously, in Cleveland, Ohio, over 200 trade unionists, religious leaders, and civil rights activists held a public demonstration. On 9 December, 400 demonstrators in Seattle, Washington, picketed the home of the honorary consul, leading to 23 arrests. Since virtually all of the protests involved civil disobedience, and occurred without physical confrontations with police, most of the religious community quickly lined up behind the FSAM at both local and national levels. Religious supporters included the United Church of Christ Board of World Ministries, the National Association of Muslim Mission, and the National Conference of Catholic Bishops. Conservative evangelicals were left in the cold. The Reverend Jerry Falwell fumed that "if we aren't [in South Africa], the Soviets will take over." But few leading clergy were listening.

As the protests increased the Reagan Administration first tried to minimize their significance, announcing that they would have absolutely "no impact" on Reagan's constructive engagement approach toward South Africa. "The real losers in this are the black community," blurted one White House official to the press. But sensing a sudden shift in public opinion, most members of Congress and local elected officials sided with the FSAM. Senator Gary Hart refused to be arrested, but did read strong statement deploring apartheid before protesters at the South African Embassy. Senator Lowell Weicker, a leading Republican member of Congress, was arrested in January. Thirty-five conservative Congressional Republicans, Reagan's firmest supporters, issued a public statement criticizing the "failure" of constructive engagement. At local levels, FSAM supporters in 44 state legislatures introduced legislation demanding divestment of public funds from banks with ties to South Africa. The National Conference of Black Mayors, which includes over 300 cities, voiced support for public divestment. In a widely publicized visit to South Africa, Senator Edward Kennedy expressed sharp opposition to the Botha government's repression of trade unionists and leaders of the United Democratic Front. Although criticized in the US press for attempting to gain political leverage for his anticipated presidential campaign in 1988, Kennedy nevertheless was able to focus international attention on human rights violations in South Africa. Under such pressure, President Reagan agreed to meet with Bishop Desmond Tutu, General Secretary of the South African Council of Churches and 1984 Nobel Prize laureate. Meanwhile, the FSAM organizers, led by Robinson, had organized a national board and had formulated several specific demands for the cessation of demonstration: freedom for all trade union leaders detained in recent protests inside South Africa; the end of Reagan's constructive engagement policies; and the prompt convening of a constitutional convention in South Africa to discuss the transferal to majority rule.

By mid-March, over 2,000 arrests had taken place, with the total number of protesters exceeding 500,000 nationwide. The media have tended to diminish coverage of the demonstrations, however, and have focused attention on the issue of divestment. US investment inside South Africa, $15 billion in 1984, totals 20 percent of all foreign direct investment. US corporations control 70 percent of the South African computer market, and an IBM computer helps run the stock exchange in Johannesburg. As of 1983, Mobil Oil had $426 million invested in South Africa, and a workforce of 3,577; General Motors, $243 million and 5,038 employees. American banks, led by Chase Manhattan, Bankers Trust, Chemical, and Manufacturers Hanover, had outstanding loans in South Africa. The Reverend Leon Sullivan of Philadelphia, for example, has authored the "Sullivan Principles," which advocate continued US corporate expansion in South Africa with provisions for desegregated workplace facilities, mandated equal pay for jobs, and the training of nonwhites in administrative and supervisory positions. In early February, Chief Gatsha Buthelezi, leader of South Africa's 6 million Zulus, met with President Reagan and strongly supported the administration's opposition to economic sanctions. Buthelezi declared that divestment was an example of "throwing away the baby with the bath water. There is nothing wrong with constructive engagement if it is given flesh."

The difficulties of the accommodationist postures of both Sullivan and Buthelezi are relatively simple to illustrate. First, as Free South Africa

Movement leaders have noted, only 66,000 members of South Africa's 6 million labor force are employed by US firms which have signed the "Sullivan Principles." But even according to Sullivan's own annual reports, progress along such lines is at best marginal. In the 1983 report, it was noted that white employees filled 94 percent of all new managerial posts, and that nonwhite workers "lost ground steadily in clerical-administrative programs over the last three years." About three fourths of all unskilled workers in firms signing the Sullivan Principles were Africans, while only 0.3 percent were white. Two percent of all managers were black; 97 percent were white. Economic sanctions would not appreciably increase black unemployment, but would be a powerful incentive to Pretoria to engage in serious negotiations with Mandela and the African National Congress.

A second factor relates to the negative impact of US corporate investment inside South Africa upon the American working class. The chief economic characteristic of apartheid is that rigid racial stratification of the labor force lowers the wage rate. Using May 1983 figures, the average monthly wages in all manufacturing firms was $1,290 for whites, $460 for Indians, $365 for Coloureds, and $320 for Africans. According to the Survey of Current Business, US companies averaged 18.7 percent annual rates of return on capital investment between 1979 and 1982.

How does this investment affect American workers? Researchers for the Washington Office on Africa and the Civil Rights Department of the United Steelworkers of America recently prepared a brief study on this issue. For several years, the US steel industry has experienced a state of rapid collapse. Between 1974 and 1982 domestic steel production declined by 50 percent. In 1983, the seven largest steel producers reported losses of $2.7 billion that year alone. Major industrial towns dependent upon steel productivity to generate jobs have had staggeringly high rates of joblessness. Simultaneously, the US steel industry has siphoned domestic profits and reinvested them in Third World nations where authoritarian regimes guarantee a low wage, nonunionized labor force. Imports from foreign nations producing steel now exceed one fifth of the domestic market. And since 1975, US imports of apartheid's steel have increased 5,000 percent.

South African steel is largely produced by a state-owned firm, the Iron and Steel Corporation (ISCOR). All of the major US companies which have experienced difficulties producing steel at home—ARMCO, Allegheny Ludlum, US Steel, Phelps Dodge, and others—have invested millions into apartheid's industries. Recently, Chicago's Southworks steel plant, owned by US Steel, laid off several thousand workers on the rationale that US workers weren't sufficiently productive and that the plant wasn't making profits. Then local steelworkers learned that the steel beams used to build a new state office building in Chicago had been imported from South Africa—despite the fact that Southworks produces the identical steel beams. Even more outrageous was the fact that Continental Illinois Bank had loaned money to ISCOR, which had produced these beams. In short, Chicago laborers were giving their hard-earned wages to a local bank, which in turn financed a competitor which was stealing their jobs!

There are obviously dozens of similar examples. The Phelps Dodge copper mining corporation has an abysmal record on domestic labor relations, and has recently called for wage cuts from US workers. Yet in its mine in South Africa, blacks labor for less than 40 cents an hour, at an average of 60 hours per week. Such investments buoy the apartheid political economy, oppress African laborers, and increase domestic unemployment.

For these economic reasons, the AFL-CIO has broken with tradition by vigorously supporting the FSAM. Workers in San Francisco made perhaps the most militant contribution to the FSAM. On 26 November, longshoremen in that city refused to unload cargo which had originated in South Africa. After nearly a two-week stalemate, a court injunction forced San Francisco longshoremen to unload the cargo. Longshoreman Leo Robinson explained to the press that workers comprehended the connections between trade union struggles in South Africa and in the US. "The shipping interests" force us "to unload cargo such as steel and auto glass, made by slave labor at non-union wages. It has meant that we unload steel from South Africa, which means that steel workers here lose their jobs." Robinson added, "Our conscience makes us rise above such laws. It's a matter of conscience, with us and of thinking about our brothers and sisters in apartheid-run South Africa." By March, other unions which had joined the picket lines included the American Federation of Teachers, Laborers Union, Painters Union, American Federation of Government Employees, the United Auto Workers, Seafarers International Union, the American Federation of Musicians, and the Brotherhood of Railroad and Airline Clerks.

One must not minimize the fragility of such a united front, which has attempted to link international and domestic agendas. Moderate elements within the FSAM have become increasingly uncomfortable with the spontaneous, mass dimensions of the mobilization. Some problems can be traced to Robinson's selections on the FSAM Steering Committee. Some Committee members chosen—notably NAACP leader Benjamin Hooks—have little knowledge of the anti-apartheid movement or the issues at stake. Others who were left of the Committee, such as black militant Jean Sindab of the Washington Office on Africa, might have strengthened the activists tendencies of the protests. Some Marxists and black nationalists question the utility of peaceful, almost passive protests, noting that lists of each day's demonstrators are regularly provided to the Washington, DC, police. Arrests are made with the agreement that the acts of civil disobedience are purely symbolic, and that all criminal charges are to be dropped by authorities. A few religious and political leaders have quietly but unsuccessfully opposed the role of leftists within the demonstrations. The US Communist

Party has been an active participant inside FSAM actions, and several of its top leaders have also been arrested.

Probably the major weakness of such a social movement is found in historical and theoretical orientation. Although many black Americans in earlier generations retained a strong sense of cultural and social identity with Africa, during most of the twentieth century such expressions of solidarity were muted. The principal political contradiction confronting African-Americans was produced by the rise of racial segregation. Blacks were denied the right to vote, were refused employment or service in public establishments, and were forcibly removed from white neighborhoods. Over 5,000 black Americans were lynched between 1882 and 1927, and many publicly burned. The new racial codes segregated all sports facilities, restaurants, buses, and trains. Birmingham, Alabama, even outlawed blacks and whites from playing checkers or dominoes together in 1930. Facing the reaction against racial equality, most black Americans leaders now advocated a political philosophy of civil rights and integration. Blacks were "fully American," and as such, should be extended basic civil liberties and rights shared by whites. Any connection with Africa was deliberately ignored or forgotten. Gradually, by the 1950s, most black Americans knew little about Africa's history or its people.

Yet the links between Africa and African-Americans did not disappear entirely during these years. W.E.B. Du Bois, noted civil rights leaders, sponsored an important series of political conferences which brought together West Indians, black Americans, and Africans between 1900 and 1945. In increasing numbers, African intellectuals came to the US and took part in desegregation campaigns. Nhamdi Azikiwe of Nigeria and Kwame Nkrumah of Ghana both attended all-black Lincoln University in Pennsylvania. Their respective rise to power in the 1950s was covered extensively in black American newspapers; the achievement of African independence captured the imaginations of US blacks. Congressman Adam Clayton Powell of Harlem attended the initial conference of Third World and non-aligned nations in Bandung, Indonesia, in 1955. After independence, connections across the Atlantic deepened in both symbolic and concrete ways. In both downtown Dar es Salaam and Nairobi, major streets were named in honor of Du Bois, the "father of Pan-Africanism." In South Africa, young black leaders such as the late Steve Biko developed their "Black Consciousness" movement against apartheid by drawing upon the rhetoric and tactics of the "Black Power" movement of the 1960s. Black American students and tourists in increasing numbers began to make pilgrimages to their "homeland"; US black cultural fashions and hairstyles began to consciously imitate African patterns.

Ironically, it was only with the achievement of desegregation and the granting of democratic political rights in the 1960s that black Americans could fully revive their political and cultural relations with Africa. Black mayors and elected officials began to use their offices to develop closer economic and civic ties with their African counter-parts. Yet this renewed interest in Africa obscured the fundamental differences between national liberation struggles and multiracial reforms within a representative democracy. There was, and still exists, a tendency to view the events in South Africa through the prism of the civil rights and southern desegregation experience; thus many protesters today carry signs stating that "the Ku Klux Klan is in power" in South Africa.

Tactics developed to fit a particular conjuncture of political and social forces in the early 1960s are therefore revived in an uncritical fashion, without efforts to encourage political education among the masses of protesters on the political economy of apartheid. Pragmatically, the campaign has succeeded in mobilizing an eclectic array of constituencies around an important public policy issue, but it is exceedingly problematic whether this unity, lacking deep roots, can be maintained beyond the next 12 months.

There are, fortunately, some concrete signs that FSAM has gained results. Manufacturers Hanover Bank recently announced its refusal to grant any loans to the South African government or to steel its Krugerrand gold coins unless it initiates steps to "generate improved circumstances for the whole population" of South Africa. A total of 40 American universities have divested over $175 million stocks linked to South Africa. On 4 April hundreds of thousands of US students plan to stage simultaneous protests against apartheid. And on 20 April, thousands of Americans will protest in Washington, DC, calling for the destruction of the South African regime, as well as opposition to US intervention in Central American. President Reagan may have received a sweeping electoral victory last year, yet it is clear that the progressive spectrum of American politics has taken away his "mandate." The issue of apartheid has reinforced democratic social protest in both domestic and international arenas—and promises to remain a major concern of US political life.

The Future of the Cold War

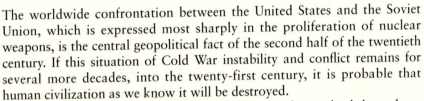

The worldwide confrontation between the United States and the Soviet Union, which is expressed most sharply in the proliferation of nuclear weapons, is the central geopolitical fact of the second half of the twentieth century. If this situation of Cold War instability and conflict remains for several more decades, into the twenty-first century, it is probable that human civilization as we know it will be destroyed.

Yet nuclear war is avoidable. The Cold War can be resolved through series of peaceful negotiations between the superpowers. But this can only occur if the advocates of peace are able to challenge the basic political assumptions and special interests which perpetuate the policies of confrontation and nuclear escalation.

The US people are bombarded daily by the media and most elected officials with propaganda which rationalizes the Cold War, and the dire necessity to spend billions of dollars on conventional and nuclear weapons. Frequently, the electorate supports those candidates who are most bellicose on the subject of Soviet expansionism. President Reagan, after all, received 66 percent of the white electorate's support in 1984; he also won 68 percent of the votes of those who have incomes above $50,000 annually, and 80 percent of the votes of all "born-again" Christians. But the far right, despite its recent electoral triumphs, has failed to create a political consensus for nuclear war against the Soviet Union. According to the research of Daniel Yankelovich and John Doble, recent public opinion polls continue to show a strong desire for peace. "By an overwhelming 96 to 3 percent, Americans assert that 'picking a fight with the Soviet Union is too dangerous in a nuclear world.' . . . By 89 percent to 9 percent," Yankelovich and Doble note, "Americans subscribe to the view that 'there can be no winner in an all-out nuclear war; both the United States and the Soviet Union would be completely destroyed.'"

It is interesting to note that the segment of the public which is most critical of the Cold War and the arms race is the black community. In opinion polls, blacks consistently favor a nuclear freeze by more than a 9 to 1 margin. Black US Representatives in Congress have repeatedly proposed the elimination of 20 to 30 percent of the Pentagon's total budget; and about 90 percent of all blacks voted against Reagan in 1984. The challenge for progressive politics in the United States, and the hope for world peace, is to expand the political perspective of black Americans to embrace a majority of the electorate.

Why is the political culture of white America so inclined to accept the rhetoric and policies of the Cold War, and why are black Americans less likely to do so? Part of the reason resides in the fear and hatred of Communism, which are embedded deeply in the popular discourse. Even among some black progressives and many liberal reformers, a kind of crude caricature of Communism is regularly projected. One example is provided by Martin Luther King, Jr., who explained his firm opposition to Communism in his 1963 book, *Strength to Love*. "Communism and Christianity are fundamentally incompatible," King observed. "A true Christian cannot be a true Communist, for the two philosophies are antithetical and all the dialects of the logicians cannot reconcile them." For King, life under Communism "stripped" human beings of "both conscience and reason. . . . Man has no inalienable rights. Art, religion, education, music, and science come under the gripping yoke of governmental control. Man must be a dutiful servant to the omnipotent state."

The atrocities committed in the name of revolutionary Marxism, from the gulags of Stalin to the irrational mass executions of the Pol Pot regime in Kampuchea, have provided some of the ideological basis for militant anti-Communism in the United States. But black Americans tend to perceive that such criticism of authoritarian regimes is distinctly one-sided. Chile, South Korea, Haiti, El Salvador, the Philippines, and other pro-US dictatorships which systematically oppress millions of people are not condemned as harshly as the Polish military's suppression of the Solidarity movement. Probably no nation in the entire world is more militantly anti-Communist than the apartheid regime in South Africa. But black Americans, and African people generally, recognize that South Africa is also a quasi-fascist state in which thousands of men and women are held in indefinite detention without charges or fair trial; where 3 million African children below the age of 15 currently suffer from malnutrition; and where the prison population is the highest per capita in the entire world. The sterile polemics of anti-Communism frequently become the justification for brutalities and an abrogation of human rights that exceed anything witnessed under most "Marxist states."

The ordeals of slavery, sharecropping, and legal Jim Crow provided black America with a special insight into the contradictions and inconsistencies of US democracy. Only through massive nonviolent demonstrations, boycotts, legal suits, and the sacrificing of hundreds of lives were we permitted a modest measure of political and economic democracy, whether inside of this country or anywhere else in the world. The Westminster model of parliamentary government and the US system represent only two flawed possibilities. The Cuban system of "people's power" includes municipal and neighborhood elections, based on a secret and direct ballot, with between two and eight Communist and non-Communist candidates for each seat. The mass constituency assemblies, women's and working people's formations created by the Grenada revolution, provide another type of noncapitalist democratic process. Political dialogue between Marxists and non-Marxists can be productive for both sides. Problems in regulating the economy, preserving natural resources, and developing new methods of production often transcend narrow ideological boundaries. Marxist states will increasingly experiment with new forms of economic pluralism—China provides only one recent example. Western capitalist democracies certainly have not evolved to their final form.

A more dangerous factor in the pervasiveness of Cold War political culture in the West is what I would term anti-Sovietism. In 1978, I was a Rockefeller Foundation fellow at Aspen Institute. General Edward Rowney, later to become President Reagan's chief arms negotiator, was a participant in my seminar. One day, quiet accidentally, the two of us were discussing Eurocommunism and the political implications of the breakdown in the monolithic Communist movement in Europe. Rowney assured me paternalistically that meaningful negotiations with Communists, and especially the Soviet Union, were almost impossible. "The Russians never experienced the Renaissance," the general observed. "They did not take part of Western culture." I inquired whether serious discussions leading to the reduction of the arms race were negated by the Soviet Union's adherence to Communism. "Communism has nothing to do with it," Rowney curtly replied. The real problem with the Soviet Union is that "they are Asiatic." President Reagan and his key advisors constantly echo Rowney's racial chauvinism when they describe the Soviet Union as an "evil empire." To perceive one's ideological adversary in such rigid, Faustian terms effectively voids any possibilities for sustained, constructive exchanges.

The proponents of peace and nuclear disarmament must overturn the demonology of anti-Sovietism among Americans. This does not mean the acceptance of every Soviet position regarding arms control, or the acquiescence to Soviet behavior or oppressive policies in Afghanistan or Poland. It does require the fundamental recognition of the reality of Soviet socialism, and an understanding that its people fervently desire peace. Cultural and educational exchanges between the American and Soviet people, if coordinated on a truly large scale, could begin to erode decades of anti-Soviet propaganda and hatred. Dialogues between US Christian and Jewish groups with Soviet religious leaders could provide tangible evidence that all Communists are not atheists. Working discussions between urban planners, trade unionists, artists, and representatives of other professions might form the foundation of greater political tolerance and understanding.

Black Americans also comprehend that peace is not the absence of conflict. As long as institutional racism, apartheid, and social class inequality exist, social tensions will erupt into confrontations. Most blacks recognize that peace is the realization of social justice and human dignity for all nations and historically oppressed peoples. Peace more than anything else is the recognition of the oneness of humanity. As Paul Robeson, the great black artist and activist, observed in his autobiographical work *Here I Stand*, "I learned that the essential character of a nation is determined not by the upper classes, but by the common people, and that the common people of all nations are truly brothers in the great family of mankind." Any people who experience generations of oppression gain an awareness of the innate commonalty of all human beings, despite their religious, ethnic, and political differences. In order to reverse the logic of the Cold War, white Americans must begin to view themselves as a distinct minority in a world dominated by people of color. Peace between the superpowers is directly linked to the evolution of democratic rights, economic development, and social justice in the third world periphery.

Black intellectuals, from W.E.B. Du Bois to the present, have also comprehended their unique role in the struggle for peace and social justice. Cultural and intellectual activity for us is inseparable from politics. All art and aesthetics, scientific inquiry, and social studies are directly or indirectly linked to the material conditions of human beings, and the existing set of power relationships which dictates the policies of the modern state. When intellectual artists fail to combat racial or gender inequality, or the virus of anti-Semitism, their creative energies may indirectly contribute to the ideological justification for prejudice and social oppression. This is equally the case for the problem of war and peace. Through the bifurcation of our moral and social consciences against the cold abstractions of research and "value-free" social science, we may console ourselves by suggesting that we play no role in the escalation of the Cold War political culture. By hesitating to dedicate ourselves and our work to the pursuit of peace and social justice, we inevitably contribute to the dynamics of national chauvinism, militarism, and perhaps set the ideological basis necessary for World War

III. Paul Robeson, during the Spanish Civil War, expressed the perspective of the black peace tradition as a passionate belief in humanity: "Every artist, every scientist must decide, now, where he stands. He has no alternative. There are no impartial observers "

The commitment to contest public dogmas, the recognition that we share with the Soviet people a community of social, economic, and cultural interests, force the intellectual into the terrain of ideological debate. If we fail to do so, and if the peace consensus of black America remains isolated from the electoral mainstream, the results may be the termination of humanity itself.

The Bitter Fruits of War

Years from now people will wonder with amazement how and why the United States became embroiled in the Persian Gulf conflict. Because despite the rhetoric in the congressional debate over granting President Bush the power to initiate warfare, and the media's constant coverage of Iraqi leader Saddam Hussein, the American people are more poorly informed about the reasons for this conflict than any other war in our history.

Let's begin with the essentials. The United States did not send its troops into the Gulf to "oppose aggression" or to defend "democracy" or to support the right of Kuwait to resist Iraq's aggression. For decades, "aggression" has been a cornerstone of US foreign policy. Eight years ago, the United States launched a massive, illegal invasion of Grenada on the false pretext that American lives were endangered. Much of the world opposed US aggression in Panama and the imposition of a puppet regime loyal to American interests. The American response was to veto several United Nations Security Council resolutions critical of the invasion.

Nor does the United States oppose "aggression" when it is committed by its allies. When Israel invaded neighboring Lebanon, bombing Beirut and killing about 20,000 people, the United States vetoed UN Security Council moves denouncing this aggression. When South Africa institutionalized apartheid, murdered and imprisoned thousands of the regime's critics, and launched invasions against Namibia, Angola, and Mozambique, the United States said virtually nothing. When Iran was our enemy a few years ago, the United States did nothing when Saddam Hussein gassed Kurdish rebels in Iraq. The Reagan administration indirectly helped Iraq obtain sophisticated weapons to use against the Iranians.

It's also difficult to characterize the former regime in Kuwait as a bastion of democracy, or to applaud the current corrupt monarchy of Saudi Arabia as a fortress for liberal values and beliefs. No one doubts that Saddam Hussein is a despotic dictator. But the same is also true of the Emir of Kuwait and the ruling class of Saudi Arabia. In Kuwait, the vast majority of the population were noncitizens, politically disfranchised. Censorship in the press was pervasive, and Kuwaiti dissidents claim that if the Emir ever reclaims power in his country again, the level of political repression will be intensified. The Saudis have a long history of torture, executions, suppression of women's rights, and an absence of democracy.

Why is the United States fighting on the side of these despots? The crocodile tears being shed for Kuwaitis murdered and raped by Saddam's troops explain nothing about George Bush's decision to send 400,000 troops into the Gulf, a force larger than the number of Americans who invaded Europe against Hitler in World War II. The basic reason is the political economy of oil, and the singular fact that Americans, who represent 5 percent of the world's population, consume conservatively 26 percent of all petroleum. The Saudis, the Kuwaitis, and the other oil-rich sheiks are actually junior partners in a corporate conglomerate system involving Wall Street, the multinational corporations, and capitalist elites in the United States and Western Europe. Dependable control over cheap and reliable sources of energy is essential to the corporate and military hierarchies in this country. That's part of the reason why George Bush thinks it is cheaper to spill American blood in the sands of Kuwait than to give up domination and control over international oil sources.

Perhaps the biggest tragedy of the Gulf crisis was the manipulation of the nation by Bush into a confrontational situation with Saddam's regime. A token American force, preferably under United Nations command, would have been sufficient to halt Saddam from attacking Saudi Arabia. Bush's secret decision to double the number of American troops in the region, announced after the 1990 congressional elections, made a negotiated settlement almost impossible. Bush, not Saddam Hussein, made the confrontation inevitable.

Pushing the world to the edge of war, every action by the Bush administration was designed to make conflict with Iraq a national obsession. By resorting to locker room boasts, vowing to "kick Saddam's ass," Bush needlessly personalized the conflict, undercutting the possibility of negotiations. By increasing the number of American troops without congressional authority, he transformed what was initially a defensive tripwire to check Iraqi aggression into an offensive force. At the United Nations, Bush refused any linkage between Kuwait and Israel's occupation of the West Bank, even though a regional security conference connecting the problems of the Middle East will be the only means to move toward peace. In Congress, Bush even asserted that he alone had the power to take the country into war, despite Constitutional provisions to the contrary.

In retrospect, years from now, the focus of inquiry on the Gulf War will not be on Saddam Hussein and the invasion of Kuwait. Rather, it will center on the domestic prerogatives of American political, military, and corporate power. All international politics is based on domestic realities. If we want to understand why war occurred, we need to analyze the system of American power. In the aftermath of the Cold War, with the collapse of Communism in Eastern Europe, the United States was in a paradoxical situation. The $300 billion military budget could no longer be justified, as domestic critics called for a "peace dividend"—increased expenditures for education, jobs, health care, and human needs. With the retreat of Soviet troops from the center of Europe, it became difficult to justify the presence of thousands of American troops across the world.

Ideologically, the demise of the Communist threat undermined the political consensus which united the forces of Reaganism. With the end of the Cold War, American conservatives no longer felt obligated to support Bush's domestic or foreign policies. By the summer of 1990, even before Saddam Hussein's invasion of Kuwait, there was significant evidence that America was slipping into a major economic recession. An external crisis was needed to divert the attention of Americans standing on unemployment lines or awaiting pink slips.

By sending American troops into the Middle East, Bush accomplished several political objectives. First, American intervention reestablished this country's central role as the world's mercenary police, suppressing Third World nationalism and preserving Western corporate and political domination. The Arab world's greatest threat is not Saddam Hussein; it is the power and exploitation of Western governments and corporations. US intervention ensures more decades of American dominance, and is a warning to all non-European countries struggling against neocolonialism.

Second, American intervention justifies expansion of the military budget and increased production of nuclear and conventional weapons, eliminating the peace dividend. Thirdly, in terms of domestic politics, it divided the Democratic Party into pro-war and anti-war camps. Pro-war Democrats were manipulated to grant Bush unprecedented authority to initiate massive warfare abroad.

In the euphoria generated by America's blitzkrieg against Iraq in the opening days of the war, the stock market soared, and oil prices fell. The American people were told that the fruits of war would be the easy destruction of an evil dictator, the crushing of international terrorism, and the reestablishment of the United States as a superpower.

Few measured the real human costs of war upon both its victors and victims—young children who must be told that their father, a young flight
lieutenant, was shot down in his F-16 fighter over Baghdad, never to return; mothers and fathers of wounded and captured soldiers who worry as
only parents can about their children and yet are powerless to do anything
about it; young men and women who will lose their limbs, or be paralyzed
or blinded by mortar fire; the thousands of American families who are behind in mortgage payments because one parent in the reserves has been
shipped out to the Persian Gulf.

Television reporters tell us about "surgical air strikes" by US bombers, a
concept both absurd and dishonest. Pilots speeding at 1,000 miles per hour,
dropping one-ton bombs guided by lasers, are not conducting kidney trans-
plants or brain microsurgery. They are obliterating families, homes, and
mosques. The 16-year-old boys in the Iraqi army are not the security thugs
who raped and murdered Kuwaitis. They are also innocent victims sacrificing their lives under American bombardments.

This unnecessary, avoidable, and indefensible war is not against Saddam
Hussein. It is in effect a massive attack against the Iraqi people specifically,
and generally against the entire Arab world. The fruits of war for the
United States will be guilt, shame, and responsibility for immoral acts of
military terrorism which equal or exceed those committed in Kuwait by
Saddam Hussein.

The only positive results of this war are the protests of those who oppose
death and destruction. People of conscience are taking a stand. In Hiroshima, survivors of the 1945 atomic bombing staged a sit-in. In Germany, 100,000 marched the day after the war began. In San Francisco,
nearly 1,000 anti-war demonstrators were arrested, the most ever in a single day in that city's turbulent history. In New York City, 5,000 protested,
tying up traffic for hours. Two major demonstrations in Washington, DC,
drew hundreds of thousands of people from across the country.

The only language the American political and corporate elite understand
is resistance. This means conducting teach-ins explaining why the war is
unnecessary. It means civil disobedience, marches, demonstrations, and political organizing, bringing together religious groups, trade unions, civil
rights, feminists, and other progressive constituencies. Creative, democratic
protest for peace abroad and social justice at home should be our focus.

Toward a Pan-Africanist Manifesto for the Twenty-first Century

Fifty years ago, black leaders from Africa, the Caribbean, Great Britain, and the United States came together in pursuit of the liberation of the Black Diaspora. In the manifesto "Challenge to the Colonial Powers," this gathering declared: "We are determined to be free. We want the right to earn a decent living; the right to express our thoughts and emotions, to adopt and create forms of beauty. We demand for Black Africa autonomy and independence." The economic vision of the Manchester Pan-African Congress was clearly and unambiguously opposed to corporate capitalism as the model for black development: "We condemn the monopoly of capital and the rule of private wealth and industry for private profit alone. We welcome economic democracy as the only real democracy."

The 1945 Manchester congress was both the culmination of a historical process of struggle which had begun a half century before and a decisive political intervention to influence the events of the time. Behind Pan-Africanism was the idea that people of African descent the world over shared a common destiny—that our forced dispersal through the transatlantic slave trade, our common oppression under colonialism in Africa and the Caribbean and under Jim Crow segregation in the United States, the exploitation of our labor power under capitalism, and the denial of political rights had created parallel contours for struggle. Our kinship was also cultural, social, and historical, and we found within ourselves the genius and grace of being which were denied us by the racist standards of the white world. By renewing our connections, we forged a consciousness of resistance which could be felt across the globe.

The perspective of Pan-Africanism was first advanced in the international context by barrister Henry Sylvester Williams of Trinidad and Tobago at the London conference of 1900. It was at this gathering that the young scholar W.E.B. Du Bois predicted that "the problem of the twentieth century is the problem of the color line." After Williams's death in 1911, the Pan-Africanist movement was continued by Du Bois. The congress at Paris in 1919, following the conclusion of World War I; the congress held in London, Paris, and Brussels in 1921; the congress held in London, Paris, and Lisbon in 1923; and the New York congress of 1927 created the context for black intellectuals, political leaders, and reformers to challenge the prerogatives and power of white colonialism. Equally important during this period was the rise of black nationalism and Pan-African militancy as represented by Marcus Garvey and his Universal Negro Improvement Association (UNIA). The UNIA mobilized and inspired millions of black working-class and poor people toward a vision of black emancipation and self-determination.

The movement to realize Pan-Africanism was directly reinforced by a wide variety of concomitant social protest and resistance struggles. We can point to the trade union movement, the struggles of working women and men, from "Buzz" Butler in Trinidad and Tobago, to Clements Kadalie of South Africa, A. Philip Randolph of the United States, and Alexander Bustamante of Jamaica. There were the struggles of generations of black women, from Ida B. Wells and Mary Church Terrell of the United States, to Amy Jacques Garvey, Amy Ashwood Garvey, and Claudia James of the Caribbean, who taught us that gender oppression divides our communities and that our sisters must be recognized as central participants and leaders of the liberation struggle. There were civil rights organizations such as the National Association for the Advancement of Colored People, which sponsored legal challenges to the barriers of segregation. And there were formations such as the Congress of Racial Equality in the United States, which adopted Gandhi's technique of civil disobedience to the efforts to outlaw Jim Crow across the southern United States.

The political context for the 1945 Manchester congress must also be remembered. The threat of fascism and the Third Reich had just been destroyed, at the cost of many millions of lives. There was the dawning of a political polarization and confrontation between the Soviet Union and the capitalist West, which would soon emerge as the Cold War. There were anticolonialist campaigns, struggles for independence, in India and Indonesia, in Vietnam and the West Indies. It was in this context of massive change that George Padmore, Kwame Nkrumah, W.E.B. Du Bois, and many others came together to craft an anti-imperialist, anticolonialist agenda for the post–World War II period.

Although we honor and recognize our debt to the vision articulated in the Pan-Africanism of 1945, we must understand that our current conjuncture in history is radically different. The challenges of the twenty-first century are fundamentally distinct from the struggles for decolonization and independence which defined the Pan-Africanism of Padmore, Nkrumah, James, Du Bois, and Garvey. The problem of the twenty-first century is the problem of the new color line: the global boundaries of inequality and exploitation between North and South; the boundaries of race, gender, and class oppression within capitalist societies; and the political struggles to redefine democracy to benefit the social needs of the majority of the world's (multicultural) people. The new color line is being transformed by the technological revolution: the role of robots, computers, and new biotechnology in transforming the structure of production; the process of capital accumulation; and the social composition of the working class. Increasingly in the capitalist world, industrial labor is disappearing, replaced by service sector, temporary, and part-time jobs at minimum wages. Living standards and real wages are declining, as wealth is increasingly concentrated in a small segment of the social hierarchy. The new technologies destroy jobs and transfer capital and the tasks of labor to the Third World, at the lowest possible wages. This process destroys labor unions, forcing workers to compete with each other and thereby driving down wages. And in racially stratified societies, black people are disproportionately victims of this technological revolution, being pushed out of industrial and manufacturing jobs and into unemployment lines, becoming the last hired and the first fired. More and more black people are being pushed out of the labor market, are being undereducated and miseducated in our schools, are lacking the skills to be competitive in a computer-driven, technologically advanced economy. Pan-Africanism must understand the political economy of cyberspace and the new inequalities it is producing.

The new color line is the permanent expansion of poverty in capitalist states and throughout the Third World, the crisis of hunger and homelessness, of famine and social disruption. And the new color line is most clearly manifested in the prisons and penitentiaries of the Western world, the black people who are harassed by the police in our communities, who are given longer prison sentences than whites who commit the identical crimes, who are warehoused inside prisons because no jobs exist for them within society. In the United States, the number of people in prisons has increased from 500,000 in 1980 to over 1,500,000 today. About 800,000 African-Americans are in prison in the United States. This represents the destruction of an entire generation of young black men. About 30 percent of all black men between the ages of 18 to 29 are either in jail, on probation, on parole, or awaiting trial. There are several hundred thousand more young black men in prison in America today than enrolled in college.

The greatest casualties in the new color line of inequality of America are African-American and Latino children and young adults. Growing up black in white America has always been a challenge, but never more so than today. To be young and black in the 1990s means that the basic context for human development—education, health care, personal safety, a nontoxic environment, employment, and shelter—is increasingly problematic. To be young and black today means fighting for survival in a harsh and frequently unforgiving urban environment.

The frightening prospects for African-American children and youths in the United States have been identified by Marian Wright Edelman and the Children's Defense Fund. Today in the United States, in comparison to white children, black children are one and one-half times more likely to grow up in families whose household head did not graduate from high school. They are twice as likely to be arrested for property crimes, to be unemployed as teenagers and later as adults, and to become teenage mothers. African-American infants are two and one-half times as likely to die in the first year of life and to be born at low birth weights. African-American young people are three times more likely than their white counterparts to live in single-parent homes, to live in group quarters, and/or to be suspended from school or receive corporal punishment. African-American young people are four times as likely to have been born of mothers who had no prenatal care, mothers who died during childbirth, or mothers were dying from HIV infection. They are five times more likely to be arrested by the police for violent crimes than are white youths. And they are nine times more likely to become victims of homicide.

The Institute for Research in African-American Studies at Columbia University, which I direct, is only six blocks away from the heart of Harlem, 125th Street. Every day, in our immediate neighborhood, I can see the destruction of an entire generation of our young people. In New York City, 45 percent of all African-American youths dwell in poverty. In Central Harlem, one out of eight households has no plumbing or toilet facilities; more than half live in buildings with more than four floors and no elevators; and one-third have no telephones. Every day in New York, an average of 70,000 children, mostly Latino and black, use illegal drugs. Black and Hispanic youth unemployment exceeds 40 percent. Pervading everything is the specter of violence. In Central Harlem, the mortality rate for children from birth through age four is almost triple that of the national average. Such statistics on black youth may be different in southern Africa, Europe, or the Caribbean, but the nature of the struggle is the same. To paraphrase Amilcar Cabral, the flower of our struggle is our youth. Pan-African liberation must make connections with the energy, anger, militancy, and idealism of our young people.

The future of Pan-Africanism as a strategy for liberation depends upon our ability to bring together young people, workers, political organizers, trade unionists, women activists, and intellectuals behind a vision of black empowerment at a global level. This means a new critical definition of the political content for Pan-Africanism. The new Pan-Africanism must challenge the structures of patriarchy within black communities and black organizations, creating a more egalitarian relationship between black women and men. We know that gender inequality is not a consequence of biological or genetic differences between women and men; women's oppression is a social construct, anchored in power, privilege, and violence against women. So long as we tolerate the oppression of our sisters, our liberation moment as black people will never succeed.

The new Pan-Africanism of the twenty-first century must take a progressive stand on environmental issues and the state of the world's ecology. We must address the utilization of the natural resources of the world; our reliance on petrochemicals and carbon-based technologies which foul the air and pollute our water; and the storage of toxic wastes which shorten the lives of our children. America's dangerous, cancerous wastes are dumped on the most oppressed people. We need a coalition strategy that creates a dialogue with environmental organizations and green political parties, linking the struggle against racism to a safe, clean environment.

The Pan-Africanism of the next century must define itself not in terms of biology, genetics, or race, but in terms of politics and social vision. Race is a category of antiblack exploitation, a product of slavery, white supremacy, and economic domination. But race today also attacks the humanity of an entire spectrum of people: the Hispanics of California who suffer under the recently implemented Proposition 187, which denies their children access to education and denies their families admission to public health facilities; the Turks in Germany who encounter rampant discrimination and neo-Nazi gangs. The struggle against racism must be fought on a global level.

Some people have argued that "our homes" are not England, Europe, or the United States; that we should identify ourselves with Africa; and that we should eventually return to the African continent. I have no doubt that we as black people are linked in history, in culture, and in resistance. There is no doubt that our work must be to liberate and unite Africa. But speaking for African-American people, we have no doubt that our struggle is also for democracy and equal rights within the United States. Du Bois taught us that African-American people were both African and American, "two souls, two thoughts, two unreconciled strivings, two warring ideals in one dark body, whose dogged strength alone keeps him from being torn asunder." We should never forget our cultural heritage, our historical consciousness of the African Diaspora; but we should never back away from the assertion that the fight of black people is central to the fight for genuine democracy inside Western capitalist society. In the United States, millions of black people provided 300 years of unpaid and exploited labor. We built that nation, and we will not be denied the full measure of our contributions and sacrifices. We are here to stay, and we will not retreat.

At the height of the Cold War, the great artist and Pan-Africanist Paul Robeson was hauled before the House Un-American Activities Committee of Congress and told that he did not belong in the United States. Robeson responded: "Our people built this country. And no fascist-minded racist will drive us out. Here I stand." And with Robeson, I say that no one will deny us democratic rights anywhere: "Here we stand." With Du Bois, I argue that the fight against racism is "a fight to the finish. Either we will uproot racism, root and branch, or we will be exterminated as a people. This is the last great battle of the West."

Our strategy for liberation cannot be the integration or assimilation of our people into the institutions of white Western domination. Our struggle cannot be based on racial essentialism, a retreat from dialogue with progressive forces outside of the black community, a turning of the principle of separatism into a narrow fetish. The Pan-African struggle is for fundamental transformation, for economic democracy, for the end of world imperialism, for the global unity of people of color and all oppressed people.

The theorists of narrow Afrocentrism, of separatist black nationalism based on the simplistic reduction of racial categories, advocate a politics of metaphysics and mysticism disconnected from the actual material struggles and needs of our people. The slogans of cultural nationalism and racial chauvinism provide no concrete analysis of our socioeconomic and political reality, of the challenges presented by globalized capitalism within a technologically changing world. Liberation must be informed by a historical analysis of real social forces, grounded in the recognition that class is the fundamental variable and issue within the organization and hierarchies of world power. In short, we should not be seeking a "black version" of the capitalist West or a segregated autonomous space wherein all black interest must reside. Our challenge is to transform the totality of the social order, to reinterpret democracy in a multicultural context, to create a new language and definitions of human emancipation and dignity beyond black and white.

Finally, we must recognize the ethical dimensions of the struggle for Pan-Africanism. The capitalist West was built upon the corpses of millions of human beings: the vast extermination of Native Americans; the genocide of the transatlantic slave trade; the brutal exploitation of our foremothers and forefathers in the sugar plantations of Haiti, Barbados, and Jamaica and in the cotton fields of the American South; the imposition of violence and terror through the apartheid system of South Africa; and the authoritarian despotism of black neocolonial regimes, from Forbes Burnham in Guyana to Mobutu of Zaire. It is the moral bankruptcy of the West, the odor of capital gains and capital punishment, which makes it vulnerable in the eyes of the rest of the world. The fight for liberation speaks to the political conscience of the world. It is not a question of appealing to our oppressors; it is a matter of recognizing that the transcendental strength of our movement has been expressed when we have made demands against our oppressors which are simultaneously politically and morally inspired.

Martin Luther King, Jr. asserted his belief that "the moral arc of the universe bends toward justice." What we fight for is not material gain simply for our own selfish interests but transformation of the structures of oppression and inequality for the entire world.

Pan-Africanism remains an essentially democratic vision: to deconstruct and uproot the inequalities of racism, to challenge the unpopular capitalist "New World Order" represented by the International Monetary Fund, the World Bank, and, more recently, the North American Free Trade Agreement. Pan-Africanism remains vital as a political framework bringing together the collective perspectives of people of African descent in our eternal struggle to assert and to affirm all humanity. Our struggle for the empowerment of the African world is, indeed, "the last great battle of the West."

PART 3

Radical Democracy
and Socialism

Why Black Americans Are Not Socialists

The chief hope [for socialism] lies in the gradual but inevitable spread of the knowledge that the denial of democracy in Asia and Africa hinders its complete realization in Europe. It is this that makes the Color Problem and the Labor Problem to so great an extent two sides of the same human tangle. How far does white labor see this? Not far, as yet.

—W.E.B. *Du Bois*, The Negro Mind Reaches Out, *1925*

Marxists have always been conscious of the symbiotic relationship between racism and capitalism. Marx himself made the point succinctly in *Capital:* "Labor cannot emancipate itself in the white skin where in the black it is branded." A half century later, W.E.B. Du Bois, radical black scholar and founder of the NAACP, observed that "more and more the problem of the modern workingman is merging with the problem of the color line." For Du Bois, socialism was an impossible goal unless anti-racist politics dominated labor organizations. "So long as black laborers are slave," he concluded, "white laborer cannot be free."[1] Thus, the relationship between race and class and the political link between racial equality and the emancipation of the working class were clearly stated a long time ago.

Although objectively, as the most oppressed section of the working class, blacks should be in the forefront of a class conscious movement for a socialist America, actually relatively few black workers, activists, or intellectuals have joined socialist organizations.

The first part of this essay explorers some of the reasons for the failure of socialism within black America, taking up the legacy of racism on the left, examining the political development of black socialists and the path they took to Marxism as differentiated from the one followed by white leftists, and noting some of the sociological factors which have retarded the development of a broad based socialist consciousness in the black community from 1865 to the present. In the second section, there is a discussion of the current black struggle and the continued gap between major black organizations and the American left.

The Racist Legacy

The history of the relationship between blacks and American white radicals is filled with broken promises, ethnocentrism, and outright contempt. Racism has blunted the critical faculties of white progressives from the colonial period to the present. Any proper understanding of black historic reluctance to support calls for socialism by radical intellectuals and white workers must begin with this twisted heritage of racism.[2]

Blacks have seen an endless series of prominent white liberal and progressive allies betray their trust and embrace the politics of white supremacy. Populist Tom Watson, the Georgia lawyer in the early 1890s, became the fiercest proponent of lynching and racist hatred the South had ever known.[3] Elizabeth Cady Stanton's call for women's right to vote at Seneca Falls, New York, in 1848 was seconded by black abolitionist Frederick Douglass. As Angela Davis notes, "Douglass was responsible for officially introducing the issue of women's rights to the Black Liberation movement, where it was enthusiastically welcomed."[4] Stanton repaid black supporters with this racist diatribe:

> As long as [the Negro] was lowest in the scale of being, we [white women] were willing to press his claims; but now, as the celestial gate to civil rights is slowly moving on its hinges, it becomes a serious question whether we had better stand aside and see "Sambo" walk into the kingdom first. ... Are we sure that he, once entrenched in all his inalienable rights, may not be an added power to hold us at bay? Why should the African prove more just and generous than his Saxon peers? ... It is better to be the slave of an educated white man, than of a degraded, ignorant black one.[5]

Birth control advocate Margaret Sanger championed black and white workers' rights, and for a time maintained close ties to the Socialist Party. By 1919, however, Sanger defended birth control as "more children from the fit, less from the unfit." In a letter to one associate, Sanger confided, "We do not want word to get out that we want to exterminate the Negro population."[6] Such was the profound racism that has underscored American politics, right to left.

An early socialist whose career parallels Watson's, Stanton's, and others was Orestes A. Brownson. Two decades before the 1848 revolutions and the publication of the *Communist Manifesto*, Brownson pursued a radical labor organizing career. A Universalist minister, Brownson was a supporter of the Robert Owen–Frances Wright faction of the Workingmen's Party. In the 1830s, he was a strong advocate of black emancipation. "We can legitimate our own right to freedom," Brownson wrote in 1838, "only by arguments which prove also the negro's right to be free." After 1840, Brownson had begun to believe that laborers "are neither numerous nor strong enough to get or to wield the political power of the State." With his renunciation of radicalism, Brownson also abandoned any support for black liberation. By 1844, he supported South Carolina Senator and slaveholder John C. Calhoun for the Democratic Party's presidential nomination. After the Civil War, he protested black suffrage, warning that black voters "will always vote with the wealthy landowning class, and aid them in resisting socialistic tendencies." He applauded Jim Crow laws, taunting his abolitionist opponents, "You will never make the mass of the white people look upon the blacks as their equals."[7]

Marxists have always insisted that the flow of social history is determined by the relationship between the subjective and objective factors—the superstructure or ideological, cultural, and political apparatuses and the base, or forces of production. But what most American socialists and Marxists adhered to was a philosophy not of Marxism—which also suggests that the relations between superstructure and base are reciprocal, one affecting the other—but of economic determinism, not unlike that of American historian Charles Beard.[8] The left economic determinists held that the base, the means of production, strictly determines the character of all other human institutions and thought. Racism was, therefore, only part of the larger class question. The rights of Negroes, per se, were no different in any decisive respect than those of Polish-American factory workers in Chicago or white miners and lumberjacks in the Great Northwest. This is not to suggest that all white socialists who held this view were racist or insensitive to racism. Eugene V. Debs made it a point of principle never to address any racially segregated audience. The Socialist Party would "deny its philosophy and repudiate its own teaching," Debs said, "if, on account of race consideration, it sought to exclude any human being from political and economic freedom." Socialist historian Albert Fried applauds Debs' enlightened views, but adds that Debs "and probably most socialists" during the early 1900s "reduced the Negro problem to a class problem. They assumed that equality would prevail in America the moment capitalism ceased to exist. Until that day they preferred to keep the race issue as far out of sight and hearing as possible."[9]

This theoretical rigidity produced two political by-products. First, militant socialists like Curaçao-born Daniel De Leon who were sympathetic to black demands for civil rights nevertheless "regarded the plight of the Negro as essentially a class issue," according to historian David Herreshoff. De Leon did not take seriously the loss of black voting rights in the 1890s, because in his own words, "the tanglefoot Suffrage legislation while aimed at the Negro ostensibly as a Negro, in fact aims at him as a wage slave." De Leon personally opposed racist legislation, but he believed "it was a waste of time for socialists to explore the differences between whites and blacks" as to their relative degrees of race/class exploitation.[10] The second and more devastating result was that white American socialists never made the issue of racism a basic point of struggle either internally or propagandistically. Thus, socialist John Sandgren was not censured for expressing the view in the Party's newspaper that blacks, women, and migrant workers "can in no manner be directly interested in politics." No one pressed for the expulsions of centrist leader Morris Hillquit and newspaper editor Hermann Schlueter for championing the exclusion of immigration of "workingmen of inferior races—Chinese, Negroes, etc."[11]

White social democrats repeatedly disappointed black leftists in their tolerance, and sometimes outright approval, of racism. In a 1911 speech before the New York City Socialist Party, Du Bois publicly attacked white leftists for refusing to combat racism.[12] In 1913, he urged the American Socialist Party to redouble its efforts to recruit blacks. "There is a group of ten million persons in the United States toward whom socialists would better turn serious attention," he declared.[13] Du Bois' campaign to force white leftists into the struggle for racial justice was effective, in certain respects. Moderate socialist/social worker Jane Addams supported Du Bois' research activities at Atlanta University. Addams and more militant intellectuals in the Socialist Party, like Mary White Ovington, William English Walling, and Charles Edward Russell, were founding members of the NAACP.[14] However, other white socialists either ignored Du Bois' call or simply restated the popular racist bigotry of the age. A typical example was Victor Berger, powerful leader of the Milwaukee socialists and head of the Wisconsin AFL, who said that "the negroes and mulattoes constitute a lower race," and were a menace to white labor. The "free contact with the whites has led to the further degradation of the negroes."[15] The Socialist Party in the South was for "whites only," and some party theoreticians expounded the view that "socialism would bring complete segregation: blacks and whites should not live in the same areas or even work in the same factories."[16]

Even some of the most "progressive" white socialists who were actively involved in anti-racist work could harbor a private hatred for blacks. For example, in December 1928, Molders Union leader John P. Frey was the

AFL speaker at a large interracial meeting in Washington, DC. Publicly, Frey supported black civil rights; privately, he was "a notorious racist." Despite the AFL's long record of racist exclusion, Frey claimed that the Federation "not only organized the negro, but brought him into the white man's unions." He added that racial prejudice against African-Americans in unions was not greater than that experienced by Italians, Jews, or Poles. Du Bois and NAACP assistant secretary Walter White denounced Frey's speech. Seeking to resolve the dispute, William English Walling counseled White to halt public attacks on Frey. As a leading Socialist Party theoretician and a member of the NAACP executive board, Walling openly fought the "color line" but privately condemned his black co-workers. In a letter to Frey, Walling described Du Bois and other black NAACP critics of the AFL as "nasty reds. Labor's attitude on the color question is 100 percent OK and it has nothing to be ashamed of." Frey's response to Walling charged that blacks themselves were to blame for their "low" representation in all-white unions![17]

From its origins, the Communist Party always maintained better relations with the black movement than the socialists. Initial black recruitment efforts were unsuccessful. During the 1920s only 200 black Americans joined the Party, but among them were some of the most gifted writers and organizers of the "Harlem Renaissance," like Cyril Briggs, founder of the revolutionary black nationalist organization the African Blood Brotherhood. The Party's real growth did not occur until the Great Depression. Communists established integrated Unemployment Councils and led "hunger marches" in dozens of state capitals and in Washington, DC. Two black Communists organized a sharecroppers' union at Camp Hill, Alabama, in 1931 that quickly mushroomed into a mass movement among black rural farmers in the state. The Party launched the National Miners' Union, which promptly elected a black Indiana miner, William Boyce, as its national vice president. Thousands of blacks supported NMU strikes and organizing activities because, in Boyce's words, "it fights discrimination, segregation, Jim Crowism and disenfranchisement." Black Party leader James W. Ford, secretary of the Harlem Section, was instrumental in organizing tenant and worker protests reaching tens of thousands of poor blacks.[18] During those years of astronomically high unemployment, vast numbers of poor blacks acquired a deep respect for the Communist Party, the first socialist organization in their experience to emphasize racial egalitarianism in theory and practice.

But subsequent Communist activity lost the Party black support. When black social democrat A. Philip Randolph organized the Negro March on Washington Movement in 1941 to pressure the Roosevelt Administration to desegregate defense plants, Communists opposed the mobilization. After Nazi Germany's attack on the Soviet Union, the Party "frowned upon any struggles that might interfere with the war effort," writes historian Philip S. Foner. Thus, black Communist spokesperson Ben Davis urged blacks to put aside "all questions of discrimination" and to "sacrifice" for the war effort. The Party's newspaper, the *Daily Worker,* told blacks to sign "no-strike pledges," and charged that black protesters involved in the August 1943 Harlem riot were "fifth columnists and profascists." The Party was silent about the immoral internment of thousands of Japanese-Americans in West Coast camps, and applauded the use of the atomic bomb on Hiroshima. "It was to be exceedingly difficult for the Communists to overcome the resentment among blacks created by the Party's wartime policies," Foner observes. "The Communists never completely erased the feeling in sections of the black community that they had placed the Soviet Union's survival above the battle for black equality."[19]

Since 1945, American Marxists have generally supported the struggle for equal rights, but their contributions to the black movement have not been decisive. White social democrats provided financial support for Martin Luther King's Montgomery bus boycott in 1955–56. Many "red diapers babies" of the New Left generation joined the Student Nonviolent Coordinating Committee (SNCC) in the early 1960s. Most white social democrats, however, were bewildered when the civil rights cause turned into a struggle for "Black Power." They thought that Malcolm X was a racist or a madman; they could not comprehend Stokely Carmichael or H. Rap Brown. Conversely, some of the younger white radicals applauded any angry black spokesperson—Eldridge Cleaver is a sorry example—without any serious analysis of the dynamics of race and class in American society. Small wonder, then, that by the 1980s, no socialist or communist organization, Old Left or New, had won over any significant number of black activists, intellectuals, or workers.

At the core of the left's legacy, therefore, is the ongoing burden of racism. In the 1920s, Du Bois characterized American social democracy and the white working class as "autocratic and at heart capitalistic, believing in profit-making industry and wishing only to secure a larger share of profits for particular guilds." After World War I and the successful revolution in Russia, however, there existed the faint possibility for a democratic movement for socialism which was antiracist. For Du Bois the logical question was: "Will the new labor parties welcome the darker race to this industrial democracy?" Reflecting critically on the United States, Du Bois had to admit that the long-term prospects were decidedly bleak:

> White laborers can read and write, but beyond this their education and experience are limited and they live in a world of color prejudice. The propaganda, the terrible, ceaseless propaganda that buttresses [white racism] . . . has built a wall which for many centuries will not break down. Born into such a spiritual

world, the average white worker is absolutely at the mercy of its beliefs and prejudices. Color hate easily assumes the form of religion and the laborer becomes the blind executive of the decrees of the "punitive" expeditions; he sends his sons as soldiers and sailors; he composes the Negro-hating mob, demands Japanese exclusion and lynches untried prisoners. What hope is there that such a mass of dimly thinking and misled men will ever demand universal democracy for men?[20]

The overwhelming majority of white American socialists have yet to confront this question seriously.

The Black Path to Socialism

A few black workers and intellectuals were attracted to socialist ideas as early as the 1870s. One of the nation's most prominent black trade unionists, New York engineer John Ferrell, was a socialist and a leader of the Knights of Labor. Peter H. Clark, the principal of the Colored High School of Cincinnati, Ohio, was "probably the first American Negro Socialist," according to Foner. During the 1877 railroad strike, Clark publicly hailed black-white unity and "called for socialism as the solution for labor's grievances." Probably the most effective black leftist before 1900 was the militant editor of the *New York Age,* Timothy Thomas Fortune. In a series of newspaper and periodical articles, Fortune demanded that "Southern capitalists give their wage workers a fair percentage of the results of their labor. If there is any power on earth which can make the white Southern employers of labor face the music," he wrote, "it is organized white and black labor."[21] Fortune called for a class struggle to liberate black Americans. "What are millionaires, anyway, but the most dangerous enemies of society?" he asked his readers. Fortune was convinced that black people had to adopt a socialist analysis to comprehend the economic forces that exploited them. "Their revolution is upon us, and since we are largely of the laboring population, it is very natural that we should take sides with the labor forces in their fight for a juster distribution of the results of labor."[22]

Lucy Parsons was one of a number of black women socialists who have been buried in the pages of history. Born in 1853, Parsons joined the Socialist Labor Party in her mid-twenties. She married a radical Southerner, Albert R. Parsons, who had served briefly in the Confederate Army. Even before her husband was indicted for complicity in the deaths of seven policemen during the Haymarket Square riot of May 4, 1886, and executed in November 1887, Lucy Parsons traveled the country in support of anarchism. Most socialist historians have ignored her writings and activities against sexism and lynching. A few have even questioned her racial identity.[23] Her contemporaries knew her as a militant supporter of the Industrial Workers of the World, and a defender of the Scottsboro Nine in 1931. Parsons joined the Communist Party in 1939, and died three years later.[24]

Some black leaders advanced socialist ideas after 1900, but relatively few joined the Socialist Party. J. Milton Waldron, a Jacksonville, Florida, Baptist minister, was a supporter of cooperatives and black-white labor unity. In 1901, he organized the Afro-American Industrial Insurance Society, and four years later joined Du Bois' Niagara Movement, the black political opposition to accommodationist educator Booker T. Washington. Politically, however, Waldron aligned himself with the Democratic Party through an all-black organization, the National Independent Political League. J. Max Barber, assistant editor of the *Voice of the Negro,* was another Niagara Movement activist who sympathized with socialist reforms.[25] In Harlem, street propagandist and black nationalist organizer Hubert Harrison had, by 1914, begun to combine the issues of race and class into a unique political program. Younger Harlem black radicals involved in union organizing, A. Philip Randolph and Chandler Owen, joined the Socialist Party. Randolph's subsequent career as the leader of the Brotherhood of Sleeping Car Porters and founder of the National Negro Congress in 1935 is, of course, well known. But for our purposes, it has relatively little relationship to Marxism. By 1920, Randolph had broken with militant socialism, and by the end of his life had become an apologist for crude anticommunism and white racism inside the AFL-CIO.[26]

Among the thousands of blacks who joined the Communist Party during the Great Depression, Angelo Herndon is, perhaps, the best known. Born in 1913, Herndon was a construction laborer and worked in the Kentucky coal mines. In 1930, he joined the Party-led Unemployment Council of Birmingham. Two years later, he was arrested and jailed for possession of Marxist literature, provoking labor violence, and trying "to establish a group and combination of persons, colored and white." The case of Angelo Herndon became a national cause for the left and many white liberals. Randolph drafted a resolution to free Herndon which was presented to the 1936 AFL Convention. NAACP attorney Thurgood Marshall supported the Herndon defense. In 1937, the Supreme Court narrowly reversed Herndon's conviction in a five to four vote. Of interest here is not Herndon's subsequent career—he broke with the Party after World War II—but the political evolution that led him to socialism. In his youthful autobiography, *Let Me Live,* Herndon explained that his "conversion" to Communism was virtually a religious awakening:

> The Negro leaders tell us that the poor white workers are responsible for our sufferings. But who controls the powerful weapons with which to spread anti-Negro propaganda? . . . Decidedly, it could not be the poor white workers who had all they could to keep themselves alive. Therefore, it could only be the rich white people who were our oppressors, for they controlled the churches and

the schools and the newspapers and the radio. . . . [To] secure their profits from human sweat and brawn they fall back upon these wicked methods of "divide and rule," divide the white workers from their Negro brothers.[27]

For Herndon and other unemployed black workers, Marxism manifested itself first in racial terms as a theory of human equality and social justice.

The most significant national black leader won to socialism during the first half of the twentieth century and who remained a militant leftist throughout his public career was W.E.B. Du Bois. As a radical journalist, he stood above De Leon, Fortune, and Randolph; as a pioneering social scientist, his voluminous writings, from *The Soul of Black Folks* (1903) to *Black Reconstruction* (1935), influenced scholars worldwide. For decades his name was the personification of the black freedom struggle in the US, the West Indies, and Africa. For these reasons his evolution as a Marxist merits considerable attention.

Du Bois viewed himself as a socialist by 1904. In his early journal, *Horizon,* and later in the NAACP publication *Crisis,* he "advised the socialists that their movement could not succeed unless it included Negro workers, and wrote that it was simply a matter of time before white and black workers would see their common economic cause against the exploiting capitalists."[28] Like Parsons, Randolph, and Herndon, Du Bois was impressed with the nonracist personal behavior of many white socialists, and probably gravitated to leftist politics because they seemed to share his burning commitment to racial equality. As early as 1908, Du Bois made this point quite clearly: "The only party today which treats Negroes as men, North and South, are the Socialists."[29] Thus, he vigorously applauded Los Angeles socialists for nominating a black man for city council in 1911.[30] African-Americans view society through the prism of race, and when they come to radicalism it is as a response to and rejection of racism and the inherent irrationality of capitalism. In August 1927, for example, Du Bois noted in *Crisis* that several blacks in Louisville, Mississippi, had been "burned alive" because of the widespread indignation at the "refusal of Negroes traveling in slow, second hand Fords to give the road to faster cars." Small wonder, Du Bois exclaimed, that some black Americans were turning to "bolshevism." Given the level of racist atrocities, he thought larger numbers of blacks would turn to Marxism.[31]

However, Du Bois' conversion to Marxism did not begin until well after the Bolshevik Revolution. Although in September 1916 he predicted that the war would create "the greater emancipation of European women, the downfall of monarchies . . . and the advance of true Socialism,"[32] when the autocracy fell in St. Petersburg six months later, Du Bois worried "whether the German menace is to be followed by a Russian menace."[33] In the summer of 1921, the black editor was criticized by novelist Claude McKay for neglecting to mention the accomplishments of the Soviet Union. Du Bois tartly rejected the slogan "dictatorship of the proletariat," and informed McKay, "[I am] not prepared to dogmatize with Marx and Lenin." He urged blacks not to join a revolution "which we do not at present understand."[34] Du Bois' leap toward the left only began in earnest with a two month visit to the Soviet Union in 1926. He was not surprised to see so many poor people, food lines, and "orphan children, ragged and dirty, [crawling] in and out of sewers." What impressed Du Bois was the Soviet government's commitment to "the abolition of poverty. . . . Schools were multiplying; workers were being protected with a living wage, nurseries for children, night schools, trade unions and wide discussion." Ever the puritan, Du Bois noted that "there were no signs of prostitution or unusual crime . . . some drunkenness, but little gambling."[35] Summarizing his experience in *Crisis,* Du Bois declared with enthusiasm:

> I stand in astonishment and wonder at the revelation of Russia that has come to me. I may be partially deceived and half-informed. But if what I have seen with my eyes and heard with my ears in Russia is Bolshevism, I am a Bolshevik.[36]

Even earlier, Du Bois believed that the essence of the socialist revolution and the most important product of Bolshevism "is the vision of great dreamers that only those who work shall vote and rule."[37] By 1931, he urged Crisis readers to study *Capital.*[38]

During the Depression, Du Bois' affection for the Soviet model of socialism grew. Visiting Russia again in late 1936, he was pleased with what he felt to be the nation's progress: "There were no unemployed, all children were in schools, factories, shops and libraries had multiplied, and there was evidence of law and order everywhere. The peasant was in close cooperation with, and not in revolt against, the factory worker."[39]

In retrospect, though, Du Bois' silence on the massive Soviet political upheavals during those years is difficult to explain. The "liberals" in the Politburo, particularly Leningrad chief Sergei Kirov, Vice Premier Rudzutak, Kalinin, and Voroshilov, were being displaced (or in Kirov's case assassinated on Stalin's orders). The "trial of the sixteen," which included former Comintern leader Grigori Zinoviev, occurred in August 1936. Former Soviet leaders Piatakov, Radek, and fifteen others were "tried" for committing crimes against the state in January 1937. One of Marxism's greatest theoreticians, Nikolai Bukharin, would be executed on false charges the following year.[40] By 1939, one quarter of the entire Soviet officer's corps was imprisoned; 1 million party members were expelled. "The Great Purge destroyed a generation not simply of Old Bolshevik veterans of the anti-tsarist struggle but of very many of their juniors who had joined the movement after 1917 and served as active implementers of Stalinism in its first phase," political scientist Robert Tucker writes. "It virtually transformed the composition of the Soviet regime and the managerial elite in all fields."[41]

Du Bois' support for Communism increased with the beginning of the Cold War. Persecuted by the federal government, his passport revoked, and his books banned from public libraries and universities, Du Bois concluded that Russia was the only hope for liberating the oppressed peoples of color across the world. He later acknowledged the crimes of Stalinism but argued that the Soviet state deserved praise for what he believed to be its positive influence on the national liberation movements in Africa, Asia, and the Americas.[42]

Since his death in 1963, no single African-American leader has emerged to articulate the socialist vision with anything approaching Du Bois' skill and power. Congressperson Ronald V. Dellums and Georgia State Senator Julian Bond are members of the Democratic Socialists of America, but neither is known particularly as a socialist among blacks. Angela Davis, the Communist Party's Vice Presidential candidate in 1980, known for her work in black and feminist history, is a prominent activist in struggles which involve poor and working-class blacks, but it is certainly questionable whether her activities are helped by her identification with the Party. Since 1968, a number of black scholar/activists, including Adolph Reed, Robert L. Allen, Damu Imara Smith, William W. Sales, William Strickland, James Foreman, and Earl Ofari, have become socialists of various ideological hues, but none has the means that were available to Du Bois to reach millions of black workers.[43]

From Timothy Thomas Fortune to W.E.B. Du Bois and those mentioned above, blacks have become radicals, socialists, and Marxists as a result of their commitment to black liberation, which usually involved protest activities and organizing in the black community. White socialists could express solidarity with the black struggle, but precious few actually incorporated militantly anti-racist politics into the core of their own writings and activities; for them, the race question has always been secondary to the class question. On the other hand, for black socialists race and class have been an interdependent dynamic. They discovered Marx on the road to black liberation.

Historical Impediments to Black Socialist Consciousness

The basic theme of black US history is the schism between protest and accommodation, struggle and compromise, radicalism and conservatism. Most leftists accept as given the proud heritage of black resistance—Nat Turner, Frederick Douglass, W.E.B. Du Bois, Sojourner Truth, Fannie Lou Hamer, Malcolm X, Martin Luther King, Jr., Paul Robeson. Yet for each of these gifted women and men, there were many African-American leaders who did not openly fight racism, Jim Crow laws, and economic exploitation. Most black Reconstruction politicians were cautious and pragmatic, ready to campaign for voting rights and civil liberties, but unwilling to call for armed self-defense of the black community and a radical divestment of the white planters' property. From 1865 until the eve of the Great Depression, over 80 percent of all black people were Southern farmers and sharecroppers. Today, we fail to appreciate the fact that, historically, blacks' sense of nationality, racial pride, and culture are essentially rural in origin. Rural attitudes toward life and labor tended to be fairly orthodox and were reinforced by the rigid code of racial segregation. Any strict caste system retards the internal social/cultural/economic dynamics of the oppressed group. New ideological and cultural currents expressed by a subgroup are repressed; the race/class interests of those in authority are often infused into the world view or "common sense" of the oppressed. Protest in any racist, totalitarian order like the US South between 1877–1960 was difficult even under the best of conditions. It should not surprise us, therefore, that the majority of black leaders emerging from such a racist society would not propose a socialist program.

Historically, the central political demand of any oppressed peasant class is the redistribution of the land. In this country, that was translated into the call for "forty acres and a mule." Those black leaders closest to the agricultural production process called for small proprietary holdings which would free blacks from the yoke of tenancy. With the migration of blacks to the Northern cities into the 1930s, this demand found its Northern echo in programs with the slogan "Don't buy where you can't work." Such policies, which it was hoped would lead to greater black employment, were supported by both the Garveyites and the NAACP, but they did not attack the root of black joblessness—capitalism. Those who migrated to the cities took their rural ideological limitations with them in the form of "black Capitalist" programs for the African-American ghetto.

The role of religion in the black community provided yet another barrier to socialism. The language of black politics has always been conditioned by the idiom of the church. Opposition to Marxism and socialism often comes from black preachers and those most heavily influenced by them. Atheism could never be popular among a peasant and working class people whose nationality and identify were forged in part through faith in their churches and in a just God. For example, on Herndon's admission into the Party's Unemployment Councils, he "bubbled over with enthusiasm" and talked to his relatives and friends "about Negroes and whites fighting together against their bosses so they might live like human beings." Without exception, his friends were aghast and warned Herndon "that I had better stay away from those Reds who were wicked people blaspheming against God."

Older religious blacks lamented that the young man had fallen into the atheist movement.[44]

Hosea Hudson's experiences with the black church were even more bitter. Born in 1898, in rural Wilkes County, Georgia, Hudson had attended church since childhood. For years, his ambition was to become a minister like his brother. When he joined the Communist Party in September 1931, he says, "I lost sight of that preaching, I lost sight of the Bible." Church-going blacks had little interest in Hudson's concern about the Scottsboro Nine case. Black ministers urged black Communists to "quit talking about" Scottsboro, and demanded that Hudson "keep that devilment out of the church." Devout friends denounced him as "a terrible something, and infidel." In his later years Hudson wrote, "We turned a lot of people away. . . . That's the way they looked upon Reds, Reds didn't believe in no God. They's dangerous." He blamed the capitalist ruling class for "whipping up the minds of people" to oppose socialism on religious grounds. But even after a half century in the Communist Party, Hudson did not escape his social and cultural origins. "I never did finally stop believing in God," he admits. "I haven't stopped believing yet today. I don't argue about it. I don't discuss it, because it's something I can't explain."[45]

Another factor responsible for the black community's indifference, even hostility to socialism was the negative influence of the small African-American petty bourgeoisie. From the 1870s to the present, the overwhelming majority of middle class black intellectuals, political leaders, and entrepreneurs have opposed socialism. Black Reconstruction politician John R. Lynch, Speaker of the Mississippi legislature in 1872 and a three-term Republican Congressperson, had no sympathy for "socialism" or "anarchism." Blacks, he felt, should strive to join interracial unions, but should repudiate violence.[46] Booker T. Washington made headlines with his caustic criticism of socialism, radicalism, and Negro participation in the trade union movement. Even Washington's liberal black critics were committed to his "black capitalism" program.

John Edward Bruce, a founder of the first black academic society, the American Negro Academy, was decidedly anti-socialist. After inviting A. Philip Randolph to speak before the Academy on December 30, 1919, Bruce judged the address "a bitter attack on all things not socialist." Bruce wrote in his diary, "I have no faith in socialism and its propagandists. It has occupied the attention of thinkers for centuries past and no three of them seem to agree as to its efficacy as a solvent for the ills of the body politic. Socialists are themselves divided and there can never be unity in division."[47] On the crucial point of a strategy for black economic development, black nationalists who supported Marcus Garvey and the staunchest of racial integrationists in the NAACP could agree: American capitalism was not structurally racist, and the desperate material condition of blacks could be alleviated through the accumulation of capital in the pockets of black entrepreneurs.[48]

Many prominent leaders of the contemporary black movement continue to "exhibit a simplistic fixation on racism and are unable (or unwilling) to delve any deeper into the American social structure."[49] Although he has since moved to a variety of socialism (Kwame Nkrumahist thought), Stokely Carmichael best represented this "fixation" in the black movement during the late 1960s. At an anti–Vietnam War conference in April 1968, for instance, the former SNCC leader claimed that Marxism was "irrelevant to the black struggle because it dealt only with economic questions, not racism." As for Karl Marx, Carmichael said that he refused to "bow down to any white man." On the question of black-white working class coalitions, Carmichael declared, "Poor white people are not fighting for their humanity, they're fighting for more money. There are a lot of poor white people in this country, you ain't seen none of them rebel yet, have you?"[50]

In the 1970s, many cultural nationalists surpassed John E. Bruce in their hostility to Marxism. "Our struggle cannot be defined as class struggle in the traditional Marxist manner," wrote *Black Books Bulletin* publisher Haki Madhubuti. "As far as skin color is concerned in the United States, if you are black, you are a slave." Cultural nationalist author Shawna Maglangbayan denounced Marxism as a "reactionary and white supremacist ideology whose chief aim is to maintain Aryan world hegemony once capitalism is overthrown. The idea of an 'alliance' with Left-wing white supremacy is a still-born infant which black Marxists fanatics resuscitate each time they muster enough force to rear their heads in the black community."[51] In fairness, it is most accurate to describe the majority of black elected officials as moderate to liberal social democrats. They do not take the anti-communist polemics of either the Reagan Administration or black cultural nationalists too seriously. However, few could be viewed historically as socialist, and in only rare instances would they be considered Marxist. The economic programs of Congressional Black Caucus members range from liberal Keynesianism to laissez-faire capitalism. On balance, most tend to agree with Du Bois' 1940 statement, "The split between white and black workers was greater than that between white workers and capitalists; and this split depended not simply on economic exploitation but on a racial folklore grounded on centuries of instinct, habit and thought."[52]

Finally, black civil society had been so conditioned by capitalism that it is difficult to find major institutions owned or run by blacks which to any degree advocate socialism. This is particularly true in the area of higher education. Historically, black colleges and universities furnish little valuable information critical of the "free enterprise system." Indeed, what is usually taught in the social sciences could be termed "non-economics": a total lack of any economic analysis critical of capitalism. Reflecting on his own education at Fisk University in Nashville, Tennessee, Du Bois wrote that "my formal education had touched on politics and religion, but on the whole had avoided economics." Courses on African-American slavery discussed the institution's "moral aspects" but never its economic dynamics. "In class I do not remember ever hearing Karl Marx mentioned nor socialism discussed. We talked about wages and poverty, but little was said of trade unions and that little was unfavorable."[53]

The inevitable result of this process of economic miseducation has been a general tendency among black intellectuals in the social sciences to relegate "class issues" to oblivion. Du Bois' series of landmark sociological studies on the Negro in America, published at Atlanta University between 1896 and 1914, illustrates this problem. The annual reports covered widely divergent topics: "The College-Bred Negro," "Notes on Negro Crime," "The American Negro Family." In only two brief volumes, published in 1899 and 1907, did Du Bois concentrate on black economic activities, and even then the works espoused no serious criticism of capitalism. A half century late, Du Bois would write that his entire "program was weak on its economic side. It did not stress enough the philosophy of Marx and Engels."[54] His scholarship on race relations, without equal at the turn of the century, was seriously flawed. "I [did not know] Marx well enough," Du Bois said, "to appreciate the economic foundations of human history."[55] Today, for most black Americans, "class" is perceived purely as a function of personal income. The notions of a "proletariat" and a "capitalist ruling class" are abstractions which have little meaning in everyday language.

The Failure of Leadership

The absence of a viable socialist presence within black America has become a critical problem in the 1980s. The election of Ronald Reagan and the electoral successes of conservative Republicans across the US in 1980 threw the black movement into disarray. Black nationalist political organizations on the left were increasingly victimized by federal and local harassment; black elected officials in Congress and in state legislatures fought desperately to maintain the number of black majority districts; civil rights groups endeavored to reverse hundreds of Reagan-sponsored initiatives reducing job training programs, public housing, welfare benefits, and health care. This political assault in the wake of the victory of the right is not limited to black concerns. The early 1980s witnessed the defeat of the Equal Rights Amendment; attacks on affirmative action for women and all minorities; a rapidly expanding federal defense budget at the expense of social programs; more overt restriction of the rights of gays and lesbians, etc. In some respects, at least for blacks, the socioeconomic and political terrain of the

early 1980s parallels the situation in the mid- to late 1890s, an era dominated by a severe economic depression, the passage of strict Jim Crow legislation, the loss of black male suffrage in the South, and the growth of white
vigilante violence. The movement for racial equality which characterized
the period of Reconstruction, from 1865 to 1877, succumbed to the control of capital and a conservative Republican–dominated federal government. Similarly, the optimism and activism that were part of the "Second
Reconstruction," 1954 to 1966, have been replaced within the black community by frustration and self-doubt.

During the earlier period, the major black figure was Booker T. Washington, founder of Tuskegee Institute, political boss of the "Tuskegee Machine," and leader of the first association of black entrepreneurs, the Negro
Business League. Washington counseled public submission to Jim Crow
laws and urged blacks to enter into a "historical compromise" with Northern capital and former Southern slaveholders against white workers. The
personification of the tendency toward accommodation within the black
community at that time, he believed that no real political gains could be
achieved through alignment with the trade unions, Populists, or socialists.
He accepted the American capitalist system as it existed and urged blacks
to take an active role in it. Black capital accumulation was the key element
of his program.

Seventy years later, during the Black Power upsurge of the late 1960s,
many young nationalists simply revived the Washington strategy and
cloaked it in militantly anti-white rhetoric. Speaking for this Black Power
tendency, black social critic Harold Cruse debated Marxists in 1967, in the
following manner:

> When we speak of Negro social disabilities under capitalism, however, we
> refer to the fact that he does not own anything—even what is ownable in his
> own community. Thus to fight for black liberation is to fight for his right to
> own. The Negro is politically compromised today because he owns nothing.
> He has little voice in the affairs of state because he owns nothing. . . . Inside his
> own communities, he does not own the houses he lives in, the property he lives
> on, nor the wholesale and retail sources from which he buys his commodities.
> He does not own the edifices in which he enjoys culture and entertainment.[56]

Washington would have embraced Cruse enthusiastically. "The opportunity to earn a dollar in a factory is worth infinitely more than the opportunity to spend a dollar in an opera house," he told his followers. "No race
that has anything to contribute to the markets of the world is long in any
degree ostracized."[57]

The coming of Reaganism has given Booker T. Washington's "black capitalism" new relevance for national black political leaders. Suffering from
historical amnesia, they do not usually attribute their own political and

economic agendas to the Tuskegee accommodationist, but since they lack political ties with the socialist movement, past or present, most have uncritically readopted the Tuskegee "self-help" philosophy as their modus operandi. Rejecting socialism, and even European-style social democracy, many now espouse a "bootstraps" program to counter high black unemployment, plant closings, and social service reductions. The failure of socialism to develop ties to the black movement has opened the door to the right in the 1980s.

Across the country, interest in black private enterprise strategy increased as the 1982 recession deepened. In Buffalo, New York, for example, a group of blacks formed the Ferguson and Rhodes American Business Careers Institute to train blacks in entrepreneurial skills. The Institute's motto, "to help those who want to help themselves," clearly evokes the spirit of Tuskegee and the old Negro Business League.[58] The Rev. Jesse Jackson's Operation PUSH (People United to Save Humanity) pressured the Seven-Up Corporation to sign a $61 million commitment to invest capital in black-owned businesses in June 1982. The Seven-Up agreement called for $10 million for the creation of black-owned Seven-Up beverage wholesalerships, $5 million invested in black-owned life insurance companies, and another $4.35 million in advertisements in black-owned newspapers and radio stations. PUSH purchased 100 shares of stock in Chrysler, General Motors, Ford, and American Motors, in order to "assure us the right and the platform to voice our concern," according to Jackson.[59] Other black political leaders joined PUSH in proposing black alliances with capitalists.

In June 1982, New Orleans Mayor Dutch Morial told a US Black Chamber of Commerce meeting in San Francisco that "a strong line of communications with bankers [is] essential for the success of black businessmen." Former aide to Martin Luther King, Jr. and currently mayor of Atlanta, Andrew Young, suggested that the decisive integration battle of the 1980s would be "the desegregation of the money markets." Jesse Jackson, however, remained unsurpassed in his "evangelical advocacy" of black capitalism. At a gathering of the New Orleans Business League in July 1982, Jackson proclaimed, "We must move from Civil Rights to Silver Rights and from aid to trade." He urged black clergy to promote the development of small businesses among their congregations, declaring that "churches are financial institutions as well as soul-saving institutions." Jackson said, "Black America does more business with corporate America than Russia, China and Japan combined. Therefore, we want our share of opportunities for risks and rewards! There's something tricky and vicious about the way we're locked out of the private sector. . . . The marketplace is the arena for our development."[60]

Various civil rights organizations applauded Jackson's initiatives, and also emphasized the necessity for aggressive black economic programs. At the seventy-third national convention of the NAACP in Boston, *Black Enterprise* publisher Earl Graves warned the organization:

> We must learn to be more dependent on ourselves, economically and politically. We know by now that as black Americans we cannot depend solely on government. We cannot depend on anyone or anything outside ourselves to provide real economic opportunity or justice. We have been standing in the same station waiting for economic opportunity, watching train after train pass us by.[61]

Following Graves' address, NAACP delegates endorsed "Operation Fair Share," a campaign of nationwide boycotts against businesses that resist affirmative action efforts.

With the recessions of 1981 and 1982, NAACP leader Benjamin Hooks authorized the creation of an economics analysis unit and a task force to assist local branches to help black small entrepreneurs and unemployed black workers. In Kokomo, Indiana, NAACP members responded to Reagan cutbacks in food stamps by organizing a food cooperative, and in Galloway Township, New Jersey, they pressured local officials to set aside half of all new municipal jobs for blacks, women, and handicapped people. In Memphis, NAACP leaders persuaded the Nissan Corporation to buy supplies for its local automobile plant from black vendors.[62]

Even with its new "economic agenda," the NAACP is reluctant to develop a militant black capitalist program. When William Perry, the NAACP president of Miami, Florida, introduced a proposal for a "Black Monday"—a plan to have blacks and whites buy exclusively from black businesses on June 28, 1982—national officers were furious. Local whites in the NAACP strongly opposed the idea, and Earl Shinhoster, Southeastern Regional Director of the NAACP, sent a testy mailgram to Perry on June 23, suspending him "immediately and indefinitely." Perry's explanation that the Black Monday "was not intended to be a boycott, just a campaign to support black businesses" did not satisfy his organizational superiors. Shinhoster argued that "any unit of the NAACP is a subordinate unit to the national organization. Autonomy [of the local branch] only extends to issues that are within the scope of the organization." Hooks gave Perry "five days to explain what happened and why his suspension should not be made permanent." Meanwhile, Perry resigned as president and promptly organized an Operation PUSH chapter in Miami. Perry informed the *Miami Times* that Jesse Jackson and PUSH "provide its local units with more autonomy than the NAACP gives its branches."[63]

The Urban League continued in its role as the right wing of the black movement. When Reagan was elected, former League director Vernon Jordan made the most pathetic concessions to the conservative trend. Reagan deserved "the benefit of the doubt," and it was "dangerous," in Jordan's words, to criticize him. Jordan was willing to wait and see whether "equality can be achieved by conservative means, to look at conservative approaches to see if they will help black people." Jordan's successor, John E. Jacob, moved the organization only slightly to the left. Jacob denounced the recent draft report of the Department of Housing and Urban Development which called for an end to federal aid to inner cities. He revived a 20-year-old proposal develop by former League director Whitney Young which called for "massive federal efforts" combined with "local public-private sector efforts" to retard unemployment and urban decay. Jacob called for joint Democratic and Republican Party efforts to encourage "investments in human capital, urban infrastructure, and economic resources needed to get the national economy moving again."[64]

In Philadelphia, on June 9, 1982, the "Hire One Youth" program was launched by the Rev. Leon Sullivan, chairperson of the Opportunities Industrialization Centers (OICs). The stated goal of "Hire One Youth" was to encourage the private sector to hire 300,000 "disadvantaged young people" during the summer and an additional 700,000 youths by the middle of 1983. "I am appealing to the patriotism of American companies, large and small, in this critical and urgent time of need to put the youth of America back to work," Sullivan explained to the press. "Immediate bipartisan action on the part of President Reagan, the Congress, and the private sector is necessary." Behind Sullivan's appeal for jobs was an omnipresent threat of urban rebellion. "America must act now to put the unemployed youth in jobs before chaos and disorder erupt in our cities," Sullivan said bluntly. "The unemployed youth problem is social dynamite and it is about to explode." Sullivan reminded corporations that a $3,000 tax credit was available to all employers who hired Vietnam-era veterans, cooperative education students, involuntarily terminated CETA workers, and teenagers from "economically disadvantaged" areas. "If every American corporation, business, school . . . puts just one [youth] to work, we can get idle youth off the streets and into the productive mainstream of the American workforce."

Sullivan's program instantly won the support of a broad segment of both political parties and corporations. A number of urban mayors, including Andrew Young of Atlanta, Bill Green of Philadelphia, Jane Byrne of Chicago, Coleman Young of Detroit, Marion Barry of Washington, DC, and Tom Bradley of Los Angeles, endorsed "Hire One Youth." Conservative political forces, including the US Chamber of Commerce, Reagan's "Task Force for Private Sector Initiatives," and Republican Governor James Thompson of Illinois, publicly supported the effort. The Seven-Up Corporation agreed to pay for Sullivan's advertising and public relations costs. For all the media hype and political support, it seems unlikely that the effort will generate more than one-fifth of the number of permanent jobs it seeks. Sullivan's OIC was a product of Lyndon Johnson's Great Soci-

ety programs. From 1964–1980, the OIC network of job training and industrial education programs received more than $500 million in federal
funds. According to one source, only 13 percent of those trained in the
Philadelphia OIC were working in training related jobs. Many of the OICs
nationwide "suffer from mismanagement and poor program performance."
Under heavy criticism since the mid-1970s, Rev. Sullivan authored the so-
called "Sullivan Principles," which provide loose guidelines to justify continued US corporate investment in apartheid South Africa. Like the
Tuskegee accommodationist, Sullivan has been a useful tool for both the
Republican Party and US corporate interests in a number of ways. For example, in early 1981, Sullivan testified before the Senate Foreign Relations
Committee in support of former Secretary of State Alexander Haig. The
anti-communist general was "necessary for America," Sullivan declared.
Since the mid-1970s, Gulf Oil and other major corporations have funneled
tens of thousand of dollars to Sullivan. It would appear, given Sullivan's
checkered history, that "Hire One Youth" was less a strategy to end black
joblessness than a program to pacify the black ghetto while maintaining the
process of capital accumulation within black America.[65]

In October 1980, two important aides to the late Martin Luther King, Jr.
endorsed Reagan—the Reverend Ralph David Abernathy and Georgia
State Representative (D) Hosea Williams. Williams said his support for
Reagan was justified because "the mounting KKK's violent activities
against blacks all across the country" were indirectly a product of the
Carter Administration. Appearing with South Carolina segregationist
Strom Thurmond, in December 1980, Williams and Abernathy announced
that they were "for the Republican platform" and supported the bizarre
suggestion that Thurmond, once a presidential candidate of the Dixiecrat
Party, serve as "a liaison officer between Republicans on behalf of minorities." As loyal members of what one journalist termed "Strom Thurmond's
Black Kitchen Cabinet," Williams and Abernathy received a "letter of introduction" from Reagan for a black trade mission to Japan in June 1982.
They met with Prime Minster Zenko Suzuki and Japanese business leaders
"to promote Japanese investments in the US by offering tax incentives to
businesses that invest in joint Japanese-Afro-American ventures." The 17-
day trade mission sparked some "interest and curiosity" among Japanese
corporations, which admitted that they had "never considered establishing
a joint-venture factory in the US with either black or white businessmen."
The entire effort may have been futile, however, because on Williams' return he was sentenced to serve one year in a Georgia penitentiary for numerous traffic violations and for fleeing the scene of an accident in 1981.[66]

The pro-capitalist economic initiatives of black managers in the private
sector have ranged from "conservative" to simply absurd. A good representative of their tendency is Joe Black, a Vice President of the Greyhound

Corporation. In July 1982, Black condemned unemployed black youth for not understanding the "thrust of the Civil Rights Movement." "Too many of them have chosen to be guided by emotion and want to believe that it was to prove that black can beat white or mistakenly think that we were to receive something just because we're black." In Black's opinion, it was time for "black adults" to "have the intestinal fortitude to tell youthful blacks that they are spending too much time worrying about the word—'racism.' When we were young, we called it 'prejudice,' 'segregation' and 'jim crow,' but we did not spend our time worrying about it." Racism was not the reason that black unemployment was at an all-time high: "Too often black college students select 'sop' courses rather than those studies that will make them competitive in today's labor market." Like Hoover Institution Professor Thomas Sowell and other black conservative economists, Black suggested that blacks' ignorance and inadequate training were to blame for their lack of employment opportunities.[67]

What almost no civil rights leader, corporate manager, or black politician comprehends is that the current economic plight of African-Americans is an integral part of a worldwide crisis of capitalism. Reaganism, its British counterpart, Thatcherism, and the conservative fiscal policies of Japan, West Germany, and other capitalist countries have escalated unemployment throughout the West. Total unemployment in all Western countries has soared from 10 million in 1971–72 to a projected 31 million by the end of 1982. Reagan's July 1, 1982, "tax cut" did not increase US corporate investment or consumer spending. Conversely, European basic industries, such as shipbuilding, steel, and petrochemicals, are "all in deep trouble," according to the *Wall Street Journal*. British unemployment exceeds 13 percent, and even Japanese unemployment is at a post–World War II record. The Western crisis in capital accumulation has forced pay cuts in workers' salaries in virtually every nation. In 1980, the average West German worker, for example, received $12.26 an hour; last year, the average salary was $10.47. In the US a similar process of capitalist austerity has occurred. Average wage increases in the first contract year for settlements made by unions covering plants of at least 1,000 workers declined from 11.8 percent in April–June 1981 to 2.2 percent in January–March 1982. The result for US black workers was entirely predictable: official adult unemployment above 18 percent; black youth unemployment, 58 percent; the projected failure of over 20 percent of all black-owned businesses in 1982 alone.[68]

The recession of 1982 illustrates with painful clarity the essential political bankruptcy of black middle class "leaders" and organizations. Unable and unwilling to advance a socialist reorganization of America's political economy, they rely on corporate paternalism and "self-help efforts," which have all been tried previously without success. Responding to the economic desperation of the black working class and poor, they offer rhetoric more suitable to the age of Washington. Without a coherent anti-capitalist alternative, it appears likely that no meaningful solution to the long-term crisis of black underdevelopment will be achieved. The distance between the black movement and the socialist vision has actually widened and may continue to do so for the next period.

None of the political problems posed here can be resolved quickly. White democratic socialists still seldom respect or even comprehend the African-American's legitimate claim to a unique national identity, culture, and tradition of struggle. White Marxists often tend to idealize the black community, ignoring tendencies toward compromise and accommodation found not only among the black elite but also within the working class. White social democrats seem to ignore racism entirely, or simply reduce it solely to a question of class. On the other side of the color line, many blacks from different classes and for various reasons of self-interest oppose socialist politics within the black community. Narrow nationalists hate Marxism because they don't trust radical whites; black entrepreneurs hate Marxism because it threatens black private capital accumulation; black politicians hate Marxism because they are committed to some form of liberal Keynesianism to conservative capitalism; and black preachers hate Marxism because it's atheistic. All of these anti-socialist sentiments are reinforced by conservative tendencies within black civil society and by the continued manifestations of racism by white workers, labor unions, and white "progressives."

We need to understand the theoretical and practical relationship between race and class. The place to begin, I believe, is with black revolutionary socialist C.L.R. James. In his truly wonderful account of the Haitian Revolution, *The Black Jacobins,* James make a comment which strikes me as the initial step toward resolving the paradox: "The race question is subsidiary to the class question in politics, and to think of imperialism in terms of race is disastrous. But to neglect the racial factor as merely incidental is an error only less grave than to make it fundamental."[69]

NOTES

1. W.E.B. Du Bois, "Problem Literature," *Crisis* 8 (August 1914): 195–196.

2. Part of the rationale for some black nationalists' fears that Marxism is a form of "left-wing racism" must be attributed to the writings of Marx himself. Marx's vicious statements about German socialist leader Ferdinand Lassalle were both racist and anti-Semitic: "It is now quite clear to me that, as shown by the shape of [Lassalle's] head and . . . hair, that he is descended from the negroes who joined the flight of Moses from Egypt (unless his mother or grandmother . . . were crossed with a nigger). This union of Jew and German on a negro foundation was bound to produce something out of the ordinary. The importunity of the fellow is also ne-

groid." David McLellan, *Karl Marx: His Life and Thought* (New York: Harper and Row, 1973), p. 322.

In Marx's letter to Friedrich Engels, dated June 14, 1853, he argued, in a comparison between black Jamaicans and slaves in the US, that the former "always consisted of newly imported barbarians," whereas Afro-Americans are "becoming a native product, more or less Yankeefied, English speaking, etc., and there *fit for emancipation.*" See Marx-Engels correspondence reprinted in Shlomo Avineri, ed., *Karl Marx on Colonialism and Modernization* (Garden City: Anchor Books, 1969), p. 454.

At one point, Marx described Mexicans as "*les derniers des hommes.*" Engels was even worse. In one work he asserted that "the Germans were a highly gifted Aryan branch" of humanity, an "energetic stock" who have the "physical and intellectual power to subdue, absorb, and assimilate its ancient eastern neighbors. Obviously, it may be unfair to judge the founders of historical materialism by the standards of the late twentieth century. But these and many other blatantly racist statements by the early proponents of socialism must give pause to many contemporary would-be black leftists. See M.M. Bober, *Karl Marx's Interpretation of History* (New York: W.W. Norton, 1965), pp. 69–70.

3. In the election of 1892, Watson drafted the Populist Party's platform on a united front between black and white farmers. "You are kept apart that you may be separately fleeced of your earnings. You are made to hate each other," Watson declared, "because upon that hatred is rested the keystone of the arch of financial despotism which enslaves you both." Biographer C. Vann Woodward declares that "Watson was perhaps the first native white Southern leader of importance to treat the Negro's aspirations with the seriousness that human strivings deserve." With the collapse of Populism, Watson turned to racism and anti-Semitism with gusto. By 1904 he favored the abandonment of the Fifteenth Amendment. In 1910 he bragged that he would no more hesitate to lynch a "nigger" than to shoot a mad dog. Even Booker T. Washington, the model of Negro accommodation, was too radical for Watson. He closed a racist diatribe against the black educator with the statement: "What does Civilization owe the negro? Nothing! Nothing! NOTHING!!!" See C. Vann Woodward, *Tom Watson: Agrarian Rebel* (New York: Oxford University Press, 1970), pp. 220–221, 374, 380, 432–433.

4. Angela Davis, *Women, Race, and Class* (New York: Random House, 1981), p. 51.

5. Ibid., pp. 70–71.

6. Ibid., pp. 212–215.

7. David Herreshoff, *The Origins of American Marxism: From the Transcendentalists to De Leon* (New York: Monad, 1973), pp. 17–18, 31–32, 39–47. Also see Arthur M. Schlesinger, "Orestes Brownson, American Marxist Before Marx," *Sewanee Review* 47 (July-September 1939): 317–323.

8. The classical statement of American economic determinist thought is Charles A. Beard's *An Economic Interpretation of the Constitution of the United States* (New York: Macmillan, 1913). Of some interest is Beard's introduction to the 1935 edition of his seminal study. Beard admitted that he was "interested in Marx when I discovered in his works the ideas which had been cogently expressed by outstanding thinkers and statesmen." However, he denounced the widely held view that his writ-

ing was influenced by Marx. Of Marxist views, he declared, "have I the least concern. I have never believed that 'all history' can or must be 'explained' in economic terms, or any other terms."

9. Albert Fried, ed., *Socialism in America* (Garden City: Anchor, 1970), p. 387.

10. Herreshoff, *The Origins of American Marxism,* pp. 159, 168–169.

11. Ibid., pp. 127, 148, 159, 169.

12. Du Bois, "The Socialists," *Crisis* 1 (March 1911): 15.

13. Du Bois, "A Field for Socialists," *New Review* (January 11, 1913): 54–57. Also see Du Bois, "Socialism and the Negro Problem," *New Review* 1 (February 1, 1913): 138–141.

14. Du Bois, *The Autobiography of W.E.B. Du Bois* (New York: International Publishers, 1968), pp. 218, 260. Mary White Ovington was among the few white socialists in the early 1900s to make the cause of racial equity central to their vision of a socialist society. See Ovington, "Vacation Days on San Juan Hill—A New York Negro Colony," *Southern Workman* 38 (November 1909): 627–634; Ovington, "The Negro in the Trade Unions in New York," *Annals of the American Academy of Political and Social Science* 27 (June 1906): 551–558; Ovington, "The National Association for the Advancement of Colored People," *Journal of Negro History* 9 (April 1924): 107–116.

15. Fried, ed., *Socialism in America,* p. 386.

16. Milton Cantor, *The Divided Left: American Radicalism, 1900–1975* (New York: Hill and Wang, 1978), p. 14.

17. Philip S. Foner, *Organized Labor and the Black Worker, 1619–1973* (New York: International Publishers, 1974), pp. 175–176. Du Bois denounced Frey's "awkward and insincere defense of the color line in the A.F. of L." in "Postscript," *Crisis* 36 (July 1929): 242.

18. Ibid., pp. 162, 191–195, 209; and Cantor, *The Divided Left,* pp. 15, 122. A valuable source on the rise of black participation in the US Communist Party is Mark I. Solomon, "Red and Black: Negroes and Communism, 1929–1932" (Ph.D. dissertation, Harvard University, 1972).

19. Foner, *Organized Labor and the Black Worker,* pp. 278–280.

20. Du Bois, "The Negro Mind Reaches Out," in *The New Negro,* ed. Alain Locke (New York: Atheneum, 1977, reprint of 1925 edition), p. 407.

21. Foner, *Organized Labor and the Black Worker,* pp. 52, 53, 103.

22. August Meier, *Negro Thought in America, 1880–1915* (Ann Arbor: University of Michigan Press, 1963), pp. 46–47; Seth M. Scheiner, "Early Career of T. Thomas Fortune, 1879–1890," *Negro History Bulletin* 28 (April 1964): 170–172. Fortune eventually came under the hegemony of Booker T. Washington's "Tuskegee Machine," renounced many of his leftist views, and quietly receded into political oblivion. See Emma Lou Thornbrough, "More Light on Booker T. Washington and the *New York Age,*" *Journal of Negro History* 43 (January 1958): 34–49; and August Meier, "Booker T. Washington and the Negro Press," *Journal of Negro History* 38 (January 1953): 68–82.

23. Albert Fried describes Lucy Parsons as "a dark-skinned Mexican" in the collection he edited, *Socialism in America,* p. 187.

24. See Carolyn Asbaugh, *Lucy Parsons: American Revolutionary* (Chicago: Charles H. Kerr, 1976).

25. Meier, *Negro Thought in America, 1880–1915*, pp. 203–204.

26. Wilfred D. Samuels, "Hubert H. Harrison and 'The New Negro Manhood Movement,'" *Afro-Americans in New York Life and History* 5 (January 1981): 29–41; Manning Marable, *From the Grassroots: Social and Political Essays Towards Afro-American Liberation* (Boston: South End Press, 1980), pp. 59–85.

27. Angelo Herndon, *Let Me Live* (New York: Arno Press, 1969, reprint of the 1937 edition), pp. iii–x, 77, 80, 82–83, 186–187.

28. Meier, *Negro Thought in America, 1880–1915*, pp. 142, 180, 186–187.

29. Du Bois, "To Black Voters," *Horizon* 3 (February 1908): 17–18. Also see Du Bois' 1911 editorial "Christmas Gift," *Crisis* 3 (December 1911). Du Bois repeats the assertion that the Socialist Party "is the only party which openly recognizes Negro manhood. Is it not time for black voters to carefully consider the claims of this party?"

30. Du Bois, "Along the Color Line" *Crisis* 2 (October 1911): 227–233.

31. Du Bois, "Postscript," *Crisis* 34 (August 1927): 203–204.

32. Du Bois, "The Battle of Europe," *Crisis* 12 (September 1916): 217–218.

33. Du Bois, "The World Last Month," *Crisis* 13 (March 1917).

34. Du Bois, "The Negro and Radical Thought," *Crisis* 22 (July 1921): 204.

35. Du Bois, *Autobiography*, pp. 29–30.

36. Du Bois, "Russia, 1926," *Crisis* 33 (November 1926).

37. Du Bois, "Forward," *Crisis* 18 (September 1919): 235.

38. Du Bois, "Postscript," *Crisis* 39 (June 1932): 191.

39. Du Bois, *Autobiography*, pp. 31–32.

40. Isaac Deutscher, *Stalin: A Political Biography* (New York: Oxford University Press, 1949), pp. 345–385.

41. See Robert C. Tucker, ed., *Stalinism: Essays in Historical Interpretation* (New York: W.W. Norton, 1977).

42. W.E.B. Du Bois, "Colonialism and the Russian Revolution," *New World Review* (November 1956): 18–22; Du Bois, "The Stalin Era," *Masses and Mainstream* 10 (January 1957): 1–5; Du Bois, "The Dream of Socialism," *New World Review* (November 1959): 14–17.

43. A representative sample of literature by recent black revolutionary nationalists, Marxist-Leninists, and democratic socialists includes Angela Davis, *Angela Davis: An Autobiography* (New York: Random House, 1974); Davis, *Women, Race, and Class;* Robert Allen, *Black Awakening in Capitalist America: An Analytic History* (Garden City: Anchor, 1969); James Foreman, *The Making of Black Revolutionaries* (New York: Macmillan, 1972); William Sales, "New York City: Prototype of the Urban Crisis," *Black Scholar* 7 (November 1975): 20–39; William Strickland, "Whatever Happened to the Politics of Black Liberation?" *Black Scholar* 7 (October 1975): 20–26; Damu I. Smith, "The Upsurge of Police Repression: An Analysis," *Black Scholar* 12 (January-February 1981): 35–37; John Conyers, "The Economy Is the Issue, Planning for Full Employment," *Freedomways* 17 (Spring 1977): 71–78; Ronald Dellums, "Black Leadership: For Change or for Status Quo?" *Black Scholar* 8 (January-February 1977): 2–5; Julian Bond, *A Time to Speak, a Time to Act* (New York: Simon and Schuster, 1972).

44. Herndon, *Let Me Live*, pp. 80, 114–115. Herndon's own writing is also filled with religious symbols and overtones. On pages 82–83, he denounces Du Bois, who

was not yet a Communist, and black Chicago Congressperson Oscar De Priest as "the tools and the lickspittles of the white ruling class. They speak with the sweet voice of Jacob, but they extend the hairy hand of Esau."

45. Nell Irvin Painter, *The Narrative of Hosea Hudson: His Life as a Negro Communist in the South* (Cambridge: Harvard University Press, 1979), pp. xiii, 23, 24, 133–135. Also see Hosea Hudson, *Black Worker in the Deep South* (New York: International Publishers, 1972).

46. John Hope Franklin, *From Slavery to Freedom* (New York: Random House, 1969), pp. 318–321; Meier, *Negro Thought in America, 1880–1915*, p. 46.

47. Alfred A. Moss, Jr., *The American Negro Academy: Voice of the Talented Tenth* (Baton Rouge: Louisiana State University Press, 1981), pp. 145–146.

48. Allen, *Black Awakening in Capitalist America*, pp. 100–101. As Allen puts it, "Garvey took Washington's economic program, clothed it in militant nationalist rhetoric, and built an organization which in its heyday enjoyed the active support of millions of black people."

49. Ibid., p. 250.

50. Ibid., pp. 250–251.

51. Manning Marable, *Blackwater: Historical Studies in Race, Class Consciousness, and Revolution* (Dayton: Black Praxis Press, 1981), p. 110.

52. Du Bois, *Dusk of Dawn*, p. 205.

53. Du Bois, *Autobiography*, p. 126.

54. Ibid., pp. 215–217.

55. Ibid., p. 228.

56. Harold Cruse, *Rebellion or Revolution* (New York: William Morrow, 1968), pp. 238–239.

57. Meier, *Negro Thought in America, 1880–1915*, p. 101.

58. "Area's First Minority-Owned Business Institute Established," *Buffalo Challenger*, 28 July 1982.

59. "PUSH Scores Again: 7-Up Agrees to Invest Money in 'Black Business': Auto Industries Next!" *Buffalo Challenger*, 21 July 1982. The major corporations are, of course, eager to provide token amounts of capital to the black middle class, if in doing so they increase their representative shares of the $125 billion black consumer market. In June 1982, Anheuser-Busch announced that it would spend $1 million in black-owned newspaper advertising. A black vice president of Anheuser-Busch made the pledge before a meeting of black publishers in Baltimore. "We are committed to the economic development of those companies which are owned and operated by minorities. [We] will expand the number of minority suppliers and contractors with whom we do business. Black support our products," he stated, "and [we] need to communicate to [black] consumers how much we appreciate their support." "Anheuser-Busch to Spend $1 Million with black newspapers," *San Antonio Register*, 1 July 1982.

60. "PUSH Leader Says We Must Move to Silver Rights and to Trade," *Omaha Star*, 22 July 1982.

61. Tony Brown, "Kennedy: Trumped-Up White Liberal," *Buffalo Challenger*, 21 July 1982.

62. Diane E. Lewis, "Is the NAACP in Step or Out?" *Boston Globe*, 28 June 1982; "NAACP Attacks Reagan, Backs Liberal Democrats," *Guardian*, 21 July

1982.

63. "William Perry Suspended from NAACP," *Miami Times,* 15 July 1982; Marable, *Blackwater,* p. 160.

64. John E. Jacob, "Formulating Urban Policy," Fort Lauderdale *Westside Gazette,* 8 July 1982; Sheila Rule, "Urban League Asks for US Jobs Plan," *New York Times,* 2 August 1982.

65. Marable, *Blackwater,* pp. 154, 165; "OIC Announces Youth Hiring Program," Fort Lauderdale *Westside Gazette,* 8 July 1982.

66. Marable, *Blackwater,* pp. 156–157, 160; "Black Trade Mission to Japan Succesful," *Pensacola Voice,* 19–25 July 1982.

67. Joe Black, "By the Way . . . ," *Buffalo Challenger,* 14 July 1982.

68. "Unemployment on the Rise Across the Western World," *San Francisco Chronicle,* 11 May 1982; Anthony Mazzocchi, "It's Time for Management Concessions," *New York Times,* 27 June 1982; Daniel Yergin, "Umemployment: The Outlook Is Grim," *New York Times,* 13 July 1982; Lauri McGinley, "Joblessness Rise Shows Economy Is Getting Worse," *Wall Street Journal,* 10 May 1982; Art Pine, "Europeans Pessimistic as Recession Appears Deep, Hard to Reverse," *Wall Street Journal,* 10 May 1982.

69. C.L.R. James, *The Black Jacobins: Toussaint L'Ouverture and the San Domingo Revolution* (New York: Vintage, 1963), p. 283.

Black Politics and the
Challenges of the Left

In the 1980s, there were two fundamental responses by African-Americans to the economic and social crisis generated by Reaganism. Their first was represented at the local level by the mayoral campaigns of Harold Washington in Chicago and Mel King in Boston, and at the national level by the Rainbow presidential campaigns of Jesse Jackson in 1984 and 1988. These electoral campaigns were the products of democratic social protest movements, the consequence of thousands of protests against plant closings, cutbacks in housing, health care, and jobs, racial discrimination in the courts, and political process at the local level. The Jackson campaigns were a revolt against both Reaganism in the Republican Party and the capitulation of the Democratic Party to the repressive policies of the Reagan administration. In capitalist societies with parliamentary governments, the Rainbow campaign would have been expressed as a multiracial, left social democratic party, a political formation calling for the state to eliminate racial discrimination and disparities of income between people of color and whites and to expand federal expenditures for human needs, employment, and education. Jackson's discourse was grounded in a tradition of resistance and the previous struggles against Jim Crow, a heritage which defined politics not simply as an electoral phenomena, but as the struggle for power on a variety of fronts. In effect, the Rainbow campaign called for a progressive social contract, a positive relationship between the people and the state which would guarantee full employment, universal health care, and housing; safeguard civil rights; and create the material and social conditions for a more democratic and egalitarian order.

The black petty bourgeoisie supported Jackson's effort along with the African-American working class and the unemployed, but for different reasons. The poor and working class had been hit with a severe deterioration of wages, the expansion of drug traffic in their neighborhoods, and the collapse in public transportation systems, health care, and social infrastructure. Voting for Jackson was a protest against Reaganism, racism, and the political domination of the two-party system. The black middle strata mobilized for different reasons. In the period 1979–87, African-American managers and professionals actually had larger income increases than whites with identical educational backgrounds and vocations. (Conversely, the rate of income growth for blacks in all other vocational categories was much lower than that of whites.) Much of the gain to this new professional/managerial stratum had come from affirmative action policies of the federal government. More than half of all black college graduates have jobs tied directly to public-sector spending. Reaganism represented a very real threat to the fragile gains of the middle class elite. The Democratic Party's failure to vigorously contest cutbacks in economic set-asides for nonwhite entrepreneurs, the nonenforcement of affirmative action and equal opportunity legislation, and the destruction of the Civil Rights Commission also alienated and outraged most middle class blacks. They saw Jackson as a symbolic advocate of their own interests.

In the quarter century since the passage of the historic Voting Rights Act of 1965, the number of black elected officials has soared from 100 to 6,700. The overwhelming majority of these are elected from majority black constituencies. The principal reason for this is that most whites simply will not vote for a black candidate, regardless of his/her political program, party affiliation, or personality. This means that in virtually all cases, African-Americans never consider running for statewide offices or in congressional or mayoral races in which whites constitute more than 60 percent of the electorates. Consequently, since middle class black politicians look to black workers and the unemployed for votes, they are usually forced to articulate a social democratic–style agenda to win popular support. Their own immediate class interests are not fully served because the weight of the black petty bourgeoisie is very small compared to that of other classes within the black community.

The second response to the economic and social crisis is a form of electoral accommodationism. "Accommodation" is historically a gradualistic response within African-American politics which seeks reforms by cooperation with the white corporate establishment, collaboration with the more conservative elements of the major parties, and an advocacy of private self-help and the development of a minority entrepreneurial stratum. Booker T. Washington was the architect of accommodation during the era of Jim Crow, the first prominent advocate of "black capitalism." Nearly a century later, in a period of expanding racial segregation and manifestations of racist violence, in a political context of pessimism and defeat for the black left, and in the social chaos spawned by drugs and the decay of social institutions, the political space for a new type of accommodationism has developed. The new accommodationists seek to articulate the interests of sections of the white middle class and corporate interests, rather than the black community. The accommodationist reformers still use the discourse of the civil rights movement, but lack any political commitment to civil disobedience or disruptive activities to achieve more equal rights and economic justice for the black working class. Unlike Booker T. Washington, this new leadership of the black middle class does not have to embrace legal racial segregation to win white support, but it does have to espouse a compromising approach to black political and economic development and to do nothing to challenge the brutal class oppression and social deterioration in the urban ghetto. This neo-accommodationist approach can be described as "post-black politics."

The November 1989 elections of David Dinkins as New York City's mayor and Douglas Wilder as Governor of Virginia symbolize this second approach, despite the fact that both victories have been widely applauded as triumphs over American racism. To be sure, Dinkins is a progressive Democrat on many issues, and no doubt he is preferable to both former mayor Ed Koch and the Republican candidate in the general election, Rudolph Giuliani. The more moderate Wilder was clearly superior to the anti-reproductive rights, conservative demagogue he opposed in Virginia's gubernatorial election. However, neither election represented a fundamental advance for the masses of black working class and poor people, nor advanced a progressive or left social democratic strategy which might push the boundaries of bourgeois politics to the left.

Both candidates, and especially Wilder, ran essentially mainstream-oriented campaigns, rather than constructing broad-based coalitions of black, Latino, and white workers, liberals, and leftists, on the model of Harold Washington's campaign. Both had recognized years ago that their own electoral constituencies of African-Americans were too small to provide the necessary core for successful bids to high office. Over a decade, they cultivated political records which would place them well within the moderate mainstreams of their respective political cultures in order to appeal to white liberal to centrist constituencies.

This was especially the case with Wilder. After the mid-1970s he effectively remade himself in the image of the classical Southern patriarch—conservative, pro-corporate, anticrime, and abundantly safe. He couldn't cross the color line personally, but he would do so in terms of his political image. So Wilder sought to become a Southern version of Los Angeles mayor Thomas Bradley, a moderately conservative politician who was "post-black"—beyond identification with race. Wilder reversed his opposition to the death penalty. He backed away from his earlier advocacy of granting the District of Columbia full statehood rights, which in effect would place two African-Americans into the US Senate. Moving away from liberal Keynesianism in economic policy, Wilder opposed any changes in Virginia's rigid "right to work" laws, which prohibit compulsory membership in unions within individual businesses.

After four terms in Virginia's Senate, Wilder was successfully elected Lieutenant Governor, the state's second highest office, in 1985. Almost immediately speculation began concerning his chances for governor, since Virginia prohibits incumbent governors from seeking reelection. One of Wilder's chief difficulties was maintaining his natural base among the African-American electorate, which had strongly supported the insurgent presidential campaigns of Jesse Jackson in both 1984 and 1988, while reassuring white voters that he was just as conservative and pro-business as any Southern white politician. Wilder placed one foot in each of two dramatically divergent political cultures, recognizing that both were necessary for him to achieve his goal. He praised Jackson personally, but took pains to distinguish the charismatic campaigner's liberal-left agenda from his own. He defused the critics by suggesting, somewhat falsely, that Jackson's electoral mobilization represented symbolism without substance. "Jesse runs to inspire," Wilder observed. "I run to win."[1]

The political terrain of New York permitted Dinkins to assume a more liberal ideological posture than Wilder's. Nevertheless, he made several strategic political compromises to secure the support of the white upper middle class, and especially Jewish voters who had supported neoconservative mayor Ed Koch in the Democratic primaries. Dinkins distanced himself from Jackson politically, and reminded white voters that he had denounced black nationalist leader Louis Farrakhan. Dinkins' lieutenants shunned efforts by Brooklyn's Arab-American Democratic Club to hold a fund-raising event, for fear of alienating the Jewish electorate. Campaign manager Bill Lynch told Arab-American leaders "not to seek to be visibly associated with the candidate," but Dinkins staffers added that they would still accept their financial contributions. In effect, New York City's Arab-American community of 100,000 was disavowed by a "liberal" who had worked closely with them in the past.[2] After his election, Dinkins and his associates refused to honor promises of appointments to several black progressives and nationalists who had been pivotal in mobilizing African-American voters.

Rather than denying the reality of race, Wilder and Dinkins sought to "transcend" the color line, offering generous platitudes of how racism had supposedly declined in significance during the 1980s. The problem with this perspective is that all the evidence suggests that white voters still remain highly race conscious, far more so than African-Americans or Latinos. Since black Democrats can never hope to escape the burden of racial prejudice entirely, they must address the issue squarely and without rhetorical subterfuge. The strategy of declaring victory against racial prejudice may produce some short-term victories, but it will only reinforce white supremacy within the electoral process in the long run.

A second, and paradoxical, problem challenges black political activists, community leaders, and civil rights advocates. They must now ask themselves, "What has the African-American electorate actually won?" Once safely in office, will Doug Wilder's administration actually produce more government jobs for Virginia's blacks, or a more aggressive affirmative action policy than that of the previous white Democratic governor? Will Wilder's conservative support for right to work laws advance the interests of African-American blue collar, semiskilled, and unemployed workers? How will a Wilder administration provide better health services, public welfare, and quality education to the most dispossessed classes when he campaigned specifically on a "no tax increase" platform?[3] Can Dinkins really empower the African-American and Hispanic neighborhoods at the expense of the corporations, real estate developers, and banks? How can Dinkins' economic and social policies really be significantly to the left of those of former mayor Ed Koch, when before the election, the black Democrat named Koch's former deputy mayor Nathan Leventhal to lead his transition team? With the exception of Dinkins' educational policy group, most of the transition planning team were clearly more conservative than the new mayor's electoral constituency.

The Dinkins-Wilder victories represent unique problems for both Jesse Jackson and more generally for the American left. Jackson's strategy in 1984 was essentially to build a broad-based coalition of forces representing roughly 80 percent of black America, combined with small fractions of the Latino, progressive white, and labor constituencies. Jackson stood for a liberal/black revolt against the failure of the Democratic Party to mount a strong opposition to the social devastation of Reaganism.

The 1988 Jackson campaign was different in many ways from the 1984 experience. First, it was much more an electoral effort than a social protest movement in electoral form. In 1984, the vast majority of black elected officials had opposed Jackson, or only belatedly embraced the Rainbow; in 1988, they were generally out front, and used their influence to steer the movement toward the safe boundaries of acceptable bourgeois politics. Consequently, the black nationalists, Marxists, gay and lesbian activists, left environmentalists, and others exercised less leverage in setting the Rainbow's agenda than they had previously. There was also a subtle change in Jackson, particularly in the wake of his stunning defeat of Dukakis in the March 1988 Michigan caucuses. The best evidence indicates that Jackson actually believed that he could be the Democratic Party's nominee, or failing this, that he might achieve the Vice Presidential nomination. Even people on the left argued that Jackson might pull off the electoral upset. Ron Daniels, the head of the Rainbow, was transferred to the electoral campaign. The Rainbow itself as a national independent political force was not developed, and today it remains a political shell rather than a viable formation.

When the inevitable occurred, and Dukakis got the nomination and shifted to the right, Jackson and the Rainbow were not prepared to advance a coherent program of critical support for the Democratic nominee, while developing their own apparatus to the left of the party. After the election, Ron Brown's promotion as head of the Democratic National Committee and the year-long speculation about Jackson's potential challenge to Marion Barry in Washington's mayoral race indicate that even the more progressive elements of the black leadership placed their individual upward mobility ahead of the empowerment of the black masses as a whole.

Both the Democratic Socialists of America and the Communist Party, in different ways, have pursued a strategy of moving American politics to the left by working with Democratic Party liberals. The hope has been to polarize the Democrats in such a manner that either the conservatives (e.g., Sam Nunn, Charles Robb, Lloyd Bentsen) purge the left, or the liberals force out the right. We have to recognize that neither of these options exhausts the possibilities. Most of us have not anticipated an ideological shift among many African-American or Latino politicians, using racial solidarity rhetoric to ensure minority voter loyalty, but gradually embracing more moderate to conservative public policy positions, especially on economic issues.

But the left must establish an independent identity, organizationally and programmatically. An inside-outside strategy which supports progressive Democrats must also be prepared to run candidates for public office against both Democrats and Republicans, especially in municipal and congressional races. The left must establish a network bringing together progressive local constituencies around projects which define politics as a struggle for empowerment, not just in electoral terms. It must recruit the thousands of young people who were politically developed through the anti-apartheid mobilizations of the mid-1980s and involved in the Jackson campaign. At a minimum, such a network would require a statement of principles for operational unity, a national publication, and the local autonomy necessary for groups to engage in independent non-electoral, community-based struggles.

Along with the development of institutions, the left and the black move-ment must reassess the potential weaknesses and strengths of mounting yet another national presidential campaign behind Jackson. We need to be clear that Jackson will never be awarded the Democratic Party's presiden-tial nomination, even if he wins every primary and caucus. The rules will be changed to deny him victory—or even more drastic measures will be taken. Moreover, the Democratic Party will never be transformed into a left social democratic, much less socialist, formation. There is too much history, ideo-logical baggage, and domination by sectors of the ruling class for progres-sives to achieve a transformation from within. More than channeling our meager resources into a costly, labor-intensive national campaign, we des-perately need to reinforce our organizational capacity for non-electoral as well as electoral struggles at grassroots levels. Socialism and black libera-tion cannot be achieved merely by electing a socialist president. It requires the careful and difficult construction of 1,000 black, Latino, and progres-sive formations and local movements in cities, towns, and rural areas.

A socialist labor party in the traditional sense would be premature, at least at this point, but an effective network or loose progressive confedera-tion could accomplish much. But we cannot build consensus for social jus-tice and fundamental, structural changes within the political economy sim-ply by continuing to tail liberals, even those like Jackson. We must demand a greater political price from such politicians for our critical support; and if it is not forthcoming, we must be prepared to employ our resources else-where. The selection of the "lesser evil" election after election is in the long run self-defeating. We should engage in a "war of position," the building of the political culture and structures of radical democracy, not advocating traditional Keynesian liberalism. There will never be a distant "war of ma-neuver" against capital so long as American Marxists act like liberals, be-cause liberals will inevitably act like Republicans in order to get elected. A radical, democratic vision of social change, socialism from below, but in a popular discourse which the majority of blacks, Latinos, feminists, and the American working people readily understand, must inform our political practice and strategic decisions for the 1990s.

NOTES

1. Michael Oreskes, "Black Candidate in Virginia: Campaign Is Not a Crusade," *New York Times,* 3 November 1989. Also see B. Drummond Ayres, Jr., "Black Vir-ginia Politician Takes Run at History," *New York Times,* 16 April 1989; and Tom Wicker, "Drama in Virginia," *New York Times,* 3 November 1989.

2. James Zogby, "Dinkins Has Locked Arab Americans Out of His Campaign," *City Sun,* 18–24 October, 1989; Celestine Bohlen, "Arab Group Says Dinkins Shunned Their Bid to Help," *New York Times,* 19 October 1989; and Howard

Kurtz, "Arab Americans in New York Say Mayoral Nominees Spurn Support," *Washington Post,* 16 October 1989.

3. Immediately following his election, Wilder urged Democrats to move to the right ideologically and programmatically. Democratic presidential campaigns must support the "values of the overwhelming majority of the people in this country," including the "free enterprise system" and "holding the line on taxes." See Robin Toner, "Enter the Mainstream, Wilder Tells Democrats," *New York Times,* 14 November 1989.

24

Toward an American Socialism from Below: Beyond Stalinism and Social Democracy

The recent social turmoil in Eastern Europe, the Soviet Union, and China has symbolized for many the end of the socialist ideal. We are witnessing the death of the Communist system, as symbolized by the authoritarian, single-party regimes inspired by Stalin. We have entered a post-Leninist period of political change, requiring those who still call themselves "socialist" to rethink old dogmas, and to reconsider the meaning of socialism for the twentieth century and beyond, in both capitalist societies and state collectivist social formations.

Although Karl Marx's theoretical critique of capitalism helped to provide an economic analysis which informed the development of emerging working class movements in Europe a century ago, the critical weakness of Marxism was its lack of a coherent political strategy. The mass social democratic parties eventually gravitated toward a reformist perspective, favoring incremental reforms within the capitalist system. The great achievement of Lenin was the invigoration of Marxism as a militant strategy for proletarian power. He was convinced that the working class, by itself, would not transcend a trade union political consciousness and political reformism. A highly centralized, disciplined force was essential to achieve socialism, particularly in an autocratic society without democratic traditions.

Lenin's emphasis on the importance of a tightly organized, highly motivated party contributed to an underestimation of the authoritarian dimensions of this approach to socialist transformation. Without a firm guarantee to protect minority rights and the expression of diverse opinions, as well as the direct election and accountability of party leaders by the general membership, democratic centralism degenerates into a dictatorship.

What is commonly termed Stalinism has been the dominant authoritarian pattern of state development and rigid economic organization under the terminology of Marxism-Leninism in peripheral capitalist social formations, beginning with Russia in 1917. The essential characteristics of such regimes included extreme concentration of authority in the hands of an arrogant ruler and a privileged bureaucratic elite, the centralization of all economic decisions by the state, the absence of an independent legal structure of civil liberties, no separation between the Communist Party and the state apparatus, and severe persecution of anyone who dissents. Perhaps most fundamentally, Stalinism was distinguished by its reliance on extreme coercion as a normal or regular aspect of the implementation of public policies. As socialist scholar Issac Deutscher observed, "The root difference between Stalinism and the traditional Socialist outlook lay in their respective attitudes towards the role of force in the transformation of society." The gulags, forced labor, and the extensive secret police networks were not marginal or accidental, but essential to the character of Stalinist regimes.

Since the secret speech by Nikita S. Khruschev to the Communist Party's Twentieth Congress in 1956, Communists have attempted to separate themselves from the legacy of Stalinism. Theoretically, historians of the Left may attempt to continue to distinguish between the actual political record of Lenin himself, and his commitment to revolutionary democracy, and his Stalinist political descendants, from Ceausescu to Honecker in Eastern Europe, to Bernard Coard in Grenada and Menguistu in Ethiopia. But in actual practice, Leninism itself, including the theory of the vanguard party and the strategy of seizing power outlined in *State and Revolution,* is no longer viable.

Trotsky's famous prediction of nearly a century ago in his polemics against Lenin's concept of the party has been realized in country after country: "The party organization [substitutes] itself for the party as a whole; then the Central Committee." This is not to provide some type of historical justification for the political tradition of Trotskyism, or the theory of the Permanent Revolution. Gramsci's complaint about Trotsky, that he was "a cosmopolitan—i.e., superficially national and superficially Western or European," can be amplified toward his political theories. Nevertheless, his basic instinct on the potential tyranny within the abuse of democratic centralism remains valid.

End of Illusions

During the 1960s and early 1970s in the United States, thousands of activists who came from the Black Liberation movement, and struggles generated by anti–Vietnam War activism, feminism, trade unionism, Latino, gay-lesbian, and other social contradictions, became attracted to Marxism-Leninism. We saw in the examples of Cuba, Grenada, Guinea-Bissau, Nicaragua, and Vietnam the elements of what might be realized within a socialist America. We struggled against dogmatic, "race-based" nationalism and sexism within the African-American and Latino movements, calling for the utilization of a class analysis. We advocated the development of Left formations or parties within this country which would employ key elements of the Leninist organizational model, because we were convinced that this approach would promote the building of anti-capitalist politics throughout the society.

In this process, many of us frequently tended to employ a political discourse and style which were not grounded in the political culture and organizational histories of the American working class or national minorities, but informed more by what we read or had personally seen in Communist or socialist states. Even those of us who were not Maoists in the 1960s and 1970s, for example, could not be untouched by what seemed to be examples of revolutionary democracy inside China during the Cultural Revolution.

The end of these illusions began a decade ago, when the massive crimes of the murderous Pol Pot regime in Cambodia became apparent to the world. It was difficult even for American Maoists to deny the reality of more than one million deaths and the dictatorial social engineering which dispersed the country's urban populace into the countryside's collective farms. For me, a decisive political turning point came with the murder of Maurice Bishop and the collapse of the New Jewel Movement in Grenada. Bernard Coard's version of Marxism—a contempt for the will of the Grenadian masses, the utilization of terror, military coercion, and murder, the control and manipulation of the mass organizations—seemed to represent a cruel distortion of the vibrant democratic ideals of revolutionary socialism. In Africa, some of the most repressive and anti-democratic regimes on the continent became identified with Marxism, among them the brutal dictatorship of Sekou Toure in Guinea. Inside the Soviet Union itself, the Brezhnev years culminated in a dreary despotism of party privilege, the suppression of dissent, and the absence of human rights.

Social democrats and not a few revolutionary socialists dealt with the vast chasm between Marxist rhetoric and reality by hastily denying that Communist states merited the term "socialist." State collectivism or "state capitalism" was not "real" socialism, despite the stated connections between Marx and Lenin with the official ideologies of such regimes. The problem with this formulation was its historical dishonesty. The political lineage between Lenin, Stalin, Mao and Pol Pot was historically real, despite the fact that Lenin's revolutionary democracy had little directly in common with the senseless brutality and appetite for slaughter of the Khmer Rouge.

Three generations of the active suppression of the American Left—from the Palmer Raids of post–World War I to McCarthyism in the 1950s—have made it difficult to promote Marxism to American working people in an open manner. This is not to say that workers are not sympathetic or supportive of the programs or specific interventions of the Left; indeed, the political culture of the African-American working class is essentially left social democratic, extremely supportive of anti-imperialist politics abroad and fundamental socio-economic reforms at home. But such support is not harnessed within the framework of an American socialist movement, but within more vaguely populist formations or progressive entities, such as the Rainbow Coalition.

While American working people have witnessed declining wages, runaway plants, and depressed living conditions, they do not resort to socialist categories to comprehend or explain their own daily oppression. When American working people hear the term Marxism-Leninism or Communism, many immediately think of the Berlin Wall, and the thousands of citizens from the German Democratic Republic (East Germany) who for years desperately attempted to escape to what they perceived to be "freedom." They may think of the USSR's policies of anti-Semitism and the political suppression of national minorities; the long lines of consumers in the cities waiting for rationed goods and produce; the extensive perks and privileges of the Soviet Communist bureaucrats who live luxuriously at the expense of the oppressed and deprived proletariat. They might ponder more ominously the millions of victims of forced collectivization, ethnic/national genocide, and authoritarian errors in state planning fostered by "socialist states" from China to Romania.

These contradictions are not the inventions of McCarthyism, but social realities stemming in part from the social model of development implied by the hegemonic ideology of a statist version of Marxism-Leninism. For all the genuine accomplishments of such regimes, including universal education, rapid improvements in health care, housing and social welfare, universal employment, and enlightened rural development, the crimes are also just as real, massive, and inescapable for revolutionary socialists. It is not sufficient for us to stand outside of these contradictions and assert that these crimes have no relationship or relevancy to "socialism." With the collapse of the Stalinist regimes in Eastern Europe, and particularly with the bloody excesses and terror of the Ceausescu dictatorship in its final days, such crimes are real, massive, and inescapable for the Left.

Social Engineering and Class Hierarchies

The actual historical record tells us that there is nothing uniformly progressive about the transition from one social formation to the next, whether the change is from feudalism to capitalism, or capitalism to socialism. Post-capitalist social formations exhibit traits of the old order, along with the goals and organizational characteristics of new orders yet to be built. The public ideology may be formally Marxist, yet the actual political culture within neighborhoods or family life may be closer to the *ancien regime*, still filled with sexism, racism, anti-Semitism, and backward ideological tendencies. Still, post-capitalist societies can be on balance progressive at least in the sense of creating structures which maximize human initiative and self-realization within a collective social process.

Amilcar Cabral and Walter Rodney, to cite only two examples, were revolutionary socialists who comprehended that socialism had to express a deep commitment to democratic decision-making procedures, and respect the elements of strength within the traditional, organic culture of the people. Both opposed mechanistic Marxism or the distortion of historical truths within political education. As Cabral explained to his party cadre, "We must practice revolutionary democracy in every aspect of our Party life." Yet for every Cabral, there are many other examples of Marxist theorists and parties which helped to consolidate versions of what can be termed socialism from above, authoritarian societies which negated democratic procedures, and employed terror and violence as normative tools for social control.

Despite the obvious political differences, there are also fundamental parallels between social democracy and Communism as two versions of socialism from above. Both have promoted extensive social engineering and class hierarchies. The social democrats elevate into office technocrats and apolitical professionals who have little direct contact or sympathy with the masses of workers. Both have historically repudiated socialist principles in favor of power. For the social democrats to win elections within political cultures and social systems deeply rooted in individualism, materialism, and the primacy of private interests above the common welfare, they have generally jettisoned their theoretical beliefs to curry favor within the middle classes.

From the German Social Democratic Party of the early 1900s to Michael Manley's People's National Party in Jamaica today, social democrats have rejected their own modest socialist agendas, betrayed their constituents' in-

terests, and moved to the right once in office. At best, these parties degener-
ate into a form of liberal social welfarism, guaranteeing the continuation of
the capitalist market system, and most of the inequities of poverty, racism,
and class exploitation which exist within these social systems. Finally, like
the Stalinists, many social democrats have been capable of gross violations
of civil liberties and human rights, particularly against the Marxist Left.
One can begin with the murder of Rosa Luxemburg during the Social Democratic regime in postwar Germany in 1918, and continue through the
murder of Walter Rodney by the agents of social democratic dictator For-
ber Burnham in Guyana in 1980.

Socialism from Below

Many conservative commentators have used the events in Eastern Europe
to argue that the struggle between capitalism and socialism is over, and that
capitalism has won. To be sure, the Communist states are in crisis. Yet
Western capitalism and imperialism are also in crisis. Capitalist social formations still experience periodic economic crises, expressed in cycles of expansion and recession. Capitalism remains a social system which creates
vast disparities of wealth and privilege between those classes which own
the means of production, finance, and real estate versus those who depend
upon their own labor power for survival. Capitalism is still responsible for
the perpetuation of institutional racism and ethnic violence, which fracture
the potential for political solidarity within the workers' movements. As
Malcolm X correctly observed a quarter century ago: "You can't have capitalism without racism. And if you find [anti-racists,] usually they're socialists or their political philosophy is socialism."

Capitalist societies which are characterized by democratic elective institutions have capitalist democracy, but not genuine democracy. A genuine
democracy must be identified with the elimination of social class exploitation and social oppression, and the elimination of poverty, social insecurity,
racism, substandard health care, and unemployment. Effective political
democracy is impossible without social justice and economic equality.

Some American Communists recently have suggested that we must take
from the best of both the Leninist political tradition, particularly its sharp
critique of imperialism and its emphasis on political strategy, and the best
of the political tradition of social democracy, such as its respect for political
pluralism and civil liberties, and its tolerance for diversity within the gov-
erning party. The argument suggests that the division of the international
socialist movement after World War I and the Russian Revolution can be
bridged. Already, the Hungarian and Italian Communist Parties are changing their names, and may soon become members of the Socialist International. But it would be a mistake to embrace a synthesis of both versions of

socialism from above. We must transcend the contradictions of both Communism and social democracy, and articulate a radical democratic vision of socialism which speaks a language which can be readily understood by the oppressed. We must go beyond both Lenin and Eduard Bernstein. Instead of socialism from above, we need socialism from below.

The approach of socialism from below in the United States would emphasize the necessity to develop networks of locally based progressive formations, organizations engaged in anti-racism, feminist, trade union, peace, environmental, gay/lesbian rights, and/or other progressive sectors. Here the Left can play the decisive role as a social catalyst, charting a new social contract, which would help the American people to redefine their relationship between themselves and the capitalist state. What do working people have a right to expect from the government? Military expenditures, which have soared to $305 billion in 1990, are destructive to the development of communities, increase unemployment, and undermine reforms in education, health care, and housing.

Justice and Freedom

American socialists must establish a non-sectarian public identity to the left of traditional liberals which calls for fundamental structural change to address society's real problems. We must advocate certain socioeconomic prerequisites for full participation in a democracy, such as the human right to a job or guaranteed income; the human right not to starve in a land of agricultural abundance; the human right to clean, affordable housing; the human right to free public medical care for all; the right to check the ability of corporations and businesses to move out from cities; the human right to quality public education. As socialists we need to state clearly that while capitalism promotes the unequal distribution of income, we would favor programs which reverse the concentration of wealth and privileges within one social class. We must declare that environmental decisions should not be by-products of the capitalist profit motive, but that the state must set tough and progressive goals to maintain and preserve natural resources.

We must insist unequivocally that the battle for racial justice is being lost, that all American working people lose when blacks' median incomes are barely 55 percent those of whites, or when black unemployment remains above 13 percent nationally. We need to make the fundamental link between crime and poverty. In Chicago today, five out of six black males age 16–19 actively in the labor force are unemployed. Black unemployment for males age 20–24 in Chicago is 50 percent. The real median incomes of almost all blacks except professionals and managers have fallen sharply since 1979 relative to whites' income.

Poverty and unemployment contribute to the growth of crime and drugs. There are currently 674,000 men and women in federal and state penal institutions. The answers are not in more police, prison construction, and the application of the death penalty. The decline of urban crime and the proliferation of drugs will come about only with the social and economic development of central cities, a domestic plan for reconstruction which can only be financed by the cancellation of billions of dollars from the military budget. The Left must be in the forefront in advancing a national blueprint for social development and an American economic "perestroika."

The Left must break with the Stalinists' and social democrats' fascination with tail-ending American liberalism in general, and the Democratic Party in particular. We must utilize an inside-outside approach to electoral politics, a strategy which critically supports liberal and progressive Democrats when they run against conservatives, but also develops the organizational capacity to contest elections as independents wherever possible or feasible. It would be dangerous to allocate most of our resources to electoral politics in the short run; in the next three to four years, the Left needs to develop a political network and structures which promote democratic resistance and socioeconomic struggle primarily at the local level. Regardless of Jesse Jackson and the Rainbow Coalition, the Democratic Party on its own will never become a socialist or left social democratic party—the trend of the 1980s, if anything, illustrated that the bulk of the Democratic Party is moving to the right. Socialism from below means developing a Left presence within the grassroots, local struggles or working people, the homeless, the unemployed, and racial minorities. It means building coalitions between community-based forces which are engaged in all different types of civil disobedience, strikes, and social agitation. The American electoral system was never designed to facilitate the development of social protest against the interests of capital. The liberals' strategy of supporting progressive candidates like Jackson without a concomitant agenda for non-electoral political struggle may in the short run "humanize" the system, but not transform it.

American societies must learn from the insights of non-socialist activists in various social reform, environmentalist, and religious organizations in our efforts to reach broader constituencies. We must cultivate a new, radical identity, clearly distinct from the failed examples of Stalinism and social democracy, which associates socialism with the values of social justice, pluralism, racial and gender equality, and freedom. The American Left has permitted the Right in this country to expropriate and distort many of the symbols of democratic struggle, particularly the theme of human freedom.

However, given the lessons from the rich heritage of the African-American liberation struggle, we should have no ambiguity about the positive and liberating value of the concept of human freedom. Freedom does not have to be defined as free markets, or the freedom of the corporations to raise prices and lay off workers. Freedom can be projected as the freedom from hunger, poverty, illiteracy, unemployment, and police brutality. Freedom can be the right to advocate a new, democratic social and political reconstruction of the existing order.

Freedom must be essential to both our methods and definition of the term "socialism." As Rosa Luxemburg reminded us: "Freedom only for the supporters of the government, only for the members of one party, however numerous they may be, is no freedom at all. Freedom is always and exclusively freedom for the one who thinks differently." We must criticize any government or party, and especially the "Left," which sanctions censorship, terrorism, political imprisonment, or any violation of human rights. Without dogma or illusions, socialism may become the democratic vision of the future.

Remaking
American Marxism

A new political orthodoxy now unites American liberals and conservatives alike: the Cold War is over; the century-long conflict between capitalism and socialism has finally ended, with capitalism triumphant. The death of both Marxism specifically and socialism in general is now widely taken for granted. The proof of this, one African socialist theorist recently observed, is the example of the Berlin Wall. "The fact that pieces of the wall were sold rather than distributed freely," Wamba-dia-Wamba observed, "underlines the reality that capitalism has won."

The apologists for capitalism now argue that the collapse of the Soviet socialism model was inevitable on economic, political, and even moral grounds. They argue that freedom in the political sphere, the unfettered competition between parties in an electoral system governed by laws, is directly dependent on a market-driven economic system, or free enterprise. Such views are now advocated by many of the new political forces in Eastern Europe and the USSR. Earlier this year, an economist elected to the Leningrad city council declared that his country must move quickly "from Marxism-Leninism, through socialism, to Reaganism."

These recent political upheavals have provoked sharp debate throughout the international left. The current debate over perestroika which appears to be developing within the Communist Party USA has erupted with much greater intensity in other left parties. The majority of the largest bloc within the British Communist Party has effectively disintegrated. Other parties have questioned their political ideology and in some instances have moved to rename themselves, identifying with the concept "democratic socialism."

Within the United States, the collapse of the Soviet socialist model in Eastern Europe, combined with the unexpected defeat of the Sandinistas in the 1990 election in Nicaragua, has created an unmistakable climate of self-doubt, disillusionment, and even defection from the left. A small number of former leftists are saying that capitalism has been proven correct by historical events, that socialism was an illusion or a fraud. But the vast majority of these leftists have not capitulated to Milton Friedman and Ronald Reagan. Instead, some are taking refuge in what can be described as pre-Marxian forms of socialism. They say that classical Marxian theories, the labor theory of value and dialectical materialism, are no longer valid. In a manner reminiscent of the Frankfurt School Marxists of the 1930s, those theorists whose search for a humanistic socialism in the face of Stalinism led backward to Hegel and Kant, or to the writings of the young Marx, they are resuscitating versions of utopian Marxism as "post-Marxism" or "post-modern socialism."

Others have moved away from identification with the very concept of socialism. Some argue that this is a tactical necessity, particularly within the United States, which has a political culture which is profoundly individualistic, entrepreneurial, and influenced by anti-socialist discourse. Because of McCarthyism and anti-Sovietism, the argument goes, we need to advocate socialist objectives without actually calling ourselves who we really are.

A more sophisticated version of this position is what might be termed "radical democratic" theory, best represented by the work of theorists Samuel Bowles and Herbert Gintis. They argue that Marxism neglects many non-class forms of oppression, that "socialism" as a political term does not embrace the complexity of the goals they project for democratic change, and that liberal capitalism can be gradually transformed into a version of economic democracy, or a "post-liberal society." The problem with many of these formations is that they obscure the fundamental factor which creates and recreates new economic and social contradictions within any capitalist society. That primary factor, which prefigures all others in the first instance, which sees the range of possibilities and outcomes, is the class contradiction. All capitalist market political economies have certain common characteristics: great concentrations of power in the hands of corporate minorities, great stratifications of poverty and wealth, the utilization of racism, sexism, and other factors to segment and divide working people.

Liberalism, by whatever name, seeks to humanize an inherently irrational, wasteful, and inhumane social system. It tries to reduce, but not eradicate, great concentrations of poverty and homelessness. Liberalism attempts to bring representatives of women and people of color into positions of representation, but it does not speak to the transfer of power to oppressed social classes victimized by capitalism. Liberalism wants to interpret the problems of the world, and to create an environment of greater fairness; but the point is not to interpret, but to change the world. In this post-modern period it is no longer popular to relate the truth, the reality that capitalism is "class struggle." It always has been, and so long as corporate capitalism dominates our economic and social system, it always must be. Our challenge is not to liberalize the existing system, but to transform it radically, building a democratic and humane society.

The dynamic and unprecedented changes in the Soviet Union and Eastern Europe must be understood against the problematic of revolution in the twentieth century. Since the 1960s, there have been a series of political mobilizations against capital, which have assumed many different forms—such as the 1968 urban revolts in France, national liberation struggles in Latin America and Africa, and the black liberation movement within the United States. All of these movements were either negated or accommodated with the interests of capital. Many of these failed social struggles were perceived as efforts to revitalize the political strategy of Marxism-Leninism.

We have to recognize the fundamental problems created by the transformation of the Soviet Union toward a market economy. It means rethinking everything we have assumed about the bipolar character of international relations and the basic forces within the political economy of capitalism. Within the Soviet Union, only two outcomes now seem probable—either the victory of a regulated market economy with the state in control of the commanding heights, dominated by a social democratic–styled Communist Party, which is essentially represented by Gorbachev; or a much more decentralized liberal capitalist social formation, with a disintegrated Communist Party, and with comparatively few restrictions on private capital, which is the model which appears to be developing behind Yeltsin. But even in the first scenario, the international implications of this rapid restructuring of the state socialist system have meant the repudiation of the theory that class struggle determines international relations. Gorbachev's adviser Yakolev has said as much. The shift by the USSR away from the theory of socialist orientation, or the noncapitalist path in Third World revolutions, the insistence that the Third World must come to terms with imperialism and that armed struggle is a historical relic, represent a challenge to non-European, anticapitalist formations throughout the globe. The Soviet Union's support for the strangulation of Iraq, its eager desire to develop closer ties with Israel, despite the continued struggles of the *intifada,* its notification to Cuba that it must pay in hard currency and at world prices for materials, are all indications that anti-capitalist and anti-imperialist forces will be at a serious disadvantage. The entire politics of non-alignment, as envisioned nearly half a century ago by Nehru, Nkrumah, and Nasser, has been rendered obsolete by the collapse of the Soviet bloc. Multinational capital will have an easier time exploiting Third World countries, demanding nonunionized labor, and higher profit margins.

But the events of the past year indicate that the transition from capitalism to some viable post-capitalist political economy is far more difficult to achieve than any of the classical theorists of Marxism ever anticipated. The major strategy employed in these revolutions against capital—the establishment of a socialist dictatorship through a single party state, with state ownership of the central means of production—has failed. However, one can make the case that the emergence of Soviet-allied states in Eastern Europe was not revolutionary, but actually preempted the possibility of the construction of a genuinely democratic socialist society. Dissatisfaction with the bureaucratic communist regimes was so great among various social classes and political groups that when Gorbachev refused to guarantee the Brezhnev doctrine of military intervention to buttress local political establishments, these authoritarian states crumbled overnight. Working class outrage against bureaucratic privilege was mobilized by sectors of the petty bourgeoisie and consolidated into a reactionary social force capable of taking state power. The calls for freedom and democracy were not linked to empowerment of working people, but rather to the construction of new forms of capitalist privilege. We can see clear evidence of this in Poland, where current projections of unemployment exceed 2 million by January 1991.

But we have not witnessed the final act of this evolving political drama. Capitalists know that the Eastern European and Soviet working classes will be bitterly disillusioned when they see exactly how market economies really work. In Latin America and Africa, there will be a massive political reaction to the imposition of economic austerity and cutbacks in social expenditures by conservative regimes. New forms of resistance to capital, strikes, labor unrest of all types, are inevitable. Capital's hope is to consolidate political formations and alliances with the most privileged social classes in Third World countries, consolidating conservative political formations which will suppress working class dissent. In Eastern Europe, this scenario exploits the revival of reactionary forms of ethnicism, anti-Semitism, and social intolerance, which are utilized to divide workers. In Poland, such an authoritarian role may be played by the darling of the west, Solidarity's Lech Walesa.

The collapse of the Berlin Wall represents an end to a period of political history. But does it also mean the collapse of our theoretical and critical approaches to an understanding of social and political forces which continue to shape the world? In other words, is Marxism, as a method of social analysis, still relevant in addressing political reality? It is a sad measure of these times that the question must even be asked. In New York, more than in any other city in the United States, the contemporary contradictions of capitalism are blatant and self-evident. Conservative estimates place the number of the city's homeless at 85,000; hundreds of thousands lack adequate shelter and employment; several million lack adequate health care and have seen an erosion in their standard of living.

Will class struggle still exist in this post-modern, post–Cold War period? I would argue that class struggle is still relevant when the top 1 percent of all US income earners receives more than the bottom 40 percent. Each year, families earning more than $50,000 receive almost $40 billion in government-sponsored subsidies in the form of mortgage interest exemptions, capital gains deferrals on housing sales, and other tax abatements. Meanwhile, the vast majority of families cannot afford to purchase a home, and in New York City alone there are 170,000 families on the waiting list for public housing. Real unemployment rates for African-Americans, which would include the "discouraged workers" not counted by the Bureau of Labor Statistics, exceed 20 percent.

Far from representing a triumph of capitalism, the end of the Cold War reveals more clearly to working people that anticommunist demagoguery masked the essential class inequalities within US society. In the 1980s, real median income of the upper 1 percent doubled, to $500,000 household income, while the incomes of working people declined. Even Kevin Phillips, the conservative guru, recognizes in his book *The Politics of Rich and Poor* that the United States is on the verge of a major political transformation pitting the rich against middle to low income Americans.

Everyone knows that the Soviet Union is experiencing a deep economic and political crisis. But from a Marxist perspective, we know that the United States is also in crisis. Our crisis can be seen in the statistical realities of growing human suffering and inequality—3 million homeless, 38 million without any medical insurance, millions in substandard housing, millions of children denied proper nutrition, millions of middle income families forced to work multiple jobs just to maintain a reasonable standard of living, collapsing bridges and highways due to inadequate support for the infrastructure, millions who are functionally illiterate or unable to work in a computer-oriented labor force. This economic, social, and educational crisis reinforces our belief that the socialist alternative continues to be both relevant and politically necessary. Our challenge is to rethink our socialist vision, advancing a political strategy which is more appropriate to the practical problems and realities of this historical conjuncture. But by remaking our political approach, we must not abrogate or abandon our intellectual and political identity as socialists.

How can we revitalize socialist politics and strategy for the 1990s and beyond? Briefly, I would suggest several points of departure, which should be explored seriously by the US left. First, instead of emphasizing electoral politics above all other political activities, we should refocus our organizing efforts on the practical problems experienced by the vast majority of working people and people of color in the central cities. The basic problematic for political engagement for the early twenty-first century will be: What constitutes an economically productive, socially pluralistic, and democratic urban community? I am not suggesting a hasty updating of Saul Alinsky's community organizing strategy. The current socioeconomic crisis of the cities is qualitatively different from the problems experienced a generation ago. Many basic conflicts with capital no longer occur in the workplace, although struggles against job discrimination and for full employment remain absolutely critical. But most manifestations of oppression occur in what can be termed the "living place," or the urban, post-industrial community.

Struggles over housing, health care, child care, schools, public transportation, and economic development all revolve around the future of the post-industrial city. The urban poor and working classes, combined with the unemployed, are, in effect, second class citizens, denied access to a quality of life which a minority of white, affluent Americans take for granted. Questions over public investment, reindustrialization, and the restriction of the right of capital to move across state and national boundaries will increasingly impact millions of Americans. The left must be in the forefront of shaping the national agenda in the definition of what constitutes a humane, progressive living place.

Second, we need to think about a socialist politics which has something innovative and creative to say about the environment. There is no coherent Marxist approach to the question of pollution abatement, ozone depletion, or a host of other environmental concerns which will assume increasing significance in the twenty-first century. In the United States, in the wake of Three Mile Island and Chernobyl, most socialists are strongly opposed to the construction of nuclear power plants. But other Marxists throughout the world have been identified with nuclear energy and other efforts at energy production which have culminated in ecological disasters. There is no identifiably Marxist approach to the issues of agricultural production and food distribution, population growth and reproductive rights, disarmament and economic conversion. It is not enough for us to criticize the policies of Western capitalism, but to develop an environmental politics of the left which addresses the root causes of ecological problems.

Third, US Marxists must seriously rethink their whole approach to electoral politics, and particularly their explicit or implicit faith that the Democratic Party will one day become "humanized," reformed from within, and transformed into a social democratic or anti-capitalist social force. I have recently been criticized, curiously, by both the Communist Party, in the pages of the *People's Daily World,* and reportedly by members of the Democratic Socialists of America's executive committee, on this very point. On this issue, the late Michael Harrington and Gus Hall were largely identical. DSA has operated as the extreme left wing of American liberalism, trying to make socialism respectable to Congressional liberal Democrats. Similarly, Communists have consistently supported political liberals, such as Detroit's Mayor Coleman Young, and even post-black candidates like Virginia's Governor Douglas Wilder, whose political agendas are hardly progressive. Both approaches fail to comprehend the class nature of the US electoral system; or, in other words, both DSA and the CPUSA have used non-Marxist approaches to the questions of politics.

The Democratic and Republic Parties have maintained a coalition government of national unity for decades, a Likud-Labour style marriage, operating more from consensus than competition. Both national parties now have a vested interest in maintaining this electoral partnership, which is the principal reason that the Democrats have ceased to function as a loyal opposition in anything but name. Many Democrats recognize that they could probably win the presidency by the route advocated by Jesse Jackson—expanding the electoral base to include millions of non-voting blacks, Latinos, poor, and working class voters and advancing a US version of left social democracy, attacking the power of corporations. This would force the Democrats into a truly antagonistic relationship with both the Republican Party and virtually all elites in corporate America. It would also require the organizational restructuring of the party, something that its bureaucracy strongly opposes. Most Democratic leaders would rather lose a presidential election and cooperate with a George Bush and Bob Dole than permit radical leaders to emerge within their ranks.

Both parties are dominated by sections of capital, and have a fundamental commitment to private enterprise, regardless of the destructive human consequences for the majority of US working people. Rather than a new deal from a stacked deck, we need a new game altogether.

Black and white progressive activists must revive the traditions and tactics of non-electoral political protest. This requires new institutions of creative resistance. For example, "freedom schools," open multiracial academies held during late afternoons, and on weekends for secondary school and college students, could offer a public protest curriculum. Learning how to organize street demonstrations, selective buying campaigns, civil disobedience, and reading about the personalities and history of American protest, would help to build a radical consciousness among this generation of youth.

Changing the rules requires innovations in the electoral process itself. The traditional plurality system in US elections gives the victory to the candidate with the most votes. This system is not only easily manipulated by corporate interests, which co-opt both major parties and suppress third party efforts, but by its nature manipulates public preferences into predictable outcomes. In multi-candidate, citywide elections, in which minority constituencies represent one-third of the total vote, or less, it becomes virtually impossible to elect candidates who represent their interests. Two results are predictable. Either the turnout rate of blacks gradually declines in national elections, which has occurred for the past 15 years, or candidates emerge who are more conservative, thus politically palatable to the white upper middle class and corporate interests. A third, better option would be to restructure voting procedures so minority interests can be expressed democratically.

Civil rights attorneys in several states have successfully pushed for changes in local elections which would give each voter several votes in each multi-candidate race. The votes could be clustered behind one candidate or shared in blocs with coalition partners. The result would be that minorities and working class constituencies would have a much better opportunity for winning authentic representation in citywide races, yet this system doesn't discriminate against white majorities. The left has to be in the forefront of campaigns to democratize the electoral process.

Fourth, the US left must rethink its current organizational forms, its political language, its general strategy, and even its historical memory, if it is to remain relevant to the struggles ahead. We must begin by asking ourselves, What has given historical force to the idea of socialism? Why have so many millions of activists fought for this nebulous political concept, which has generated both constructive accomplishments and monumental crimes, and which now for many seems abstract and irrelevant? The expression of any politics presumes a set of values. Beneath the socialist idea is a core of egalitarian and humanistic values: the human right to creative, productive work; the right to accessible and dependable health care; the right to decent housing; the right to public education; freedom from oppression based on race, gender, or ethnicity; the elimination of great concentrations of power and privilege in the hands of a tiny minority; and the democratic empowerment of those who historically have experienced the burden of exploitation and oppression.

The political expression of these values has created a number of political formations. Some who share these values have called themselves Communists or Marxist-Leninists; others have joined democratic socialist organizations or labor parties; and still others have belonged to a host of other formations, inspired by the writings and political examples of China's Cultural Revolution, or Leon Trotsky, C.L.R. James, and others.

Once political organizations are created, they generate their own unique internal dynamics, which help to perpetuate the formation and those personalities in leadership positions. To justify their continued existence, formations emphasize their distinct theoretical and programmatic differences with other groups which share their general outlook. This pursuit of political purity fragments the possibility for cooperative relations among groups. The left cannot afford this type of destructive sectarianism. The political events which once divided the international working class movement in the early twentieth century are being rapidly superseded. Before the twenty-first century, it will become less important whether one belongs to the Democratic Socialists of America, or the Communist Party, or any other social organization, than to grasp and build upon those basic principles which unite us, which give our political practice a creative vision and progressive orientation, which challenge the capitalist system of power and privilege in this nation.

We must look forward to a day when there will be a single democratic and pluralist socialist formation in the United States, a national organization with the capacity to influence millions of Americans. It would be based on a common program of Marxist principles and politics, drawing upon the positive elements of both Marxism-Leninism and social democracy. But in the immediate years ahead, diverse elements of the left must engage in intense dialogues, identifying areas of common political concern, and constructing practical unity by joint activities. The US Communist Party has its own unique organizational history and a rich legacy of struggle, particularly with the anti-racist and labor movements. Members of the Democratic Socialists of America, particularly those close to the Democratic Party, would have to overcome years of anti-Soviet and anti-Communist thinking. Both formations would have some difficulties relating to militants who had formerly belonged to the Socialist Workers Party, or to activists who were part of the new Communist movement of the 1970s. There are ancient, personal animosities and political grievances going back decades between individuals within similar groups, which in some instances will never be bridged. We can only respond to these realities by reminding our comrades of C.L.R. James's observation: "Revenge has no place in politics."

At this preliminary stage, the call for regrouping and rethinking is the recognition that our political conjuncture has been changed fundamentally by recent events; that the old political and organizational categories of the past century no longer adequately reflect these latest trends; and that the dynamics of capitalist exploitation within this country still require the existence of an active, militant, Marxist left. Unity, if it occurs, must evolve dialectically, through the common participation of various groups in political conferences, publications, the construction of institutions and political campaigns. Regrouping also suggests that critical elements of both Marxism-Leninism and social democracy are essential as the basis for the new unity. Marxist-Leninists in America were far more successful than social democrats in building progressive movements among the unemployed and workers in the 1930s and 1940s. They made impressive contributions to the mass democratic struggles against racial segregation. Communists recognized the critical importance of national liberation struggles in Asia, Latin America, and Africa, and were crucial in mobilizing Americans against apartheid. But these strengths were undermined by the Marxist-Leninist's tendency to devalue the process of democratic decision making, and to rely on authoritarian methods. The Communist Party not only refused to work cooperatively with others who called themselves Marxists or socialists, but actively attacked them. Conversely, socialists in the Norman Thomas–Michael Harrington tradition had a healthy respect for political pluralism and ideological diversity, and recognized that the vital link between democracy and socialism destroyed by Stalinism was central to their definition of politics. Yet the social democrats tended to relate to the interests of labor leaders more than the concerns of the rank and file, they did little to develop links with people of color domestically, and they did not comprehend the importance of supporting national liberation struggles as part of the larger struggle for socialism. Democratic socialists underestimated the repressive capability and characteristics of the capitalist state. A synthesis of strengths from both political traditions could form the foundations for a far more effective socialist movement, if we agree to enter into a protracted process of practical collaboration and discussion. A theory of revolution which is truly organic and appropriate to the unique conditions of the United States could emerge from this process.

Finally, we must constantly return to the challenges which exist in our society today, and which will exist in the twenty-first century. Does capitalism have the capacity to end racism and sexism, to abolish hunger and illiteracy, to eliminate homelessness and unemployment, to reconcile vast disparities of wealth and income between antagonistic social classes? No way. Unless we consolidate a national formation with sufficient numerical strength in membership and political clout, which openly and unambiguously calls for democratic socialism, we will become increasingly marginalized and isolated from the broader currents of protest. We must cease looking backward, mired in outdated political feuds and formulations, and grasp the new challenges and opportunities which may exist. We must, in short, dare to have historical imagination, and dare to be Marxists. If we do so, the so-called death of socialism in 1989–1990 may one day transform itself, Phoenix-like, into a new birth.

26

Toward a New
American Socialism

Americans who identify themselves as "the Left"—independent progressives, radical feminists, democratic socialists, Marxists, and others—have never lived in a more depressing, challenging, and potentially liberating moment.

With the collapse of the Cold War and the demise of the Soviet Union, the immediate reaction was "capitalist triumphalism" all over the world, but especially in Europe and the United States. Many social democrats repudiated their commitment to the liberal welfare state and adopted the rhetoric of the free market, the *laissez-faire* entrepreneur. Communist parties in the West fragmented or disintegrated as many Marxists renounced any identification with historical materialism.

The surprising defeat of the Labour Party in last spring's general election in Great Britain, combined with growing mass movements inspired by racism and anti-Semitism, from Germany to Louisiana, reinforced the general perception that the world's center of political gravity had shifted fundamentally to the right. Western liberals weighed the mounting evidence and announced their latest version of the Lesser Evils Thesis—that even traditional liberal goals were unrealizable in the immediate future, that anything just barely to the left of Reaganism/Thatcherism was preferable to being held hostage by the militant Right.

But before we deliver a solemn eulogy to socialism, let's re-examine the corpse. Internationally, in recent months, the Left has won several important electoral victories without sacrificing its principles. In New Zealand

and Guyana, socialists have won. In Mexico, the Democratic Party of the Revolution of Mexico has won millions of adherents and is now poised to challenge the government's pro-corporate policies. The Workers Party of Brazil is the largest democratic, popular force in Latin America's largest nation. In Haiti, it required the brutality of a military coup to overthrow the popular electoral Lavalas movement of Jean-Bertrand Aristide. Even in Nicaragua, the Sandinistas stand an excellent chance of being returned to power in the next national elections. In Europe, the situation is less optimistic for the Left, but not entirely bleak. Last November, ex-communists were swept into power in Lithuania. And inside the United States, that same spirit of political unrest which has erupted into socialist and labor movements elsewhere simmers just below the surface of our political culture.

Part of the reason for the new worldwide activism of the Left is the radically different international environment in the aftermath of the Cold War. The decayed factories of the Rust Belt, the doubling of the number of homeless Americans within a decade, the 37 million-plus who have no health insurance, the 1,500 Latino and black teenagers who drop out of school every day—these stand as graphic illustrations of the failure of rampant militarism and Cold War economics. If the USSR's disintegration symbolizes the bankruptcy of Stalinist communism, that is no reason to believe that American capitalism has solved its problems.

What can the Left do?

What's required is not a blanket rejection of Marxism as a critical method of social analysis but a fundamental rethinking and revision of "socialist politics."

The Leninist vanguard-party model of social change, evolving in the context of a highly authoritarian, underdeveloped society devoid of any tradition of civil liberties and human rights, has finally been thoroughly discredited. The idea of seizing state power by violence in a computerized, technologically advanced society is simply a recipe for disaster.

But if socialist politics is defined specifically and solely as a radical project for democratic change, what set of political perspectives and concepts can guide the renaissance of the American Left? What is still worthwhile and valuable in the concept of "socialism" for a new generation heading into the twenty-first century?

For starters, we should examine the practical problems confronting American working people and racial minorities and respond with a series of political interventions that actually empowers the oppressed.

And we should advance our political agenda in concert with larger, stronger currents for social change in America—feminists, people of color, trade unionists, lesbians and gays, environmentalists, neighborhood and community organizers, and many others—recognizing that we socialists will play, at best, a secondary role in the struggles immediately ahead.

My vision of a new American socialism will certainly not be the same as that of others on the Left. My objective here is not to present a theoretical blueprint, but to build a framework for dialogue among democratic socialists across organizational and ideological boundaries. All too frequently, the disorganized, fractious Left has made its sectarianism a red badge of courage, refusing to speak to others who share 90 percent of its own politics because they differ on the remaining 10 percent. But we can no longer afford to dwell in the political ghettoes of ideological purity.

We must champion a renewed commitment to internationalism—espousing global solutions to global problems. Critical environmental issues cannot be fully addressed at the level of the nation-state, but predatory corporate capitalism has the destruction of the biosphere on its agenda.

And we must link the question of the environment with labor issues, recognizing that the export of US industrial and manufacturing jobs to Third World nations is not just a capitalist search for lower wages but also a desire to avoid pollution controls and health and safety standards.

With a new vision of socialism, we must rethink the character of capitalism and the means by which the corporate-dominated economy can become more egalitarian and democratic. Our economic system is based on private greed and public pain, but it is also much more flexible, dynamic, and creative than earlier generations of Marxists, including Marx himself, ever imagined.

The immediate task for American socialists is to support and build strong workers' movements and to defend the rights of trade unions. But we must also help create transitional economic structures that address working-class needs and build solidarity across the boundaries of race, ethnicity, and income, giving people a concrete understanding of what economic alternatives are needed.

We should establish a clearer public identity for "socialism," outlining in a common-sense manner our theoretical and political boundaries—and how our politics differs from that of our ideological second cousin, "liberalism."

A new American socialism must make a clear and unambiguous distinction between our politics, values, and vision, and those of American liberalism. Irving Howe has defined "democratic socialists" as "the allies of American liberalism," pressuring "liberals to hold fast to their own ideas and values, without equivocation or retreat." Howe argues that liberals and socialists alike share "an unshakable premise of our politics that freedom is the indispensable prerequisite for social and economic progress." By "freedom," what Howe really means is "liberty," in the context of classical

Western European political philosophy. Howe described his commitment to
the struggle for human equality as secondary to his faith in liberty. Within
his scenario, there are a logical continuity and cordial ideological kinship
between socialism and liberalism.

The problem is that there are too many historical examples in which
both liberals and social democrats have sacrificed their high ideals of liberty
and equal justice upon the altar of expediency. During the Cold War, thousands of workers were expelled from unions, lost their jobs, or were imprisoned, at the urging of most liberals and not a few liberal socialists. The
Communist Control Act of 1954 made membership in the Communist
Party a crime and stripped the Party of "all rights, privileges, and immuni-
ties attendant upon legal bodies." Even Howe wrote that the "Congressional stampede" to outlaw Communist and Marxist ideas illustrated that
Democrats and Republicans alike were prepared "to trample the concept of
liberty in the name of destroying its enemy." Other prominent instances in
recent history in which liberals repressed radicals include the Kennedy Administration's surveillance and lack of support for the desegregation movement and, more recently, the capitulation by many congressional liberals to
key elements of Reaganomics.

I believe that the single, defining characteristic of socialism, the prerequisite from which all else flows, is the commitment to human equality. An individual's personal liberty to speak freely is insignificant if one doesn't own
or have genuine access to the press. An individual's freedom to vote means
little if one is unemployed, homeless, hungry, or poor. The unequal distribution of wealth under capitalism—in which the top 1 percent of all households has a greater net wealth than the bottom 90 percent—makes liberty a
function of power, privilege, and control.

In a typical American election, more than 80 percent of the citizens who
earn more than $50,000 annually vote; only 44 percent of all African-
Americans, 35 percent of Latinos, and 38 percent of the unemployed voted
in the 1988 Presidential election. The affluent and comfortable classes logi-
cally recognize that they have a stake in the outcome, and they exercise
their franchise. Without material and social equality, the political consequences are always unequal, unfair, and discriminatory, despite the existence of legalistic freedoms.

The essential socialist project is about equality—efforts promoting the
empowerment of working people and other oppressed sectors of society,
and the redistribution of power from the few to the many.

And that's not liberalism.

If "equality" and "empowerment" are what socialists should seek—not
the "equal opportunities" under capitalism and "greater social fairness"
sought by liberals—then we must rethink our relationship with the Democratic Party and the character of our interventions within the electoral arena.

For several decades, many democratic socialists have supported the liberal wing of the Democratic Party, attempting to shift its political center of gravity to the left. Michael Harrington's "Democratic Agenda" efforts more than a decade ago developed some productive relationships between socialists and key liberals in Congress and within organized labor. Unfortunately, the emergence of Bill Clinton and the neoconservative Democratic Leadership Council clearly shows that the Democratic Party will never become a social democratic or labor-oriented party. Ideologically and programmatically, the current Democratic leadership occupies the space once reserved for "moderate Republicans"—Wendell Willkie, Jacob Javits, or Charles Percy, for example.

Harrington never really understood that the natural political behavior of liberals is cautious, timid oscillation: When strong social protest movements are in the streets, liberals will drift to the left; with the rise of Reaganism in the 1980s, they scurried to the right. As Stanley Aronowitz observed in *The Progressive* in 1986, "The Democrats are not an alternative to the Republican conservatives. At best, they slow down the most retrograde aspects of the GOP program; at worst, they bestow legitimacy on conservative goals, leaving their constituents bothered and bewildered."

Harrington's well-meaning mistake was modest, compared to the profoundly flawed electoral strategy of the American Communist Party. For more than four decades, Erwin Marquit recently observed, the Communist agenda "never went beyond progressive politics." The "implementation of the Party's program was reformist in content and sectarian in form." It extended nearly uncritical support to liberals and progressives in the Democratic Party but viciously attacked Marxists outside its own ranks as the "phony Left." Finally, some Trotsykist-oriented parties and formations have denounced for half a century any relationship with progressives inside the Democratic Party, elevating sectarianism to the level of political principle.

A number of independent Marxists and progressives have been critical of all of these approaches to electoral politics. Arthur Kinoy's characterization of the two-party system as being "controlled by the powerful corporate, industrial, political, military establishment" is essentially correct. But the task of the Left is to work "inside" and "outside" of that system, Kinoy argues.

My own inside-outside approach to electoral activism rests on four key political activities:

•We must work for and support progressive and liberal Democrats, strengthening the party's liberal wing but making clear distinctions between their politics and ours.

- We must support the development of nonsectarian, popular third-party efforts, such as the pending formation of the Vermont Progressive Party led by that state's member of Congress, Bernie Sanders.
- We must aggressively work toward structural reforms within the electoral system. These would include fair ballot access for third parties and independent candidates; permitting candidates to have "cross-endorsements" or "fusion" between small third parties and the major capitalist parties, as advocated by the New Party; proportional representation in local races and ultimately in Federal elections; and, most importantly, public financing of elections, to take the corporations' and the capitalists' special interests out of the public's decision-making process.
- We must do much more to expand the potential electoral base of the Left by engaging in voter education and registration campaigns. Part of the success of the Rainbow Coalition in 1984 and 1988 came from registering hundreds of thousands of new voters, most of whom were African-Americans, Latinos, students, working people, and the poor.

And we must integrate these four approaches to promote a more radical, multicultural definition of democracy, giving the Left a more clear-cut identity in electoral politics.

We must also link progressive electoral endeavors to ongoing social protests and democratic movements of the oppressed within American society. We must work in collaboration with progressive and left-wing leaders and activists, and groupings within the trade union movement. This must be central to our practice as socialists.

There is a direct, inescapable connection between working-class organizing, antiracist activism, and the empowerment of people of color. The vast majority of African-Americans, Puerto Ricans, Chicanos, and other people of color are, after all, working-class women and men. And the emphasis in labor organizing should be in workplaces with the highest concentration of workers of color.

Extreme conservatives on the Republican Right are searching for a new political and ideological framework for their assault on American working people, racial minorities, and the poor. The collapse of Soviet communism has meant that sterile anticommunism and red-baiting are much less effective in attacking their political opponents. And that's why the Right has moved aggressively to connect a number of cultural and social issues: opposition to "political correctness" and multicultural education on campuses; advocacy of vouchers and use of public funds for private schools; homophobic state referenda such as the recently passed constitutional amendment in Colorado banning local ordinances that protect lesbian and gay rights; legislative initiatives to void women's freedom of choice on abortion; attacks on affirmative action as "quotas."

The role of socialists is to get into the thick of the debates on all of these issues. By joining broad, mass organizations fighting for women's rights, against homophobia, for academic pluralism and multicultural education, we increase the capacity of oppressed people to resist, and we strengthen democratic currents throughout society.

The struggle to define the Left and to build movements for radical democracy will fail, though, unless progressives squarely confront the issue of race. Marx himself always recognized the importance of the race question to the politics of socialist transformation: "Labor cannot emancipate itself in the white skin where in the black it is branded."

Historically, racism has been the most decisive weapon in the arsenal of America's ruling elites to divide democratic resistance movements, turning fearful and frustrated whites against nonwhite working people. Today, we live in a nation in which nearly 30 percent of our population is Latino, American Indian, Arab-American, Asian/Pacific American, and African-American. By the middle of the twenty-first century, the majority of the working class will consist of people of non-European descent.

The Left must ask itself why most socialist organizations, with the exception of the American Communist Party, have consistently failed to attract black, Latino, and Asian-American supporters. It must honestly and critically confront the fact that most radical whites have little or no contact with grass-roots organizing efforts among inner-city working people, the poor, or the homeless. The Left should be challenged to explain why the majority of the most militant and progressive students of color in the hip-hip contemporary culture of the 1990s have few connections with erstwhile white radicals and usually perceive Marxism as just another discredited "white ideology."

Part of the Left's problem is the rupture between the theory and practice of social change. A good number of white socialists have the luxury to contemplate "class struggle" in the abstract. People of color and working people don't.

I didn't become a socialist because I was seduced by the persuasive materialist logic of Karl Marx. Nor did I equate the "freedom" of liberal socialists like Irving Howe with the gritty struggles for "freedom" which were the political objective of W.E.B. Du Bois, Martin Luther King, Jr., and Malcolm X. Socialism is only meaningful to African-Americans and other oppressed people of color when it explains how capitalism perpetuates our unequal conditions and when it gives us some tools to empower ourselves against an unfair, unjust system.

That's not a metaphysical enterprise but a practical, concrete analysis of actual, daily conditions. A social theory is useful only to the degree that it helps to explain reality, to the degree that it actually empowers those who employ it. And the day-to-day reality lived by millions of African-Americans, Latinos, and others along the jagged race/class fault line beneath American democracy is the continuing upheaval of social inequality and racial prejudice. Socialists must find a way to speak directly to that reality holistically, not as an afterthought or an appendage to their chief political concerns.

As vice chairperson of the Democratic Socialists of America from 1979 to 1984, I helped to create DSA's National and Racial Minorities Commission and raised my own funds to sponsor DSA's first gathering of socialists of color, which was held at Fisk University in Nashville in 1983. I also edited and largely financed a short-lived DSA publication, *Third World Socialists*. But much of DSA's leadership was unenthusiastic about the publication, and the national organization committed relatively few resources to working with Asian-American, Latino, or African-American activists. The growing student groups linked to DSA on college campuses had serious difficulties recruiting students of color.

To their credit, DSA members were prominent in support of the Presidential campaigns of Jesse Jackson in 1984 and 1988. DSA's Antiracism Commission does excellent work, and DSA honorary chairperson Cornel West, my good friend, is one of the most influential intellectuals within the black community today.

Nevertheless, unfairly or not, DSA retains a basically "white identity" which it has never been able to overcome. The reason for this is simple.

No American socialist organization has ever been able to attract substantial numbers of African-Americans and other people of color unless, from the very beginning, they were well represented inside the leadership and planning of that body. When that does not occur, individual radical intellectuals such as West might be affiliated with a socialist group, but that affinity remains marginal and secondary to their political endeavors. When forced to make a hard choice of priorities between the "socialist project" and "black liberation," the vast majority of black activists throughout the twentieth century have chosen the latter.

Fortunately, some leftists are trying to learn from the errors of the past. A majority of the national executive of the Committees of Correspondence consists of people of color. The New Party, which has initiated organizing efforts in nearly 20 states, has a rule insisting that 40 percent of all leadership groups be people of color. A precursor chapter of the New Party also elected African-American activist Jackie Kirby to the Pine Bluff, Arkansas, City Council in 1991. Activists of color were prominent in the leadership of the People's Progressive Convention held at Eastern Michigan University in Ypsilanti last August.

A new socialist vision must be identified with peace and the resolution of social problems without resort to force or violence, unless absolutely necessary. I am not a pacifist. But W.E.B. Du Bois taught me the essential connection between peace and social justice.

"Peace" in the context of race relations means the empowerment of people of color, the reduction of racist language and behavior, and ultimately the obliteration of the very idea of racial categories. Peace is not the absence of social tensions and class conflict but the achievement of social justice and equality of conditions for all members of society.

This is a period of political rethinking and organizational realignment within the Left.

The former League of Revolutionary Struggle, which was notable on the Left for its predominantly Asian-American, Latino, and African-American composition, has split in two political directions: the majority tendency, which has moved sharply away from Marxism-Leninism and produces the *Unity* newspaper, and the minority grouping, the Socialist Organizing Network. The Network is now engaging in collaborative discussion with the Freedom Road socialist organization, which in turn publishes the very impressive publication *Forward Motion.*

The former Line of March organization developed into the nucleus of the journal *Crossroads,* which has played a central role in the theoretical and organizational reconstruction of a wide section of the Left. A new theoretical journal, *Rethinking Marxism,* has become an important forum for many radical scholars.

A number of national conferences on the Left in the 1980s and early 1990s have also brought activists and socialist intellectuals together into productive dialogue. These have included the annual Socialist Scholars Conference in New York City, closely associated with DSA; the Midwest Radical Scholars Conference in Chicago, initiated by veteran leftist Carl Davidson; the Activists of Color conference in Berkeley in April 1991.

The National Committee for Independent Political Action, based in New York, has brought together a number of well-respected community organizers, progressives, and socialists such as radical law professor Arthur Kinoy and Alabama's Gwen Patton, a former leader of the Rainbow Coalition.

And perhaps the most important step toward a new type of nonsectarian Left unity has been the creation of the Committees of Correspondence, the merger of those Marxists who recently left the US Communist Party with a number of independent socialists and activists. The leadership of the Committees embraces an unprecedented range of women and men who have struggled, in various formations and socialist parties, for a democratic society: former Communist Party leaders Angela Y. Davis, Charlene Mitchell, and Kendra Alexander; former Socialist Workers Party Presidential candidate Peter Camejo; lesbian activist Leslie Cagan; Chicana activist Elizabeth Martinez; Arthur Kinoy and Carl Davidson.

In recent months, some have suggested that the next stage of Left unity should be the development of a "socialist united front" among various American socialist groups. The election of Bill Clinton and the Democratic Party's repudiation of key tenets of its traditional liberalism certainly help this process by pushing the Democratic Party's public policy boundaries to the right, leaving a growing political vacuum on the Left.

But I believe that such a front is premature. Certainly there needs to be greater dialogue and practical cooperation among socialist organizations and progressive, independent political movements. This process should begin with joint projects, local conferences, and collaborative activities among a wide range of groups that share a commitment to socialism and democracy.

Nothing is more urgent than establishing practical joint activities and discussions between the two largest entities on the Left, the Democratic Socialists of America and the Committees of Correspondence. Such unity should be based on the democratic right "to agree to disagree" on certain questions, to respect the organizational autonomy and integrity of the various formations, but to seek areas of cooperative relations and joint action, striving for greater consensus about the character of our socialist vision for American society. Unity which rests on such practical accomplishments today may culminate in a unified, but pluralistic and democratic, socialist organization in the future.   .

But the central questions confronting the Left aren't located within the Left itself but in the broader, deeper currents of social protest and struggle among non-socialist, democratic constituencies—in the activities of trade unionists, gays and lesbians, feminists, environmentalists, people of color, and the poor. We must accept and acknowledge the reality that, for the foreseeable future, the essential debate will not be about "capitalism versus socialism" but about the character and content of the capitalist social order—whether we as progressives can strengthen movements for empowerment and equality within the context of capitalism.

This means advancing a politics of radical, multicultural democracy, not socialism. It means, in the short run, that tactical electoral alliances with centrists like Clinton, within the Democratic Party, are absolutely necessary if we are to push back the aggressive, reactionary agenda of the Far Right. Bush's defeat last November was critical for the Left; it allows us to raise a series of issues, from the adoption here of a single-payer national health system like Canada's to the enforcement of civil rights initiatives. As the focus of national policy debates shifts from right to center, progressive and democratic forces have a better chance to influence the outcome. And as we move national policy toward radical democratic alternatives, we establish the preconditions necessary for building a democratic socialist America in the next century.

Finally, our new vision of socialism must not approach the question of social transformation as a project that is essentially oppositional, but as a collective, protracted task filled with hope, affirmation, and human aspirations. The theoretical history of the Left is basically a rich, if often contradictory, legacy of criticism. Marx's *Kapital* was not a blueprint for the construction of a socialist, democratic society; it was a trenchant, brilliant critique of the inequalities and class contradictions of capitalism as an economic system.

But there was also something mechanistic in this projection of a socialist future—the idea that impersonal, amoral social forces and economic factors will determine the outcome of history. Marx himself explained that the working class had "no ideals to realized." Many communists interpreted this to mean that undemocratic measures which grossly violate human rights and morality could be justified in constructing a future society that was perfectible in principle.

In a different way, white social democrats generally shared this contempt for the ideals and human aspirations of working people, focusing instead on the utilitarian mechanics of winning elections and running governments. A century ago, Edward Bernstein, the very first "socialist revisionist," proclaimed, "To me that which is generally called the ultimate aim of socialism is nothing, but the movement is everything."

It is here that the insights of the Black Freedom Movement most sharply contradict the theoretical and political legacy of white socialism. As Martin Luther King, Jr. observed, every truly profound movement for human liberation is driven by a "revolution in values." Much of the world's continuing social unrest and class struggle exists because the means of power are radically severed from the ends—by both the Right and the Left.

"We will never have peace in the world," King insisted, "until men everywhere recognize that ends are not cut off from means, because the means represent the ideal in the making, and the end in progress."

To achieve a truly just, egalitarian society, we must actualize our ideals in our daily political endeavors and activism with the oppressed. And we must do so with a sense of urgency, because there is nothing preordained about our ultimate victory.

In the words of Albert Einstein, "The existence and validity of human rights are not written in the stars."

As socialists, we must be critical of the government and its policies, opposing such American adventures as the invasion of Iraq, protesting cutbacks in education, health care, and other areas of human need. But the politics of criticism is an act of negation. We cannot construct a political culture of radical democracy simply by rejecting the system. We cannot win by saying what we are against. We must affirm what we are for.

"It was as a Socialist, and because I was a Socialist," Michael Harrington observed years ago, "that I fell in love with America. In saying that, I am not indulging in romantic nostalgia about youthful days on the road but rather underlining a political truth. If the Left wants to change this country because it hates it, the people will never listen to the Left and the people will be right. To be a Socialist—to be a Marxist—is to make an act of faith, of love even, toward this land. It is to sense the seed beneath the snow; to see, beneath the veneer of corruption and meanness and the commercialization of human relationships, men and women capable of controlling their own destinies."

Harrington was right. America has an incredibly rich history of radical democratic protest. The socialist critique can only succeed as an extension, not a departure, from that heritage of Frederick Douglass, Fannie Lou Hamer, Vito Marcantonio, and Cesar Chávez. We have a political responsibility to speak to that tradition, to identify with the working people of this land, to express their dreams and hopes.

Not long ago, I left Los Angeles airport at the crack of dawn, traveling eastward across the land. The sun peered across the horizon, illuminating the ground's features thousands of feet below. The view from above was familiar, but also, in some new way, unexpected and awesome: the snow-capped mountains, the bone-dry basins, the craggy plateaus; the twists and curls of Colorado River, cutting its path to the sea. I was moved by the great spectrum of physical diversity, the overarching beauty and simple grandeur of our continent.

And the vast richness and diversity which are our land struck me to the core as I pondered the plight of millions of people who labor and love, dream and build, study and reflect in countless cities, towns, and villages. These are the people who lack adequate shelter, who sleep in the alleys, subway tunnels, and parks. These are the people standing in innumerable unemployment lines, desperate for work in order to feed and clothe their children. These are the voiceless people who have lost faith in politicians' promises, who have seen their real incomes reduced over the past dozen years, who yearn for effective solutions to their problems.

These are the tens of millions of Americans who tremble at the first signs of illness or physical adversity in their children, because they lack medical insurance. They are the millions of women who accept in silence sexual harassment at their places of employment for fear of losing their jobs during a recession. They are lesbians and gay men whose rights are under assault by homophobic referenda. They are African-Americans and Latinos who are denied bank loans because of their race, whose job applications are rejected, whose children die at twice the rate for whites, whose sons and daughters are in prison, whose hopes have been destroyed.

This is the landscape of our humanity, its fears and frustrations, its desires for a better life. American democracy is an unfinished project, and its central creative power is found in the talent and energies of its working people. Yet millions of Americans find themselves divorced from the reality of equality and empowerment, and the promise of a better life. They stand in isolation from the comfort, the power, and the privileges of an upper class which is determinedly dedicated to the preservation of the economic status quo.

It is the task of American socialists to call for a new social contract for this country, a common understanding about the principles of power and human development, cutting across the rainbow of cultural and social class, of ethnic diversity. What if we challenged the idea that virtually all corporate, political, educational, and cultural leadership must be selected from a narrow band of white, upper-class males? What if we employed the full power of government to provide the basic human needs—universal health care, decent shelter, quality education for our children, improved public transportation facilities, and the right to a job or guaranteed income—for every citizen? How much would all of our lives be enriched, how much more productive?

To revitalize our cities, to put people back to work, to create a social environment without the discrimination of race, gender, and sexual orientation, to improve the quality of public schools, to address the growing crisis of our deteriorating environment, we Americans desperately need a new vision of what democracy could be. To be a socialist is to pursue this radical democratic project: taking back the power from the upper class which dominates the state and the corporations, empowering the people to fight for full human equality in all aspects of daily life.

I have no doubt that the current glorification and triumphalism of capitalism will continue, at least in the short run. But as the South African expression goes, "Time is longer than rope." The fundamental reasons for class struggle still exist. Our challenge is to grasp the new problems and concerns of oppressed people and to transform their awareness of the issues into a political culture and consciousness favoring radical democratic alternatives, aimed at fighting corporate capitalism.

So long as corporate greed continues to destroy the environment, so long as several million Americans are homeless, so long as anti-Semitism, racism, sexism, and homophobia are manipulated to divide neighborhoods and communities, so long as factories shut down overnight and corporations hold cities as economic hostages in their demands for concessions, the vision of socialism will continue to be relevant and essential to the construction of a truly egalitarian, democratic America.

About the Book and Author

Through public appearances, radio and television interviews, and his many articles and books, Manning Marable has become one of America's most prominent commentators on race relations and African-American politics. *Speaking Truth to Power* brings together for the first time Marable's major writings on black politics, peace, and social justice.

The book traces the changing role of race within the American political system since the Civil Rights Movement. It also charts the author's striking evolution of political ideas, moving toward a political analysis of multicultural democracy, social justice, and egalitarian pluralism.

Manning Marable is professor of history and director of the Institute for Research in African-American Studies at Columbia University.

Index